Tony Thompson is a forme
of the *Observer*. Having secu
killers, armed robbers, drug
police officers and customs
unique insight into the innermost workings of
Britain's criminal underworld.

BLOGGS 19

The Story of the Essex
Range Rover Triple Murders

Tony Thompson

sphere

SPHERE

First published in Great Britain in 2000
by Warner Books
Reprinted by Time Warner Paperbacks in 2004
Reprinted by Time Warner Books in 2006
Reprinted by Sphere in 2008 (twice), 2010, 2011, 2013

A CIP catalogue record for this book
is available from the British Library.

ISBN 978-0-7515-2241-9

Typeset in Stone by M Rules
Printed and bound in Great Britain by
Clays Ltd, St Ives plc

Papers used by Sphere are from well-managed forests
and other responsible sources.

MIX
Paper from
responsible sources
FSC
www.fsc.org   FSC® C104740

Sphere
An imprint of
Little, Brown Book Group
100 Victoria Embankment
London EC4Y 0DY

An Hachette UK Company
www.hachette.co.uk

www.littlebrown.co.uk

For Emma

Contents

'HMP Woodhill. Protected Witness Unit (PWU): Designed to hold prisoners who are giving evidence or assistance to the police in cases of serious crime. All inmates are known to staff simply as "Bloggs" followed by a number. Their true identity and reasons for being in the PWU are known only to senior management at the prison.'

The Prisoners' Handbook

Acknowledgements

I am eternally grateful for the help and assistance of Linda Christie, Todd Austin and numerous police officers, customs officers and members of the underworld who are, as ever, too shy to allow themselves to be mentioned by name. I would also like to thank Caroline Dawnay, Alan Samson and Rosemary Scoular (not forgetting Vanessa and Annabel!) for their unyielding support and patience.

'If you want to know the truth'

'If you really want to know the truth, the whole truth that is, then yeah, I'd have to agree that there were times when I should have realised that something was wrong; times when it should have been blindingly obvious that the stories I was being told didn't actually make much sense. But it's all too easy to look back with hindsight and spot the clues that you missed along the way. When you're right in the thick of it, it's a hell of a lot harder to be objective. And when two of your closest friends get into your car, just seconds after they've brutally murdered three people, and – even though they're all covered in blood and bits of brain – they start laughing and joking, giggling like a couple of schoolboys who've just seen their first naked woman, well then it's fucking hard to accept that you've unwittingly become part of their crime.'

On 15 May 1996 Darren Nicholls, a little known petty criminal from Braintree, Essex, disappeared from the face of the earth. The arrest of the stocky thirty-year-old electrician two days earlier after 10 kilos of cannabis were found in the back of his Transit van had only barely made the local news, but less than twenty-four hours later, Nicholls had become the man who everybody wanted to talk to.

Detectives from the drug squad were standing by to quiz him about a further 50 kilos of cannabis that had been found sitting at the bottom of a lake; officers from Scotland Yard's anti-corruption squad wanted to know about his links with a policeman they were investigating for conspiracy to pervert the course of justice and other criminal offences; while officials from HM Customs and Excise wanted to know about numerous trips abroad that Nicholls had made, during which hundreds of kilos of drugs had been smuggled into the country.

But first in line were the Essex murder squad. They wanted to talk to Nicholls about the bodies of three drug dealers that had been found in a Range Rover in a quiet lane in Rettendon a few months earlier. Patrick Tate, Craig Rolfe and Tony Tucker – all three well-known local villains – had each been blasted in the head with a shotgun at point-blank range. Their faces were so distorted that, had their fingerprints not been on file, they would have been almost impossible to identify.

Compared to the three dead men and Jack Whomes and Michael Steele – the men who would later be accused of killing them – Nicholls was a nobody: a bit player in the Essex criminal underworld that includes everything from hitmen and gun runners to car thieves and fraudsters. Nicholls was about as close to the bottom of the ladder as it was possible to be, but soon after the police arrested him they realised they had a prize beyond measure.

Nicholls had worked closely with both the killers and the killed. He knew exactly how their extensive and wide-ranging criminal operations worked and understood the elaborate techniques they employed to avoid capture. He was on first-name terms with all their contacts throughout Britain and Amsterdam. He knew of their plans to expand into Europe; he knew who supplied their drugs and their weapons. Most importantly, he knew exactly who had pulled the trigger on the night that Tate, Tucker and Rolfe died. If the police could persuade him to talk, to switch sides and turn grass, they knew that Nicholls could be the key to a string of convictions.

As it was they hardly needed any persuasion at all. As he stared at the blank walls of his police cell in the hours following his arrest, Nicholls knew that even if he didn't talk, the men he once considered to be his friends would hunt him down and kill him, just as they had hunted down and killed others who had stood in their way.

Today, if you take a trip down to the Public Records Office, you'll find no trace of Darren Nicholls. His birth certificate and marriage licence have both been deleted. His National Insurance number has been withdrawn, his passport details destroyed. All his bank and building society accounts have been closed down, along with all his old store cards and hire-purchase loans. His driver details have been erased from the computer at Swansea and he no longer appears on any electoral roll.

Even his criminal record is no more. Every possible path that someone might use to try to track him down has been blocked. It is as if he was never born.

And it is just as well. In the run-up the murder trial where Nicholls was the key prosecution witness – according to the police the most important supergrass since Albert Donoghue betrayed the Kray twins in July 1968 – the price on his head rose to a spectacular £250,000. All avenues were explored: his mother and brothers were watched and followed to see where they might lead; friends and neighbours were approached in pubs and clubs and pumped for information or offered bribes; letters proclaiming that Nicholls had won free holidays and the like were sent to his old address in the hope that they would be forwarded on and he'd reveal himself, all to no avail.

At first, Nicholls and his family felt secure in their police safe house, surrounded by panic buttons, alarms and video cameras. But the longer they spent on the witness protection programme, the more he felt that police promises to look after them when it was all over were little more than a sweetener to ensure Darren gave evidence at the trial. Nicholls never expected a life of luxury in some fancy foreign villa but the reality – a handshake and directions to the nearest dole office – fell short of even his worst expectations.

Nicholls desperately needed to talk it all through, but there was no one around. His wife was too angry with him, the police were too busy. It was only when he heard that one of the senior officers on the murder case was so fascinated by what had gone on that night that he planned to write a book about it that Nicholls himself found a solution. After all, he was the one who had been there; he was the one who had seen the blood-stained hands and smelt the smoking barrels; he was the one who had suffered the nightmares and would have to life with the guilt and the fear. If anyone was going to write a book, surely it should be him.

The anonymous phone call to my office, promising to tell me the inside story of the Essex triple murders, came out of the blue. Nicholls had persuaded his police bodyguards to take him to a bookshop and he had made straight for the true crime section where he spotted a copy my first book, *Gangland Britain*. During that first call he refused to tell me who he was or anything about what he might be able to tell me about the killings, only that he was certain I'd be interested. Intrigued and, with hindsight, feeling a little reckless, I happily followed his complex instructions, which seemed to come straight out of a Hollywood movie – drive to this service station; drive around this roundabout three times; park down this side street; pick up the ringing public telephone; and so on. I later found out that Nicholls and his minders had tailed my car for several miles to ensure I was alone. Nearly four hours after my journey began, I found myself searching for a space in the car park of the Romford branch of McDonald's. As my car drew to a halt, a cautious-looking Nicholls tapped on my window.

I have always been fascinated by supergrasses and police informers. The life of a professional criminal is fascinating enough on its own, but the life of someone who betrays their friends and gives up everything to save themselves is all the more fascinating still. Just how do you live under a new identity? How easy is it, overnight, suddenly, to become someone else? How can you live with yourself knowing that you are free only because your evidence sent others to jail?

That meeting in the McDonald's car park was to be the first of many with Darren Nicholls during which he slowly, carefully and occasionally emotionally began to recount the story of his involvement in the Essex crime scene in one of the most notorious murder cases of recent times and in Britain's little-known witness protection programme.

This is that story.

Tony Thompson

1

'I've got a gun at home. If anyone tried to rip me off, I'd blow their fucking brains out'

Darren Nicholls was nearly five years into a career with British Telecom when he came to the conclusion that he must be doing something very wrong. He'd made himself available for overtime and out-of-town shifts; completed his projects on time and on budget; spent spare evenings studying for exams and assessments; and was always respectful to his bosses. Despite this, Nicholls had repeatedly been passed over for promotion and his meagre salary had only barely risen.

That was bad enough, but what really got to him were some of the people he'd grown to know across his home county of Essex: people who never seemed to do very much but always had a hell of a lot to show for it. Some would claim to be builders but as far as anyone could remember had never actually built anything. In fact, if they tried to do so much as dig a hole in their back garden, they'd make such a mess of it they'd have to get someone else to come round and sort it out. Others said they earned their living as market traders but they'd never leave their houses before noon and then only to head straight for the betting shop or the pub.

They would always get the best tables at the local restaurants, never had to queue to enter the most fashionable clubs and were always weighed down with grotesque gold jewellery – inch-thick bracelets dangling from their wrists and chains that hung around their necks like glittery nooses. In winter they'd jet off to the Canary Islands or the Caribbean for weeks at a time; in summer they'd spend their afternoons cruising around the grounds of their palatial homes on a £10,000 sit-down lawnmower or they'd hook up their jet-skis to their BMW or Merc for a run down to the beach.

And as Nicholls watched them, worked for them and occasionally drank with them, so he became increasingly dissatisfied with his own life and dreamt of the day when he too might have money to waste.

In a bid to improve his lot, Nicholls quit his job and set up in business for himself. At first he prospered and was making more money and working fewer hours than ever before, thanks to a contact with a major property firm that would build an estate full of houses and then hire Nicholls to do all the wiring. But then as the eighties drew to a close the property market started to slow down and the firm decided to bring Nicholls in only once a home had actually been sold. As sales started to dry up, so did his income.

NICHOLLS I remember New Year's Eve 1989. Me and my wife Sandra, my mate Ron and his wife all went out to try and celebrate. We had seven quid between us. We'd spent it all by 8 p.m. and just spent the rest of the evening feeling miserable. Everyone else was living it up and it felt like we were only barely living. That was the night I said to myself, fuck it, I just can't handle this any more. I've got to do something. I've got to do anything.

Nicholls started off small, breaking into telephone boxes – sweet revenge against his former employers.

NICHOLLS In the old-style payphones, the cash box was held

on with a couple of high tensile steel bolts. Now these bolts, they're really strong in certain directions: you can't cut through them at all and if you tried to lever the box off, you'd be there until the cows came home and all you'd end up with would be a house full of cows. But the bolts can't take being stretched, so I worked out that if you put a hydraulic car jack underneath the box and pumped it a few times, the bolts would just snap and the cash would be yours in less than thirty seconds.

The very first time I did it, I was well nervous. Me and Ron had driven out to this phone box in the middle of nowhere to put my theory to the test. I wasn't sure if it was going to work so I got down on the floor for a better view of what was happening. We jacked, higher and higher, and suddenly there was this fucking enormous crack as the blots snapped. And the box fell off the wall, right on my head. Knocked me out cold. Ron just cracked up, pissed himself laughing. When I came round about half a minute later, he was still at it, rolling around the floor and giggling his head off.

Now this box was seriously heavy, weighed an absolute ton. We really thought we had struck gold. We could hear all these coins moving about and the weight of it was just unbelievable. We thought we had motherloads. When we finally got it home and got the thing open it was a bit of a shock – there was exactly £3.30 inside.

But once we realised how easy it was, we went round and within a week we did every remote telephone box we could find across the whole area. It wasn't big money – I think the most we got out of one box was about £100, but I was so desperate that anything was better than nothing.

After that it became a bit of a craze. A couple of other mates joined in (so we wouldn't always use the same vehicle) and once we'd done all the remote phone boxes it became a bit of a game to see who had the most front. We'd end up going into the town centre in the middle of the day, pulling up in a van, running into a payphone, pumping the jack, grabbing the cash box and driving off.

A couple of us nearly got caught. BT started putting little micro-switches into the money box so when they fell off the phone would send a signal back to base saying it was out of order. And whenever they got that signal, they'd send a police car out because they knew there was a good chance someone was trying to jack the cash box off. More than once I was in the van with a cash box in the back on my way home and I'd pass a police car, all lights and sirens, on its way to where I'd just been. It had started to get boring but whenever that happened, I always got a real buzz.

I'd considered breaking the law loads of times before but I was always too scared to actually go through with it. Once I started doing it and realised that I wasn't nervous at all, I just got carried away. I was spending virtually all my time just looking for things to nick. Me and my little firm were on a roll. We starting taking lead off the roofs of buildings, breaking into factories and stealing their generators – anything for a bit of extra cash.

And because I hadn't been caught I just started escalating into bigger and bigger things.

One of the guys I met through doing the phone boxes had a mate who managed a large department store in London. He tipped us off about when they had a good load in the safe and gave us a map of the alarm system and the keys to the front door.

The place had this special alarm system, which would only let one person in the store at a time and then only if they walked a certain route. So once we got through the shutters and the front door, the three of us had to stand really close together and walk in time like our feet were tied together. We'd got about halfway through when we heard this sound from the front. It turned out a bunch of girls out on the piss could see us through the window. They thought it was the funniest thing they ever seen but we had to keep going to fool the alarm system. I don't know what they thought we were up to but they didn't bother to call the police. When we finally got to the safe, there was £10,000 in it, so that was a real result.

I was trying to keep Sandra out of it but once I started making proper money rather than just a bit of extra change, she demanded to know exactly what was going on. She was horrified at first but then when I started spending some of the money I'd made on her and on the kids, she'd calm down for a little while and then get all panicky again. She was always saying to me, 'You're gonna go away, you're gonna go away.' But it got to the stage when I just couldn't do without it. Once you find out just how easy it can be, it becomes impossible to walk away from.

Pretty soon I was doing something every week. Moneywise, things were a lot better than they were, but greed soon starts to take over. The problem with the petty stuff is that it doesn't pay very well, especially when you're sharing it with two or three other people. It's like the people who earn £15,000 a year but are always broke and reckon that, if only they earned £18,000 a year, then they'd have loads of cash to spare. But as soon as they get to eighteen grand, they start moaning about how they need a few more grand. Crime's just the same. You do one robbery, make a little bit and then do a slightly bigger one. And the whole time you try to convince yourself that if you could walk away with twenty-five grand, then you wouldn't need to do it any more.

It was around this time that I got some part-time cash work on this farm in Braxted, repairing bits of machinery and keeping the generator running. As well as doing general farming, the guy had a few old barns on his land, which he rented out as cut-price business units. I got quite friendly with one of the guys who rented one, Mickey Donnelly, who, along with his brother John, had a reputation for being a bit of a hard case. There were all sorts of stories floating around about his exploits and I'd heard that a couple of years earlier Mickey had been working this scam, which involved gold-plating old pennies to make them look like sovereigns and then using them to rip off jewellers. I knew he was up to something dodgy in his unit on the farm – after all he was paying £300 per week to rent what amounted to little more than big garden shed – but I didn't know what. He was friendly enough but whenever I used to try to talk about exactly what he was doing, he always got really cagey about it. I thought the coin thing sounded like a brilliant idea and, if he was still doing it, I wanted to get involved.

Then one day I got back from the pub to find the whole farm absolutely swarming with police. There were helicopters, dozens of vans, sniffer dogs – the lot. It turned out that Donnelly had been using his shed to run a little amphetamine factory.

Donnelly ended up getting seven years. That sounded like forever to me but apparently it didn't bother him a bit. He was far more worried about the fact that the people who had put up the money to let him make the drugs were now seriously out of pocket and were threatening to make his life hell. Even though he was in prison, he was desperately looking for a way to earn some cash.

In the end, he arranged with his brother John, who worked as a printer, to run off some counterfeit money. A lot of the people who'd had been working with Donnelly on the amphetamine had either been locked up or scared off so he needed some extra pairs of hands to help distribute it. That's when I got a message that Donnelly wanted to see me. He was on remand at Chelmsford at the time. I'd never been to a prison before. It was strange, exciting, a bit of an adventure really, going through the gates and all that. The thing is, though, you can never really work out how the other person feels. You sit there, they come out, have a cup of tea and a chat and a bun and then go off, and you sit there thinking, 'Well, this ain't so bad, I don't know what all the fuss is about,' because after a few minutes you forget where you are and it all seems normal.

When I saw Donnelly he sat me down and started to give me a lecture. It was like something out of *Goodfellas*. He was saying stuff like, 'Okay, Darren, here's the rules. The first one is the most important one all right? You never grass up your mates. Do you understand? Okay. Next, you never say anything to the police. Do you understand? Good. Okay now, if you're willing to accept these rules, then you can join our little gang. But remember, if it all goes wrong, then you're gonna end up in here with me. And if you do end up in here with me and I find out you've crossed me, I'll fuck you up. I'll do you. And if I can't get to you to fuck you up myself, I'll get someone else to do it for me.'

About a month earlier, I remembered that I'd seen a story in my local paper about a guy who had been caught with some counterfeit money, and I managed to dig it out down at the library. This bloke had been caught with about £50,000 worth of moody twenties and it was his first offence so he'd been given a suspended sentence and a bit of a fine – basically he had his wrists slapped. I knew it was illegal, but it didn't seem to be a crime that anyone took particularly seriously so I decided to go for it. As far as I was concerned, I didn't have much to lose.

Once I'd made my mind up, I just steamed into the whole thing. John was turning out these first-class tenners. They had a watermark and even had the metal line in them. The paper was a bit of a let-down – it always is – but they were good enough to fool change machines and things like that, so they were a good buy.

The first run was just £30,000 and the deal I was getting was that I could buy the finished notes for £2 each. I was taking up to £4,000 at a time but selling it in smaller amounts, usually £40 for £100 worth. So I was doubling my money and doing okay out of it. The next run was going to be a lot bigger and the Donnelly brothers decided to get a friend of theirs, Martin Cymblist, to join in. He'd been made redundant from some job up North and was desperate to earn a bit of extra cash so he could afford to move back to Essex. Because there was so much cash being produced, the whole thing escalated. I was selling it to people who were selling it to people who were selling it on again. The stuff was moving like hot cakes and the money was rolling in.

But the thing about money is that the more you earn, the more you go out and spend. I don't know what I did with all my new-found wealth but I think a lot of it ended up going down the pub. I was just wasting it, probably because I thought I'd be able to keep on selling it for a while.

The money was coming in quite steadily so I started giving out small amounts of credit rather than getting cash in advance like I normally did. One bloke, Billy Horn, took £20,000 off me and sold it to some blokes who were caught trying to pass them off in some shops in Raleigh. They'd all got picked up before they had a chance to give Billy any of the money they'd made, so I was out of pocket.

Horn was a weedy little git and I think he was shit scared of me. He was terrified that I was going to do something terrible to him so he came round and explained that he knew some people who still wanted some money and that he'd put me in touch with them so that I could make back what he owed me.

He arranged a meeting for later on that week at the Nag's Head in Brentwood and introduced me to these two blokes. They were both fairly young lads who dropped a few names from the Basildon crime scene, people that I'd heard of but have never actually met. The two of them seemed really confident, cocky, like they did that kind of thing every day of the week and before too long I started to feel bit intimidated.

They had some big drug deal coming up and they were planning to pay for the goods with the moody cash. They were pushing me the whole time, saying they wanted to buy all the money I had, every single note, and they wanted to know if there was any more in the pipeline.

I started talking big to try to impress them. And it seemed to work. We started talking about the rip-off they were planning and they said to me, 'So, don't you ever worry about being ripped off?' I just laughed and said, 'Listen, right, I've got a gun at home. If anyone ever tried to rip me off, I'd blow their fucking brains out.' I was talking bollocks of course – I was just trying to act tough – but it seemed to do the trick. They almost looked impressed. They were saying, oh yeah, great idea mate, nice one and stuff like that. I remember it was around then that I started thinking they were a pair of right wankers.

But business is business. In the end we settled on £250,000 of counterfeit tenners. Now I knew that, for that amount, I could buy them for £1.50 a note. I was selling them on for £2.50 each, so in one fell swoop, I was gonna make twenty-five grand. Fucking A. Now one of Donnelly's friends, a bit of a top crim called Jason who I'd got to know quite well, didn't like the sound of it. Too good to be true, he reckoned. He was one of those guys who was living a lifestyle that first made me want to get into crime and he was really, really good at it. He'd been at it for years and made a fortune, but had never got so much as a parking ticket.

When I went to collect the money I started telling him about it. He took me to one side and said, 'This isn't right. I'm gonna come along. You won't see me, but I'll be there checking the whole thing out.'

The big day came and I got down to the venue – a hotel at the South Mimms motorway service station – about half an hour early. About ten minutes before the guys were due to turn up, I went to the toilet and as I was standing there having a piss, Jason appeared next to me. He leaned over and whispered, 'You, mate, are fucking nicked. That place is packed full of Old Bill. I'm really sorry, but you are nicked. I told you this deal was no fucking good. If I was you, I'd get on the blower to your mates right now and tell them to get the fuck out of there. It's a trap.' Then he turned around and walked off.

I looked around the foyer and I couldn't see a hair out of place. There were some blokes in suits checking in, some teenagers playing on the fruit machines, a couple of couples who couldn't keep their hands off each other and loads of staff milling around. I kind of figured that the way Jason had managed to avoid trouble was by being extra cautious, extra paranoid all the time. I found it really hard to believe what he'd told me but I decided to play it safe anyway.

I didn't have the money on me; it was in a car in the car park. I called the guy who was looking after it and told him to drive to the Trusthouse Forte in Brentwood. 'If it isn't a trap, I'll call you a bit later and tell you to come back,' I told him.

Martin Cymblist was also there. I didn't have the cash to pay for all the notes in advance so he wanted to be there at the hand-over to make sure he was going to get his cash. With the money gone I felt a lot safer so I carried on waiting but half an hour after the guys were supposed to be there, they still hadn't turned up. I dialled up the mobile number they'd given me and when he answered I said, 'Where the fuck are you, you've let me sitting here on my own like a right prick.' He was really apologetic, saying, 'I'm just outside, sorry, I got held up, I'll be with you in two seconds.'

I put the phone down and at that same instant, I felt something hard and cold jab me in the ribs and something grab me around the throat and pull me to the floor. Before I had time to say, 'What the fuck,' I realised it was the barrel of a rifle in my ribs and the hand of some dirty great copper around my neck. I was surrounded by police and every one of them was pointing a rifle at me. They were screaming, 'Get your fucking hands up, where's the gun, where's the fucking gun?'

They searched me and dragged me to my feet then took

me outside to look in my car. As we walked out, half the fucking foyer walked out as well. Jason was right. The businessmen, the teenagers, the snogging couple – even half the staff – every single one of the fuckers was Old Bill. They'd been watching me the whole time.

There were just as many police outside the hotel as there were in the foyer, so they'd seen the car with the money leave and followed it. We all got picked up and ended up on remand at Chelmsford.

Over the next few days I found out what had happened. One of Billy Horn's cousins had grassed him up after being arrested and Horn himself had ended up down the nick. To try and get off himself, he decided to offer me up to the police as the next person up the ladder.

The two blokes he set up the meeting with were, of course, undercover cops and the reason I had what seemed like the entire armed fucking response team aiming at me down at South Mimms was because of the big-mouth boast that I'd made at the Nag's Head a week earlier.

But that wasn't the end of the grassing. Later that day, John Donnelly got arrested, even though he'd been nowhere near the deal. Someone had obviously talked but we couldn't work out who it might be. Everyone in the gang – me included – was insisting that they hadn't said anything to the police at all.

They remanded us all to Chelmsford, where I knew that Mickey Donnelly would be waiting for me just as he said he would. I managed to avoid him for a few hours, during which time I'd heard that he had given Cymblist a right load of verbal, so much so that the bloke was now refusing to come out of his cell and was requesting a transfer. I was terrified that I was going to get the same treatment. All I could think was, fuck, I'm dead. Donnelly cornered me during the afternoon and asked me to walk with him in the yard. When no one else was around he said quietly, 'Look Darren, I know you've kept quiet. You did what you had to do and kept quiet. That's fine. You've got nothing to worry about.'

I only spent a week on remand before I got given bail on condition that I signed in at Epping police station every other day. Once I got out I felt really relieved – not at being out of prison, but because of what Donnelly had said. In some stupid way I felt really proud of myself. I'd obeyed the rules: I'd kept my mouth shut, hadn't grassed anyone up and was ready to face the music, to take whatever punishment was coming my way.

For the first time in my life, I felt like a proper criminal.

2

'The thing is . . . everyone thinks you're a grass'

On 19 November 1992, eight months after he had been caught in the police sting, Darren Nicholls appeared before Chelmsford Crown Court, along with Martin Cymblist and John Donnelly, on a charge of distributing counterfeit currency.

NICHOLLS We were all pleading guilty so the whole case was going to be over in a day. All the judge had to do was hear our mitigation and then hand out our sentences. I'd been out on bail for ages and was trying not to think about what might happen. Because it was my first offence, my barrister had been talking about the possibility of a community service order. I wasn't quite that confident. I was pretty sure that I was going to spend some time in prison, but I really didn't think it was going to be very long.

When I got to court my mum was waiting for me outside. She'd been quite ill in the run-up to the trial – she'd had an operation a few days earlier – and she was still in absolute agony. She was looking really unwell and really upset and took me to one side and gave me an envelope.

'Listen son,' she said. 'I don't want to see you go away. Here's some money – it's not much but it's all I've got. And here are the keys to my car. I want you to make a run for it. Go on. Clear off. Just don't let them find you.'

I was tempted. I was so tempted. But I thought I'd be better off doing a couple of months in prison rather than risk getting into even more trouble. Besides, the week I'd spend on remand in Chelmsford hadn't been that bad. I thought I could handle it. 'Nah, Mum, I've done wrong and I've got to be punished. That what you've always taught me. I'll just go and get it over with and before you know it, life will be back to normal.'

I went and stood in the dock and the judge started his spiel, then gave Donnelly – who was basically seen as being in charge of the whole operation – four and a half years. Donnelly was well pleased with that and so was I – I thought perhaps we had a really lenient judge and I was going to walk. But then he gave Cymblist, who had been responsible for cutting the notes up and adding the metal line, four years. Cymblist just collapsed and started crying like a baby. He'd given evidence against me and Donnelly in the hope that he'd get off, but because the two of us had both pleaded guilty, Cymblist couldn't get any credit.

I'd been told that I'd get roughly half of what Cymblist got, so I was still pretty hopeful. When the judge started talking about me it was as if he and I were the only people in the courtroom. I was watching his lips really closely, listening to every word he was saying and just waiting, urging him to two years, two years. And then he did, only it came out wrong. It sounded like three years. And I was thinking, 'Eh, what's he on about?' It just didn't sink in. I just stood there, couldn't speak, couldn't say a fucking word. I looked around the courtroom and saw my solicitor with his head bowed, packing away his papers, my mum crying, looking at the floor and shaking her head really slowly. And then I got taken down to the cells. It didn't hit me proper until about two minutes later. Then I wanted to scream and shout and smash the doors in, but there was no point. It was all over. I wanted to kick myself – I should have taken up my mum's offer and just pissed off out of there. Sometimes I still wonder how different my life would be now if I had.

My mum came to see me in the cells, putting on a brave face. I told her not to worry and that I had learned my lesson: 'I know 81 per cent of people with convictions reoffend, but I aim to be one of the 19 per cent.' She managed a weak smile and then she was gone. Sandra didn't come to the court. I didn't want her to be there. I knew she'd take it really badly if she was there when I went down.

When my mum told her about it, she just cracked up and cried and cried. I tried to call her later that night but she didn't want to speak to me. She just kept saying how much I'd let her and the kids down.

Darren Nicholls spent a few days back at Chelmsford Prison where he had been on remand but was then transferred to HMP Hollesley Bay in Suffolk.

NICHOLLS I soon learned that being on remand is nothing like serving a full sentence. On remand, everyone thinks they're going to get off or get bail or be transferred. No one expects to be there for too long. Being in prison proper is different. It doesn't matter whether you've been sentenced to six months or six years. As far as you're concerned, you're there forever.

I had an easier time of it than some. I don't smoke or take drugs and for a lot of people, they are the things that keep them going. When they have to go without, it really fucks them up and they end up in a right state.

Friends would visit and give me cigarettes and I'd just end up giving them out to people. They always ask what I wanted in return and I'd say, 'Nothing, they're no good to me, you might as well have them.' Big mistake.

You see, I had no idea how an inmate was supposed to

act, so I just went around being polite and friendly to
everyone and expecting them to be polite and friendly back.
I'd take an interest in what they were doing, ask questions,
make small talk and then give away a few more cigarettes –
anything to pass the time. I even spent hours chatting to the
screws. Pretty soon, I found myself being blanked by
everybody. It wasn't until John Donnelly took me to one side
one day that I realised exactly what was going on. 'The thing
is Darren,' he said with a grin, 'everyone thinks you're a
grass.'

Up until a couple of weeks before Darren Nicholls arrived,
Hollesley Bay prison had been a youth custody centre.
Although the inmates had changed, the vast majority of staff
had not and were slowly adjusting to working with fully
grown adults rather than hard-core teenagers.

NICHOLLS They knew they couldn't treat us the same way as
the kids, making us all line up and stand on the red line
outside the cells in the morning, but at first they went too far
the other way. The whole place was so slack it was untrue.
    Being an open prison there was no fence around it and, at
first, they said you were allowed to go walking pretty much
anywhere you wanted, as long as you were back in time for
meals and work and stuff. Loads of people started taking
advantage, really taking the piss. They'd sneak out to the
woods to meet their mates who'd hand them bottles of
scotch or lumps of puff, which they'd then bring back to the
prison and stash somewhere. Trouble was, practically
everything that was being brought back and hidden away
was being found by the screws, sometimes within a few
minutes. It didn't seem to matter how clever or complicated
the hiding place was, the screws always seemed to know
exactly where to look. Everyone was convinced that someone
in the prison was grassing people up. And as far as everyone
in my unit was concerned, that someone was me.

But it wasn't. Fact was, the screws had been at the prison for so long they knew every possible hiding place off by heart. They were just bloody good at their jobs. One of them said to me that he always found it really funny when new inmates came in because they'd spend months working out the best place to hide something and then he'd come along and find it in the blink of an eye, because it's always the same best place that every other bod for the last thirty years has hidden his stuff.

That wasn't the only thing putting me in people's bad books though. A lot of the blokes on the wing reckoned I wasn't enough of a trouble-maker. If the screws asked me to do something, I did it because I thought that was what you did. I didn't know any better. Everyone thought I was a right arse-licker, a sort of prison teacher's pet.

Donnelly, 'cos he had a bit of form and knew how to behave, was getting on well with everyone. He put in a few good words for me, telling them that I wasn't the kind to grass and that I'd kept my mouth shut about his case. That helped a bit – at least I could stop worrying about being jumped on in the gym and getting the shit kicked out of me – but a month into my sentence I still hadn't made any real friends. Then, just before Christmas, everything changed.

We were all in the canteen waiting for lunch when the chefs came in and started serving up a load of absolute crap. Now normally, I'll eat anything, anything at all, without complaint. But this stuff was just shit. It turned out that they had planned something else but it had all gone pear-shaped so they had knocked something together at the last minute. It was this well dodgy-looking stew with loads of half-cooked potatoes, bits of vegetable and lumps of fat floating about in it. It looked and smelled disgusting. I wouldn't have given it to a dog. We refused to eat it and demanded something else.

At first everyone was really into the protest. We were all shouting and banging the tables with our cutlery, standing on the chairs and making a right racket. But then, as it got to the end of the lunch break, the screws started threatening people that if they didn't get back to work they'd be in big trouble.

At Hollesley Bay, every prisoner gets given some job. You do the job and you get paid – not very much – but enough to buy the odd phone card or a few stamps. If you don't work, if you refuse, you get thrown out of the nice, soft open prison and sent to a hell-hole called HMP Highpoint, which is so awful everyone takes the piss and calls it Nicepoint.

Once the screws started mentioning that, the protest started to fall apart. But a few of us, me and about three others, refused to budge. If the food had been okay I wouldn't have made such a fuss but the way they had treated us was right out of order. I was just standing up for what I believed in.

One of the other protesters was a bloke from my landing who had spent most of his time giving me the cold shoulder. He was a big bloke, not a bodybuilder type but certainly not someone you'd want to mess with 'cos he always looked a bit fierce. From the things he said and the way he acted around the prison, you just knew he was really bright, really ultra-clever. When the protest had started, everyone straight away voted him the spokesperson and all the way through he'd been the one shouting loudest about how out of order the whole thing was. He'd been around a while and you could tell that he just didn't give a fuck. The last thing he was gonna do was let the screws intimidate him.

Eventually the Governor himself came down, apologised and promised to look into it. As none of us had eaten, he sent down some fresh rolls with loads of ham and cheese. As we were stuffing our faces and celebrating our victory, the bloke leaned over and held out his hand. 'Michael Steel. But you can call me Mick,' he said.

From there on my social life started to improve drastically. Mick, who was in for drug smuggling, introduced me to the guy who had the room opposite him, Jack Whomes. He was another big bloke, six foot wide as well as tall, and looked like he probably lived in a cave. He was a sweet bloke, though, and an absolutely brilliant engineer. There was nothing he didn't know about all sorts of mechanical things. One of the easiest ways to wind Jack up was to call some part of a car engine by the wrong name, pretend you didn't know what it was. He'd always start fuming and then correct you. It was funny really, he couldn't read that well and didn't really have much to say, but when it came to certain subjects he was in a class of his own. His brother John was banged up with us at same time, having been caught with Jack on a car-ringing scam. Neither of the Whomes brothers could exactly be described as the sharpest tools in the box, but it was clear that Jack really idolised Mick, thought he was the most fantastic bloke in the whole world and would do anything for him. It was easy to see why. Mick was really clever, much cleverer than anyone else there, and he was also really interesting and funny. Being a bit older than the rest of us (the Whomes brothers were just a few years older than me while Mick was in his fifties) meant we all looked up to him like a father figure. We started spending more and more time together and, along with John Donnelly, we formed a bit of a gang.

Then a bloke called Francis Reed got sent to Hollesley. It turned out that a year or so earlier I'd sold some of the dodgy tenners to a bloke in Braintree, who'd sold about a grand's worth to Francis.

He'd driven down to Great Yarmouth and run the notes through loads of the change machines you get down at the amusement arcades and was heading back to Essex with 900-odd pound coins in the boot of his car. He got pulled up for speeding and while the police were having a quick look over the car, they found the coins. They guessed he'd been up to something but didn't know what so they let him go. About three months later, Francis was just starting to think that he might have got away with the whole thing when they came round and nicked him for distributing counterfeit currency. It turned out they'd found one of his fingerprints on one of the notes inside one of the change machines. He thought it was hilarious that me and Donnelly were at the prison and he ended up joining our little gang.

Because Hollesley had such an easy regime, everyone who had mates who were elsewhere in the prison system wanted to get them along there. After we became friendly, Mick started telling me about this friend of his that he'd met while banged up in Swaleside and how he'd written to him saying that he had to get his arse over to Hollesley Bay because it was such a doddle.

I don't know how the guy had managed to swing it but about two weeks later, Mick said that he was on his way. This bloke turned up and he was absolutely fucking enormous. When he stood in a doorway, he filled the entire thing. He didn't have arms; it was like someone had stuck an extra pair of legs into his shoulders. He was just massive. Mick was really excited and took him around introducing him to everyone. 'Here Darren, this is the bloke I was telling you about. This is Pat. Pat Tate.'

He might have been a giant but Pat was a really nice bloke. Really friendly and with a brilliant sense of humour. The two of us really hit it off and used to train down the gym together all the time. He quickly became one of the best friends that I had in the nick. People used to say that he was a violent man but I never saw no violence in him.

He was only a twelve-year-old when he first got into trouble. He'd found a wallet on the roof of a parked car with more than £300 in it. It turned out to be the fund for a police Christmas party. He blew the lot on leather jackets and a record player for him and his mates. They took cab rides up to fancy restaurants in Cambridge and then tipped the drivers what must have been the equivalent of a week's wages. When the police tracked him down – all the other boys had been bragging about what they'd been getting up to – he got sent to an approved school.

When Pat was straight, and in those early days that was most of the time, he'd talk about how awful it was. He really felt that his dad beating him – and his mother and his brother – and the fact that his parents had split up when his was five had this huge effect on him. Apparently his dad used to beat up his mum and he and Russell would jump on their dad's back to try to stop him. Then he'd start beating them up as well. I used to feel really sorry for him.

I spent a lot of time in his cell – he didn't invite many people in – and he really opened up to me. He always thought it was hilarious that he had this really nasty reputation and everyone expected him to be a real monster, but the truth was the only thing he ever got angry about was his bad back. He was a good friend, he'd always help me out whenever he could. He helped a lot of people out. He was brilliant down the gym as well. Because he was so strong and could pick anything up, you felt confident that you could take on more weight than you would on your own. If you got stuck, he'd just come over and get you out of trouble.

Because he was so big, most people were terrified of him and he took advantage of that to get his own way. None of the screws would dare to strip search him after visits and when he made it clear that he wanted a job as the assistant in the gym, they just kicked out the bloke who was doing it rather than piss him off. Mick and Pat were also really close. Pat was on a different wing but most nights he would come over to Mick's room and the two of them would spent the night laughing and joking. With Pat there, our little gang was complete. And we all knew that, if we stuck together, we were big enough and tough enough to do pretty much whatever we wanted. So we did.

Our wives would come along on visiting day and, before long, they'd all got to know each other. Sandra was quite shy and didn't like to mix to much, but Mick's partner, Jackie

Street, and Pat's girlfriend, Sarah Saunders, had known each other for a while and got on like a house on fire. They would often travel up together. Because of that she got really friendly with Mick as well and that made Mick and Pat closer. It was like one big happy family.

It seems stupid that anyone should think of the time they spent in prison as being some of the happiest days of their life, but once we were all together, that is exactly what they were to me. When the weather was nice we'd go for long walks or Pat and me would go down to the gym and work out while Whomes, Steele and the others would play badminton; we'd all watch TV together, eat our meals in each other's rooms – everything. We basically just made it easier for one another and made the time go faster. And we got away with pretty much anything.

The main things most people miss when they are inside are drink, decent food and women, but we had the lot. I managed to get myself a top job in the kitchen so at the end of each day – or sometimes at the beginning – I used to keep stuff to one side to take back to the cells later. We'd always have the best cuts from the butcher, the freshest rolls, the creamiest milk, the lot.

As for sex, we made sure we didn't go without. There was an old officers' mess building at the back of the prison, about three fields away from the main complex. When we first got there and had the freedom to walk anywhere, we'd take it in turns to go over there with our wives or girlfriends during lunch and have a quick bunk-up while the others kept a look out for guards. Mick used to go there twice a week for a picnic and shag with his partner, Jackie, and come back pissed out of his head on champagne.

We also developed a system for getting other food and drink into the place. There was no point in storing it anywhere for more than a day because we knew the screws would find it. Instead, we started getting stuff delivered. We also started a rota for visitors so that we'd get a constant

supply of spirits and other things we couldn't get out of the
kitchen. Sometimes we kept them hidden in shampoo bottles
but most of the time they were drunk so quick all we needed
to do was chuck out the empties.

One time, we ordered a £60 Chinese takeaway and a crate
of lager. We got the restaurant to put the whole lot in a taxi
and John Whomes sneaked out to the prison perimeter and
picked it up. Then we sat in the cell and had a blinding party.

There was so much booze around, we spent most of the
time completely off our faces. One of the favourite night-time
party games was shotgunning cans of lager in the cells. You
take a small can of beer – you really don't want to do it with
a large can – and lay it on its side. You then take a key and
make a really small hole at the end furthest away from the
ring-pull. Then you put your mouth over the hole and suck as
hard as you can. But because there's nowhere for any air to
escape, none of the beer comes out. Then, while you're still
sucking, you pull the ring pull and in about three seconds,
the whole can of beer goes down your throat. It's a real hit.
You basically go wooooooooow! And then do another one and
then you generally fall over, unless you get your timing
wrong or don't swallow properly, in which case you just end
up covered in beer.

The screws always knew what we were up to but just left
us alone, particularly because of Pat. No one wanted to get
on the wrong side of him.

The other thing we used to do to pass the time was talk
about all the stuff we'd got up to in the past. I'd talk about
getting knocked out in a telephone box and sitting in a hotel
lobby not knowing that I was surrounded by armed police;
Francis would talk about being pulled up for speeding with
hundreds of pound coins in his boot; and then the others
would take a turn.

Jack had a brilliant story. He used to go around nicking
bits of farm machinery – tractors, diggers and those sort of
things. One day he was driving about and spotted this really

tasty-looking tractor in the middle of the field so he made a plan to go back and nick it later on that day. He got rid of the engine and chassis numbers – anything that could be used to identify it – and sold it on to some contact of his who then sold it on to a farmer in Wales.

Now this tractor really was state of the art – it had all kind of gadgets and flashy bits on it that you don't normally get – so the farmer who bought it was always showing it off to his mates. His neighbour, another farmer, was so impressed he decided that he wanted to buy one himself. He phoned up the company that makes them and asked if he could have one of the new X400 tractors. They didn't know what he was talking about. He said, the X400, you know, it does this, it does that, it has this function and that function – the bloke on the farm next to me has one. They still didn't have a clue what he was on about but they took his details and promised to call him back. Next thing he knew, the farm next door was full of police and both farmers had been arrested. It turned out that the tractor Jack had nicked was a prototype, the only one of its kind in the world. Police managed to follow the trail back and arrest most of those involved but, by a stroke of luck, Jack managed to get away with it.

Mick also had some fantastic stories, especially the scams he used to get up to when he was younger in the sixties. The first thing he made real money from was red diesel, the stuff that farm machinery and factories that use diesel are run on. You don't pay any tax on red diesel – nowadays it costs around 50 pence a gallon while the white stuff costs five times as much. But they are exactly the same, they just add a dye to the white stuff to turn it red.

When he was just eighteen, Mick, being the clever boy that he is, worked out a way of getting rid of the dye. He went out and bought a tanker and filled it with 10,000 gallons of red diesel. He then mixed in a load of fuller's earth and let the whole thing settle for a few days. The fuller's earth took out the dye and Mick skimmed all the white diesel off the top and sold it to a couple of cab firms for a tidy profit.

It was a slow process and difficult to judge how much fuller's earth you needed so when Mick found this garage in the middle of nowhere where the bloke who ran it added the dye himself, he came up with a different approach. Mick went in with his tanker, and asked for 10,000 gallons of red. The bloke filled it up and then went to add the dye. Mick offered to give the guy a fistful of cash if the dye somehow didn't make it into the tanker. So the bloke just spilt a bit around the hinge to make it look like he'd done it and then Mick drove off. He sold the whole lot immediately for three times the price and then went straight back to the garage. And that was the beginning of a brilliant criminal relationship.

Now the trouble is that red diesel only has a few specialist uses – it's not really the sort of thing that you sell tens of thousands of gallons of in the height of summer. Yet this tiny garage in the middle of nowhere had sold more than half a million gallons of the stuff in less than three months. The firm that owned the garage launched a major investigation and the bloke got sacked while Mick got eighteen months.

Then there was Pat Tate. His whole ten-year sentence was purely down to the fact that he'd been off his face in the Happy Eater restaurant in Basildon one day. He had basically gone there after a weekend of non-stop clubbing with his girlfriend, Sarah Saunders, and got into an argument over the bill. He hit the cashier and nicked £800 out of the till. He and Sarah both got arrested and Pat was found to have loads of cocaine, speed and puff on him.

A couple of weeks later, he was at Billericay Magistrates' Court on a routine remand hearing when he gave a signal to his brother Russell and a couple of mates who were in the public gallery. They all started attacking all the police officers in the court and Pat, after getting a few kicks in himself, vaulted over the dock and made a dash for the door. There was a motorbike waiting for him outside and he jumped on and vanished. He buggered off to Spain and was doing fine for a few weeks when he made the mistake of visiting Gibraltar. He got rearrested at the border and brought back a few weeks later.

Tate also used to do a lot of armed robberies on jewellery shops. He always had loads of girlfriends and he used to give them all sorts of chains and rings and things to keep them sweet. He ended up in court over it once and this ex of his got up and started giving evidence against him. He shouted over from the dock, 'One more word and I'll fucking kill you,' and she decided she'd said enough. For some reason though, it never went any further. It was a bit weird with Pat. He seemed to have got away with a lot for no good reason. Some of the stories about what he'd done in the past didn't quite add up, but no one seemed to be that bothered. We were too busy having a good time to take too much notice.

In fact, I had such an easy time inside there was no way it was going to put me off ever committing another crime. If I had gone there and it had been absolute fucking horrendous, I would never even consider reoffending. But because I went there, did the time, made some friends and had a big laugh, it didn't bother me. It made the whole thing into a bit of a game. It meant that when I did something wrong, the last thing on my mind was going back to prison. The only thing I cared about was making sure that if I was going to risk going away again, to make sure it was for something a bit more profitable than counterfeit money.

You see films like *Midnight Express* where they hose the inmates down and people get beaten up by the guards and I'm sure that for some people, it's like that. But where I was, there were people literally desperate to get in.

There used to be stories about how when it gets to Christmas time, all sorts of tramps and old people throw bricks through windows and then stand around waiting to get arrested. And when they do, they tell the magistrate to fuck off just to make sure they get sent to prison. Well, it really happens. I met loads of them. They'd talk about the fact they got fed and it was warm and they could have a good time and, as far as I was concerned, they were right.

We actually had some people, real villains, who didn't want to leave. I remember one bloke on our landing who actually started crying when he got granted parole, begging the screws to let him say. He was going, 'I've made so many friends, I'll never have friends like it again.'

I couldn't believe what I was hearing. I was saying to him, 'Mate, you're getting out, you can get on with your life, just fuck off and enjoy it.' In the end they let him stay for the weekend so he could watch the football team from his unit playing all the others.

At first I thought it was crazy but pretty soon I sort of knew how he felt. As far as I was concerned, the friendships that we made in prison were going to last for life. You spend so much time talking, so much time together, sharing, helping, all that kind of thing, you can't help but get attached to people.

We spent virtually the whole time laughing, joking and saying that this was the way every prison should be. And like the guy who didn't want to leave, there was a little part of me which hoped it would never end, even though I knew it would have to one day.

A few months on, John Whomes was caught smuggling in one too many Chinese meals into the prison and was shipped out to Highpoint. A few weeks later Pat followed him, mainly because the screws were shit scared of him because of his size and because he was getting more and more out of control. He was still nice to me and the others, but everyone and everything else in the world seemed to really piss him off. He'd started taking more and more steroids to make himself even bigger and it was starting to affect his mind. A couple of months after he left, around May 1993, Mick received parole, then finally Jack and Fran got to the end of their sentences and were allowed to go home. And that was the end of our little gang. I still had seven months to go before my sentence ended, and suddenly I felt like my world had ended. I was all alone.

When I'd first been sentenced I was getting letters from family and friends on a regular basis, but the novelty soon began to wear off. The only letter I got in the last few months was from Mick and that was only because he'd lost a circuit diagram that I'd drawn up for him.

I was finally released on 17 May 1994. I'd made a few calls the night before but none of my so-called friends wanted to pick me up from prison. I think they were afraid that someone might see us together and they'd be tarred with the same brush as me. In the end, it was Jack Whomes who drove over and took me back to Essex

Once I was back on the outside, I started off working for my younger brother, Graham, laying patios and doing landscape work in gardens. Before I went away, we'd always been pretty close, but when I got out, we just argued all the time. It was unbearable. It turned out that he never wanted me to work for him in the first place but my mum had put him under a bit of pressure – got to look after your own and all that. I ended up quitting after a couple of weeks.

I tried setting up in business on my own but just couldn't find any customers. I didn't have any recent references and it all got a bit tricky when they asked what I'd been up to for the past couple of years.

In July, another one of my brothers, Jonathan, asked me to work with him. Again, there were huge arguments within the family. His wife and his father-in-law weren't happy about him employing someone who had a criminal record. As far as they were concerned I couldn't be trusted. I finally got work with a friend of mine, Ricky. The days were long and the money wasn't much good, but I enjoyed the work and we became close friends.

It's a shame. If the money had been better then I think I'd

have managed to stay on the straight and narrow. But as it was, I knew that I was still the same person that I always was. If the right opportunity came along, I'd be tempted all over again.

3

'I've been a fool . . . I need to finish with it.'

In the summer of 1994, as Darren Nicholls was struggling to stay on the straight and narrow, another petty criminal from Essex was also desperately trying to put the past behind him.

Kevin Whittaker seemed to be on the right track: he had managed to kick his long-term cocaine habit, he was holding down a steady, well-paid job that he really enjoyed, he had given up drug dealing, and his beloved long-time girlfriend, Alison, was expecting the couple's first child.

It was the kind of life that few would have predicted for the former tearaway whose first brush with the law had come a decade earlier at the tender age of eighteen. He and two friends – Mark Phillips and Allan Venner – drunk on a mixture of cheap lager and Pernod, had broken into the Kingswood Junior School in Basildon and started playing around with some matches. The handful of small fires they set took hold rapidly and, within minutes, two classrooms were completely ablaze. By the time the flames had been brought under control, nearly £100,000 worth of damage had been done.

Whittaker and his friends were seen running away from the school and were arrested a few days later. When the case came to court, Phillips and Venner were convicted of arson and sentenced to eighteen months each. Whittaker was acquitted but was sentenced to nine months' youth custody for his part in a series of burglaries that came to light as a result of the investigation.

After his release, Whittaker went back to living with his parents, Albert and Joan, who encouraged him to find work and to try and sort out his life. He went through a succession of menial jobs, none of which lasted more than a few weeks, and ended up spending most of his time on the dole. Despite this, he never seemed particularly short of cash. Or company.

'His friends would come round all the time and they would all have mobile phones and expensive cars, but none of them were working,' says Albert. 'Kevin had also started smoking cannabis almost all the time. I told him I didn't want it in the house, but he just carried on regardless.

'Sometimes he would disappear for a few days at a time. And then there were times when we'd get phone calls in the middle of the night. They'd seem really desperate to get hold of Kevin, but they'd only ever leave their first names, no numbers. At the back of my mind I suspected he was involved in drug dealing but there didn't seem to be anything we could do.'

According to one of his old school friends, Simon Smith, Whittaker had started dabbling in drug dealing soon after being released from prison. He started out selling tiny amounts of cannabis strictly to his friends and slowly built up the scale of his business until he was trading whole ounces at a time to everyone and anyone and making enough money out of it and the dole to be quite comfortably off.

By the early nineties, Whittaker's drug-dealing operation would have been turning a tidy profit had it not been for the fact that most of his earnings were disappearing straight up his nose. 'The first time I saw Kevin snort cocaine was at a party in Southend in 1992,' says Smith. 'A few months later, he confided in me that he was a cocaine addict, but was confident that he would be able to control it. But from what I could see, it was just getting worse and worse.'

Whittaker had many sources for his drugs but the one he favoured most was a certain Craig Rolfe, an arrogant, stocky young man who seemed determined to make a name for himself in the Essex underworld. 'I met Craig about half a dozen times in all and immediately formed the opinion that I didn't really like him,' says Simon Smith. 'It may be that was because I'm a bit quiet around people I don't know but for some reason I just couldn't click with him. He hadn't done anything wrong; it was just my instinct telling me not to trust him.'

That Craig Rolfe would end up pursuing a life of crime was as inevitable as night following day. He was born on 7 June 1969 in the hospital unit of Holloway Prison where his mother, Loraine, was serving eighteen months for making false statements.

The attractive twenty-three-year-old had been having a passionate affair with nineteen-year-old John Kennedy behind the back of her market-trader husband, Brian Rolfe, for the best part of two years. Just before Christmas 1967, the pair had eloped to Birmingham, but within a few weeks Loraine discovered she was expecting Rolfe's child and opted to return to her husband rather than stay with the jobless Kennedy. The affair continued, however, and over the months that followed Kennedy became increasingly frustrated at Loraine's refusal to end her marriage. In the small hours of Christmas Eve 1968, he decided he had had enough. He broke into the couple's house, crept up to the main bedroom and, as Brian lay asleep next to his wife, smashed his skull to pieces with three hefty blows from a bowling alley skittle.

Loraine awoke to the horrific scene to find Kennedy kneeling beside her. 'I've done this to prove how much I love you,' he said before dragging the body from the marital bed and dumping it in a van at the side of the road to make it look like a bungled robbery. Just days after the brutal killing Loraine, by then a mother of three, discovered that Rolfe had got her pregnant once more. It didn't take police long to crack the case and within a few days both she and Kennedy were arrested and charged with murder. The following March, Kennedy was sentenced to life. Loraine, who broke down sobbing in court as her lover was sent down, was cleared of murder but convicted of lying to the police to throw them off Kennedy's scent. 'I done nothing,' she screamed as she was led down to the cells.

With skeletons like those in his cupboard, it surprised no one that the young Craig Rolfe turned out to be a difficult child. He had precious little time for rules and regulations and even less time for the classroom: for him, school was just a place where you got into fights and met up with your friends; studying for exams was something that only idiots did.

By the age of sixteen, Rolfe had become a classic juvenile delinquent, rebelling against pretty much everything that society had to offer and picking up a few minor convictions along the way. He worked briefly as a tyre fitter, then as a plasterer, but the only thing he ever truly applied himself to was the study of drugs, happily sampling whatever he could lay his hands on.

It was around this time that Rolfe started dating Diane Evans, a local girl with a handful of convictions for shoplifting and cheque fraud. Eager to impress the new lady in his life, Rolfe began selling drugs in nightclubs around Basildon in earnest. The relationship was turbulent to say the least, but no matter how much they argued and fought, somehow the pair found they couldn't live without each other. Just a few months after they began going out, Diane was horrified to discover that she was pregnant. She booked herself into an abortion clinic but Rolfe – fanatically close to his mother and desperate for children of his own – persuaded her to see it through with the promise that he would look after them all. Rolfe was never going to be a criminal mastermind, but it didn't take long for him to realise that, although selling drugs was a profitable part-time business, buying them was too much like hard work and something of a mug's game. If you needed some gear, all you had to do was find someone to strike a deal with . . . and then rip them off. Powerfully built and absolutely fearless, Rolfe excelled at the task.

Craig and Diane's daughter, Jennifer, was born in the autumn of 1990. A few weeks later, Craig made a drugs sale that was to dictate the path the rest of his life was to follow.

A large, dark-haired man turned up at Rolfe's house having been told by friends that there was some good quality cocaine available. As is the custom, a small test sample was arranged. 'This is good gear, where does it come from?' asked the man.

Rolfe, high on his own supply, saw no reason to hide the truth. 'Dunno, nicked it off some pikey fucker down on the coast.'

The man was Tony Tucker, another up and coming 'face' in the Essex underworld. After getting out of the army in the late eighties, Tucker had worked briefly as a carpenter before starting up a small firm supplying doormen for clubs and bars. At the time Tucker was a small-time businessman with criminal leanings. He lived in a modest two-bedroomed house, drove a second-hand Granada and occasionally made a little money on the side. A keen bodybuilder, Tucker recruited staff for his doorman firm from gyms across the county to make sure they looked the part as much as he did himself. Tucker's timing was perfect – the second summer of love was in full swing and acid house parties and outdoor raves were all the rage. The demand for doormen grew and the security business quickly became Tucker's sole source of income. His burly lads were also in demand as debt collectors and it didn't take Tucker long to realise that, even if there was no debt, big blokes with a lot of front could still collect money. One of his earliest scams involved some stables near Basildon where he kept his horses. He sent a group of heavies into the bar of the riding school where they proceeded to smash the place to pieces and threaten the staff. The next day a concerned Tucker went to see the owner. He earnestly explained that he had heard about the trouble on the grapevine and had a good idea who was involved. Through his contacts and his firm, he could ensure the men never came back . . . and all he would ask in return would be that he could stable his horses for free for the rest of his life.

Like Rolfe, Tucker also liked to rip off drug dealers. He would slowly gain someone's confidence and then explain that, through his connections in the club scene, he would be able to shift a large amount of drugs. The idea would be to give the dealer the impression that Tucker had never done anything like it before, that he was simply doing them a favour. The last thing they would ever suspect is that he was about to stitch them up. Having acquired the drugs, Tucker would then disappear to meet with the buyer. He'd return a little later looking shell-shocked, saying that the police had raided the meeting place; he'd been forced to dump the drugs and run for it; he'd been lucky not to get arrested.

There isn't much etiquette in the drug world but one accepted protocol is that, if you are the courier, the go-between in a drugs deal and it all comes on top, then it's down to you to repay the debt. Tucker was only too well aware of this and fronted them out. He got away with it every time. Few people were brave enough to argue. To take on Tucker was to take on his entire firm.

When Tucker met Rolfe, he immediately recognised a kindred spirit and took him under his wing. At the time of the meeting, Rolfe was twenty-one and Tucker was thirty-three. For Rolfe, Tucker was the father figure he had always craved. What made it even better was the fact that Tucker was living the life that he himself was aiming for. Tucker drove either a black Porsche 928s with the number plate TT9 or his brand new Jaguar XJS. He had a large, nicely decorated house in Diamond Close, Chafford Hundred, and had a wardrobe to die for. He even had enough cash to buy his then wife a Porsche 924. Rolfe was particularly impressed with the fact that Tucker hung around with the celebrity set: he was the personal minder to and a close friend of the boxer Nigel Benn, having been at the ringside for many of his biggest fights. Then there were the fringe benefits: Rolfe's personal cocaine habit was becoming ruinously expensive but hanging around with Tucker meant there was a near constant supply for free.

Tucker benefited too: Rolfe was a devoted, willing and reliable general, happy to run around and do every mundane errand that was put before him. Then there was the admiration. So far as Rolfe was concerned, Tucker was the best bloke in the world, ever, and he made sure that everyone he met knew it. If it ever came on top, Tucker knew that Rolfe would do absolutely everything he could to protect him. He would literally take a bullet for him. And in the world that Tucker was moving in, it never hurt to have someone like that around. It was a match made in heaven.

Over the next couple of years Tucker's business grew to the point that he was turning over £5,000 each week just from providing doormen. His earnings soared even higher once the younger and more streetwise Rolfe turned him on to the idea of cashing in on the rapid growth of the club drugs scene. Controlling the doors of a club instantly means that you control who sells drugs inside. Tucker began to charge dealers 'rent' of around £1,000 per week in return for granting them exclusive access to the club.

Rolfe was rewarded with what he considered to be the perfect job, one that gave him credibility at the bank and allowed him to apply for a mortgage but one that he never had to turn up at the office for. In fact, he didn't have to do anything at all. The job – a director of Tucker's security company with a salary of £30,000 per year – existed only on paper, but to Rolfe it was worth its weight in gold.

Although Rolfe had no active role in the day-to-day business, he was closely involved in helping Tucker keep other employees in check. The reputation of both men was usually enough to ensure that all those they employed behaved themselves. On the few occasions that someone was stupid enough to step out of line, the pair ensured that the matter was dealt with ruthlessly so as to discourage others from doing the same.

One such punishment beating was caught on a CCTV camera trained on the car park of an Essex pub. The grainy black and white footage shows Tucker and Rolfe hauling the man out of the exit and pushing him hard against a wall. They poke him hard in the chest as the accusations fly, slapping him in the face to encourage him to answer. The petrified victim doesn't know which way to look or what to say, but then the first punch comes. He crumples to the ground and rolls about, clutching his face in agony. The pain grows more intense as the kicks follow, thick and fast. Then Tucker backs off, breathing hard with the exertion. Rolfe leans forward and picks the man up, propping him against a wall so that Tucker can hit him some more. There are punches to the head, kicks to the groin, elbows, knees and headbutts until the man finally collapses, unconscious and senseless. Only then do the pair walk away, safe in the knowledge that no matter who might have seen them, no one would dare speak out against them.

Another film shows Rolfe slapping lightly around the face someone who then collapses in a pool of blood. In fact the man had been slashed around the face with a Stanley knife.

In July 1994, the final part of the jigsaw that would transform Tucker and Rolfe into an unstoppable force fell into place. Pat Tate was released on parole. A childhood friend of Tucker, Tate was immediately reinstalled into the business and took charge of acquiring yet more drugs for distribution throughout the clubs and pubs under Tucker's control.

Any criminal worth his salt knows that being banged up in prison is no excuse for dropping out of the game, and so it was that Pat Tate had continued to organise highly profitable drug shipments by phone while being held at cells in numerous prisons up and down the country, aided on the outside by his brother Russell.

That, combined with the contacts he had made while serving time, made him a valuable member of the team. Ripping off dealers was fine for acquiring small amounts – an ounce there, a half kilo here – but the smart money bought the stuff in bulk from reliable sources. With Tate on board, the price of the ecstasy, cocaine and speed that Tucker was able to buy in dropped dramatically. Profits from trading in the clubs soared and the gang even started re-exporting drugs to the holiday market in Tenerife and Ibiza. Tucker, Tate and Rolfe were on their way to dominating the club drugs scene across Essex. And nothing and no one was going to stop them.

Around the time that Whittaker started dealing with Craig Rolfe, he also started up a relationship with Alison Pickton. The relationship lasted several months, then the pair broke up. But after a few months they decided to get back together again. 'Kevin told me that Alison and him were getting engaged and had set up home together in Brackley Crescent, Pitsea,' says Smith. 'It took me completely by surprise, as I wasn't even aware that they were back together. A few weeks after that, in late 1993, Kevin told me that Alison was pregnant and due to have a baby the following June. He told me that he had managed to stop taking cocaine altogether because he wanted to be a good father.'

Whittaker had also found paid work, laying crazy paving with a man called Ronnie, and for the first time in his life seemed to be genuinely stable. His parents noticed that he was working hard, looking after himself and saving to prepare for the birth of his son. They were pleased that he had finally turned over a new leaf. But then disaster struck. Around April 1994, Whittaker and Ronnie had a huge argument and he suddenly found himself unemployed and with a baby due in only a few weeks. Desperate for cash to make ends meet, the temptation to go back to his old ways was simply too powerful to resist.

Whittaker approached Rolfe, who offered him the chance to be the courier in a cannabis deal that he was putting together with the backing of Tucker and Tate. Whittaker's job was to collect the drugs from a firm in Manchester and then bring them back to London. But when the drugs arrived, there was a kilo missing.

As Whittaker was the courier, the debt was down to him. He pleaded that the Manchester firm must have made a mistake with the amount, that they were probably trying to rip Rolfe and the others off. But Rolfe wouldn't hear of it: the debt was down to him and had to be repaid. Whittaker know only too well what Tucker and Rolfe were capable of. He suspected that he himself might be the victim of a set-up, that Rolfe was just trying it on to line his own pockets. But he could never prove it and he knew that unless he got the money to pay the gang back, his life wouldn't be worth living.

Towards the end September 1994, Kevin Whittaker turned up out of the blue at his mother's workplace. 'He said, "Please can you help me?"' Joan recalls. 'I said in what way? He said he needed some money to get him out of trouble. I said what sort of trouble? He said, "I can't tell you. I will tell you one day, but I can't at the moment." I told him he'd have to come home and talk to me and his dad about it.'

Albert takes up the story. 'He sat us down. He was as white as a sheet, you could see in his eyes that he was very, very frightened. He explained that he desperately needed £2,500. He said he owed the money for drugs. He said, "I've been a fool. I need to finish with it and get out of the drug business and this is the way to do it." He said that if he did not get the money, he'd kill himself, that he would jump off the multi-storey car park or something. He appeared nervy and in trouble. I'd never seen him in such a state. He'd never talked about committing suicide before so we knew he was genuinely worried.

'It was a bad time for us. We were off on a holiday to the Far East a few days later, but I decided to help Kevin in the hope that he would come to his senses and it would be the end of it.'

On 30 September 1994, Albert made out a cheque from his Woolwich Building Society account for £2,000. Kevin had instructed his parents to make out the cheque not to him but to a Russell Tate, younger brother of Pat. At the same time they handed over the cheque, Joan gave her son £500 in cash. The following day, Albert and Joan left for their holiday. They returned three weeks later to discover that Kevin and Alison had split up and their son was now living with his friend, Simon Smith.

'Kevin ended up sleeping on the settee in my lounge,' says Smith. 'He never confided to me the root of the problems between him and Alison but he was clearly very upset by the whole incident. He wasn't taking much care of himself as far as personal hygiene was concerned. He never had a bath at my home and he wasn't washing at all. The fact that he wasn't taking much pride with his appearance was out of character, because he was a clean, meticulous person. He was even sleeping each night fully clothed. He was obviously pretty down about things.'

On the morning of Wednesday 16 November, Whittaker was preparing to leave Simon's house. 'I asked him if he wanted a lift to somewhere and he said, "No, I'm meeting someone," and walked off towards Rectory Road.' A little later, while driving his car, Smith passed a Vauxhall Corsa being driven by Craig Rolfe and spotted Whittaker in the passenger seat.

'I got back home around four in the afternoon and found Kevin asleep on the settee. He woke up and we spoke about what he had been up to that day. He explained that he and Craig were involved in a drugs deal. He said that he was getting something, Craig was getting something and that it was going to be put together to give to the same person. Kevin said he was getting cannabis but didn't say what Craig was getting. I asked him if it was a good earner and he said he was going to make a few grand.'

The following morning, Smith gave Whittaker a lift to his parents' house. Having got back from holiday they had taken charge of the situation and arranged for Alison to bring their grandson to their house each afternoon from Thursday to Monday so that their son could have access. Alison turned up a little later and Whittaker spent the afternoon playing with his son and taking a few phone calls, including one from Simon Smith.

'I planned to see Kevin and the baby that afternoon,' says Smith. 'We spoke on the phone late afternoon and he said he was waiting for a call from Craig and then planned to meet up with him. I asked if everything was all right and he said, "Yeah, I'll talk to you when I get back." When I turned up at his parents' house, they said I'd just missed him. I never saw him again.'

As the evening drew on, Albert and Joan became increasingly concerned about their son. Whenever he left them with the baby, he would always call every hour or so to check everything was okay. This was the first time he had not done so.

'Kevin had seemed fine when he went out,' says Albert. 'He did not seem depressed or anything. The split-up with Alison had upset him but he seemed to be all right. There had been times in the weeks since the break that Kevin had been down, but he had not mentioned ending it or seemed particularly stressed since he had asked for the money.'

Nearly thirty hours after he had left home, Albert and Joan's worst fears were realised at 10 p.m. on Friday evening when Detective Sergeant Sharpe and Detective Constable Mayo arrived at the house and asked whether the two of them would be able travel to the mortuary at Basildon Hospital to assist in an identification.

The body of Kevin Whittaker had been found face down in a ditch at the side of Dunton Road, Dunton, surrounded by a few odd bags of rubbish. There were no signs of violence and no obvious cause of death until a closer examination revealed five puncture marks on his right forearm and elbow. A toxicology report from the Aldermaston Laboratory found that Whittaker had cocaine, ecstasy and ketamine and lignocaine in his bloodstream. Each drug was present in high enough concentration to have caused death on its own.

Police began interviewing Whittaker's friends and family to piece together his movements up until the time that his body was found. It was only a matter of days before Craig Rolfe was arrested. On 1 December 1994, he made the following statement at Basildon police station: 'I met Whittaker at a friends flat five years earlier. Over the years I have got to know Kevin fairly well. Having said that, we were not particularly close although I have done him a few favours in the past. We have only gone out socially together on one occasion and on average I would see him two or three times a month.

'The last time was on Tuesday 15 November around the mid-afternoon when I saw him standing in a telephone kiosk in Rectory road, Pitsea, making a telephone call. I stopped the car I was driving – a blue Vauxhall Corsa – and had a conversation for approximately ten to fifteen minutes. I then drove off and left him to walk to Simon Smith's house.

'The last time I spoke to him was between three and four on Thursday the 17th when I phoned him from my home address to his father's address. The conversation lasted five minutes and I can recall that he said he had been to see his little boy that morning. At no time did he mention that he was worried about anything or that he had any problems other than the fact that he was a bit down having split up with his girlfriend.

'That evening I went out to friends. I received a call on Saturday saying that Kevin was dead.'

Rolfe's statement was supported by his girlfriend, Diane Evans, who testified that he was with her on the night and at the time that Kevin Whittaker was thought to have died. The two of them had stayed in to watch a video. Nothing out of the ordinary had happened. It was just a quiet evening in.

Once the police had finished gathering the evidence, the most likely explanation, it seemed, was that Kevin accidentally overdosed. He had probably died at the home of a friend who, terrified of being implicated, had dumped the body in a ditch. But for Kevin's parents and his close friends, that simply didn't add up. For one thing, Kevin had an absolute fear of needles. A few years earlier he had been bitten by a dog and his family tried to take him to hospital for a tetanus injection. He kicked up such a fuss that they eventually agreed to drop the idea. Then there was the fact that the puncture marks were on Kevin's right arm. Kevin was right-handed – for him to inject himself in such a spot would be physically impossible.

'There's no way my son died by accident,' says Albert Whittaker. 'It was murder.'

It would take nearly two years for the truth to emerge.

Having narrowly escaped a good hiding over the missing cannabis fiasco, Whittaker had been wary of dealing with Rolfe and Co. again. But when, in November 1994, they offered him the chance of coming in on another deal, it was too good an opportunity to miss.

A buyer had come to Rolfe asking for 25 kilos of cannabis – worth around £60,000. Rolfe didn't have access to that much straightaway but didn't want to lose the deal so he stalled while calling round everyone he knew in order to put their stashes together to make up the full amount. Whittaker knew where he could get his hands on a large amount of cannabis on short-term credit and at a discount for buying in bulk and realised that this was his chance to make some proper money for once.

Based on his contribution, he should have made at least £5,000, but once the deal was in place he was told that he was only going to be paid £2,000, barely enough to cover the cost of the drugs themselves and leaving him with no profit at all. It was then that Whittaker made the biggest mistake of his life. He complained.

Rolfe promised to sort it out and, after discussing the situation with Tucker, called Whittaker on the Thursday to invite him over to his house on the pretext of wanting to arrange another deal to boost Whittaker's profits.

At first it all seemed plausible enough. Whittaker arrived to find Rolfe, Tucker and Rolfe's girlfriend in the front room, drinking. He was offered a beer and sat down to join the conversation. But as he drank, he began to feel a little woosy, and then he found he could no longer stand properly or see clearly. By the time he realised his drink had been spiked, it was too late.

Tucker had always suspected Whittaker of stealing the missing kilo of drugs. It was he who led the inquisition. 'Like drugs, do you? Well here, have some more. Have all the drugs you want.' Whittaker was held down and injected time and time again with Special K – Ketamine – and cocaine while being bombarded with questions about his suppliers. He finally slipped into unconsciousness and his limp body was taken through the interior door to the garage where a Vauxhall Corsa had been hired especially for the task. He was driven to Dunton, where his body was dumped. The car was valeted twice before being returned to the hire company.

None of this was known when the inquest into Kevin Whittaker's death was held in January 1995 at Chelmsford Coroner's Court. Detective Inspector Peter Hamilton explained that police had investigated a suggestion of murder connected with a drugs deal but had found no evidence. The file had been closed. The court also heard evidence from Craig Rolfe, who turned up with Tony Tucker. He repeated what he had said in his statement and took the case no further. The coroner, Dr Malcolm Weir, had no option but to support the police line on the death, that the twenty-eight-year-old had all but taken his own life. Depressed after the split with his girlfriend and the loss of his job, he had started to inject hard drugs but accidentally overdosed. An open verdict was recorded.

After the inquest, Rolfe and Tucker and a few friends celebrated with a night on the town. No one could deny that they were on the up and up. No one could deny that they had ascended to new heights of criminality and were joining the ranks of the elite. The two of them had literally got away with murder.

4

'If that's all they've got, they'll never catch me'

Around the same time that her lover was dragging Kevin Whittaker's lifeless body into a ditch, Tony Tucker's teenage mistress, Donna Garwood, was desperately trying to get hold of her man to give him a special birthday treat.

The pair had met more than a year earlier at Raquels night-club in Basildon, where Tucker controlled the door staff. The pair began a passionate affair and Garwood quickly became besotted, telling friends that she had met the man she wanted to spend the rest of her life with. 'In my eyes Tony wasn't the drug baron or villain he was made out to be,' she says. 'He used to say, "They don't know me, so who are they to judge?" When we met we just clicked and that was it. He was very romantic and he showed me what life was all about. We used to go riding together and were always laughing. He was a little kid at heart really.'

Though Tucker had no intention of leaving his live-in lover, Anna Whitehead, he had become equally infatuated with wild-child Garwood. He set her up in Pat Tate's old flat in Swanstead and the two spent as much time together as they possibly could. At first he tried to keep her well away from his business dealings, rarely discussing anything when she was in earshot, but it soon became impossible. It wasn't long before the teenager knew most of Tucker's business.

Despite her tender years, Garwood took easily to the role of mistress. She got used to not having her lover on tap whenever she wanted, to meetings being cancelled at the last minute and unexpected, frantic sex sessions whenever Tucker found himself with twenty minutes to spare. She also got used to never, ever calling him at home to ensure that Anna never found out about them. Instead, if Tucker's mobile wasn't on, Garwood would call one of the other members of the team – all of whom knew about her – and ask them to pass the message on.

Although Tony Tucker, Pat Tate and Craig Rolfe were the main driving force behind 'the Firm', as their gang had come to be known, there were a handful of honorary members who were allowed to mingle in their social circle and became privy to many of their activities.

One was Bernard O'Mahoney, also known as Bernard King, chief bouncer at Raquels nightclub (though he preferred the title 'Head of Security'), wannabe villain and sometime thug who had a tendency to let his fists do the talking. A friend of Reggie Kray, O'Mahoney liked to keep the company of people a good few leagues of criminality above himself.

Another associate was Steven Ellis. Given the nickname 'Nipper' because, at just 5 feet 5 inches, he was dwarfed by his companions, Ellis was the type of bloke who gave the business of crime a bad name, having picked up a handful of convictions for silly little robberies. His greatest moment came after he broke into a dry-cleaning shop and stole a whole £100 from the till. He was caught but escaped from Southend Court, dislocating the shoulder of a policeman on the way, and went on the run. A few weeks later he was caught red-handed as he tried to break into a home-improvement centre. Crime was obviously not Ellis's strong point, but he had some useful contacts, was funny and good company, and the trio warmed to him. Pretty soon he had become part of the furniture and was tagging along everywhere the Firm went.

As the morning of Tucker's birthday, 17 November, became afternoon and then early evening, Garwood gave up leaving messages on his mobile and called Ellis to try find out where he was. Ellis, coked out of his head and in a playful mood, couldn't help making a joke of it. 'Tucker? He's probably giving his old lady one. Yeah, he's probably fucking the arse off her right about now.'

It wasn't what Garwood wanted to hear. When she eventually spoke to Tucker, she told him how much Ellis had pissed her off. By his own admission, Ellis knows the remark was well out of order, but then so was Tucker's response. 'Tony thought he was the big hard man, the one who everyone respected, and I'd embarrassed him. The most he should have done was come over and give me a slap, tell me not to talk to his bird like that, to show her a bit of respect,' Ellis said later.

Instead, Tucker, with Rolfe in tow, went on the warpath. Still buzzing after the murder of Whittaker, the pair turned up at Ellis's house, where Tucker stuck a loaded pistol in his temple and threatened to kill him there and then. Then Rolfe produced a machete and told Ellis that he going to cut off one of his hands and then one of his feet. As Ellis cowered in the corner, mumbling apologies, Tucker and Rolfe took their anger out on his house, smashing up everything apart from the television and video, which they decided to take for themselves. Finally, as a final act of savagery, both men defecated on the living-room floor and spread their shit over the walls before driving off, laughing hysterically.

Pat Tate had missed out on the first round of festivities, but once Tucker told him what Ellis had done, he was keen to join in: Tate had always suspected that Ellis had grassed him up over an incident where the Firm had smashed up a grocer's shop and beaten the owner when he tried to break up a 'friendly' food fight a couple of weeks earlier. This was his chance to get his revenge. Ellis was not to be found at his own place so Tate and Tucker decided to drop in on his parents. They threatened his father and told him they planned to cut the fingers off Ellis's fifteen-year-old sister, one at a time, until he was man enough to face them.

'There was no way I was going take that,' says Ellis. 'I can look after myself, but when they started threatening my family, that was going too far. I went out and got myself a gun and a bulletproof jacket and went after them. I was coked up and whizzed up and had it in my mind that I was going to kill them. I wasn't scared. The thing about Tucker is that, at the end of the day, he's just a bully. I've seen him shit himself when a gun is pulled on him. I've seen him get beaten up, I've heard him say, "No more, no more please." I might only be small but I knew I had to stand up to them. And I knew I had to get all three of them. If I only killed one or two, the others would come after me. It had to be all three of them.'

The exact details of what happened next vary according to whose version of events you deem most reliable. What remains certain, however, is that in the early afternoon of Sunday 20 November, Tucker and Rolfe made a complaint to the police that, as they were on their way to a Dagenham snooker hall that Tucker had booked for a birthday party, they had been confronted in the street by a screaming Stephen Ellis who brandished what looked like a sawn-off shotgun at them. With no weapons of their own, they had no choice but to make a humiliating retreat.

An hour or so later, while Pat Tate was in the bath at his £120,000 Basildon bungalow, also getting ready for Tucker's party, a brick came crashing through the window. He peered out to see what was going on and immediately saw a handgun being pointed directly at his head.

As the gun was fired, he instinctively threw his right arm up in front of his face to protect himself. The bullet entered at his wrist and travelled up to his elbow, shattering bone and tearing out lumps of tissue as it went. The would-be assassin stepped forward to fire again and finish the job but his gun jammed so he turned and fled.

Later, as he was carted off to hospital, Tate was asked by a friend if he could identify the gunman. Tate nodded and claimed, 'It was Nipper Ellis. Steven Ellis. And he's gonna die.'

News of the shooting spread like wildfire. Ellis's standing among the Essex underworld was soaring rapidly while Tate and Tucker were fast losing respect. At Tucker's birthday party later that day, only around twenty people turned up (the previous year there had been more than 200), the rest fearing a massive gun battle might erupt in its midst.

NICHOLLS I heard on the grapevine that Pat Tate had been released from prison and that someone had shot him. So remembering what a great bloke he was I rang Mick Steele to see if he had a number for him. I finally got through to Pat on his mobile – he'd taken it with him into the hospital – and he seemed really pleased to hear from me. I arranged to go to visit him the next day, taking four bottles of lager as a kind of 'Well done for not being dead' present.

Just before I left, I happened to mention to a friend, who also knew Pat but not that well, that I was going to see him. He told me to say hello and, remembering Pat's obsession with building his body, asked if I could find out if he had any steroids for sale.

I was really looking forward to seeing Pat again but within about thirty seconds of getting to the hospital, I realised that he just wasn't the bloke I used to know. He was really arrogant, noisy and right off his face on something or other.

There was this young girl there, couldn't have been more than sixteen and, right in front of her, he started saying to me: ''Ere Darren, this is Lisa. She's just here to give me a blowjob so I don't have to bother my girlfriend when she comes to visit me. Do you want one? She doesn't mind. She does it for a living. She's fucking good at it.'

Then he started ordering her about, sending her off to get

cups of tea and all that, treating her like she was a bit of dirt or something. I'd heard he was running a load of young prostitutes down in Southend and I guess he'd brought one along. Once she was away, he started going on about how he was going to set up Nipper Ellis and kill him, and how people were smuggling drugs into the hospital for him so he didn't have to go without. 'It's like a fucking party here every night. You should come by again later. My mate Tony will be here, I'd fucking love the two of you to meet.'

When I mentioned the mutual friend who wanted the steroids, Pat suddenly got really excited. 'How much does he need? You tell him as much as he wants, I can get them for him. I can get fucking truckloads. Does he just want steroids? I can get the lot. E's, whizz, Charlie, puff. Tell him no matter how much he needs, I can get it. I'm the man.'

Maybe it was the drugs he'd taken. Maybe it was because I hadn't seen him for such long time that I'd forgotten what he was really like. Or maybe getting shot in the arm had affected his brain. Either way, the bloke in the hospital wasn't the Pat Tate I remembered. He'd gone from nice bloke to total wanker.

Later that same day, Mick rang me up and asked me to go over to his bungalow in Aingers Green as he had some work for me. I'd spoken to Mick a couple of times since I'd been released and I'd bumped into him once, but this was the first time we'd had a chance to catch up properly. We were standing in his kitchen and he asked if I'd seen Pat and what I'd thought of him.

'Listen Mick,' I said. 'No offence right, because I know the guy's your friend and all that. But I really didn't like him. He wasn't the same Pat I met at Hollesley Bay. He seems to have turned into a bit of an arsehole.'

Mick just laughed then asked if I'd mind going over to his mum's house in Point Clear to have a look at her central heating, which was playing up. Once we got there, it was obvious the whole lot needed to be replaced and Mick paid me to do the work. We spent a lot of time chatting over the next few days and, in some stupid way, it was a bit like being back inside. I felt like we were becoming mates all over again.

No one had seen or heard of Nipper Ellis since a couple of days after the shooting. Before he had gone to ground, he had left a message on Tony Tucker's answering machine: 'Hey you cunt, this is Steve Ellis. I've fucking just shot Pat Tate and you're next. Now fucking leave my family alone you fucking wanker.' The Firm, desperate not to lose face, were desperate to lure Ellis out in the open. They changed tactics. Rather than threats, Tucker left a sympathetic message on Ellis's machine saying that there was no point in any more violence. That Pat wanted him to come and visit him at Basildon hospital so that the whole thing could get sorted out. Even Ellis wasn't stupid enough to fall for that one and stayed well away. A couple of days later, a nurse making up Tate's bed while he was in surgery found a handgun hidden under the mattress. Tucker had smuggled it in and the plan was that, the second Ellis stepped through the door, Tate would execute him and then the gun would be immediately smuggled out and destroyed.

But it wasn't to be. After the gun was found, Tate had his parole revoked and was sent back to finish his sentence, furious that he had ended up going back to prison because he'd been the victim of a serious crime and was trying to protect himself.

A few days later, Ellis was arrested in possession of a Smith and Wesson handgun. He was also found to be wearing a bulletproof jacket. Although he was the main suspect for the attempted murder of Pat Tate, forensic tests showed that his gun was not the same one. Instead, Ellis was charged with illegal possession of a firearm and a few weeks later sent to prison, where he continued to receive death threats from friends of Tate on an almost daily basis.

NICHOLLS I was seeing quite a lot of Mick now and would

often drop in on him if I was in the area. About a week after Pat had gone back to prison, Mick called me up and asked me to go round to see him. I found him at Tate's house, where he was building a low wall and laying a driveway in the front, just as a favour to his friend.

Mick said he had something to show me and we both went to sit in the front of his car. He then pulled a bar of cannabis resin out from a bag and asked whether I thought I could sell it for him. Now, believe it or not, I'd never touched cannabis in my life. My wife smoked it all the time but I'd never even tried it – I was always more of a drinker than anything else. I told Mick that I really didn't think I could do anything but he told me to take it anyway and see how I got on. If I had no luck, I could just give it back to him. If I did sell it, however, it was down to me to fix the price. Mick wanted £600 for the bar. Anything else I made was mine to keep.

As I was leaving, Mick explained that Pat Tate had been working on some drug importations and, now that he'd gone back inside, he'd asked Mick to look after them for him. If I did manage to sell the stuff, there was plenty more available.

I went back to Braintree and made a couple of phone calls and a couple of appointments. And that was it: I had become a drug dealer. Not only that, I seemed to be pretty good at it. It turned out that virtually everyone I knew either smoked dope or knew someone who wanted some. Once I'd put the word around, people starting coming in out of the woodwork all over the place. I'd let them try a little bit and once they realised it was good stuff, they all buy some. I'd sold the lot within a couple of hours and made about £200 profit.

Any doubts or dilemmas I had about getting involved in the drug trade vanished the moment I felt that money in my hand. I took Mick at his word so far as the supplies were concerned and went to see him the next day. And the next and the next.

Mick Steele also offered Nicholls work of a more conventional nature, though even that eventually revolved around drugs. Having rented a little factory unit in Brightlingsea, Steele asked Nicholls to wire it up for him. He explained that was buying a boat so that he could get back into smuggling and he needed the unit to make a few adjustments.

The boat was a 21-foot black and orange Humber Attack, a type that Steele had owned before and knew well. Once in the unit, his first job was to build a trailer so that he could tow the boat around with his truck. Steele could have bought one for about £2,000, but he decided to build one himself so it would meet his exact specifications.

It was the same with the boat itself. Having bought it for £13,000 cash (in a false name through a friend to prevent customs from finding out), Steele ripped out the insides and built his own seating and navigation console from sheets of stainless steel. Then he bolted on a 150-horsepower Yamaha engine and built some extra fuel tanks, again from stainless steel. The tanks were pressure-tested to ensure they wouldn't leak and baffled to prevent the fuel from slopping around too much. Finally he sprayed the whole lot dark metallic blue. 'I saw it when it was finished and it looked absolutely brilliant,' says Nicholls. 'It was a total work of art.'

Despite dropping hints like crazy, Nicholls wasn't asked to take part in the sea trials. Instead Steele took Jack Whomes and Jackie Street down to Clacton and put the boat through its paces. It performed brilliantly, the only cloud on the horizon being the engine, which, while powerful, used far more fuel than expected. An extra tank would be needed. At one point in the trials, Jackie Street needed to use the toilet, so Steele docked his boat at the marina so she could use the one in the nearby yacht club. While he and Jack were waiting, they started chatting to a man on the other side of the jetty who had a smaller, less powerful speedboat.

'I like your boat,' said the man. 'What do you use it for?'

'Diving. Made all the console and the tanks myself,' said Steele. 'Your boat's pretty good too. What do you do with that?'

'Ah, this is the firm's boat,' the man replied. 'We're testing this one to see what it can do and how fast it is.' As he spoke, three other men in dayglo waterproofs walked down the jetty and got into the man's boat.

'What is it you do?' asked Steele.

'I'm a customs officer,' came the reply.

It soon became Steele's favourite anecdote and a constant source of amusement. 'If that's all they've got,' he would tell whoever was willing to listen, 'they'll never catch me.'

Smuggling with a boat was a return to the old ways for Michael Steele.

He had started out in the early eighties with a 33-foot motor cruiser, which he would sail over to Ostend once a fortnight or so with his friends Peter Corry and Paul Gwinnett. Once there, he'd buy up to a ton of Old Holborn from a small tobacconist shop near the harbour, load it in the boat and then sail back to Britain. A skilled navigator, Steele had no trouble finding his way from Belgium to a remote part of the Essex coast in the middle of the night and he never even came close to being caught. It became such a regular thing that the harbour master knew all the gang by name (he thought they were simply moving the tobacco up the coast to another shop) and Steele, ever the ladies' man, ended up having an affair with the wife of the shop's owner.

Once the route and technique were well established, Steele switched to smuggling cannabis. Steele rarely bought the drugs himself. Instead, he worked as a kind of import agent, smuggling on behalf of others and charging them £330 per kilo, regardless of the size of the load. For the sake of easy mathematics, he preferred to bring cannabis into the country in loads of 333 kilos. That way, each trip netted him and the rest of the gang a cool £100,000.

Customs had been aware of Steele since 1987, when they received a tip-off about his tobacco smuggling, but it was only when Steele used the profits from his cannabis trips to invest in a £38,000 single-engine Cessna and started making lots of short flights to Holland that customs decided to take action. Having discovered that Steele was now a major player in bringing tons of cannabis to the east coast, Operation Waterski was launched and Steele became the target of major surveillance operation.

But 'Mickey the Pilot', as he had come to be known, was too clever for them. Realising that he was being watched, he devised a cunning plan to outwit his pursuers. With pressure on their own resources, customs couldn't afford to follow Steele all the time: the plan was to catch him red-handed flying in a consignment of drugs so all that they had to do was watch his plane. Steele's next move was a master stroke. He bought a second plane and kept it at a different airstrip. He would leave his house and see the customs car tailing him in his rear-view mirror. Then, as they saw he was travelling in another direction from the airstrip, they would break off the pursuit and leave him be. Within just three hours, Steele could fly from the other airstrip to Holland, pick up a consignment of drugs, land in a field somewhere in East Anglia and be back at home with customs thinking that he had probably just popped out to the supermarket or something.

Steele's humiliation with customs finally came to an end in May 1989 as Steele arrived at the Albert pub in Colchester to hand over his latest consignment, which he had transferred from his plane into a white Fiat van. A two-man team in a single car had tailed him since he had landed, but a split second before the back-up could arrive to arrest him Steele spotted the officers and sped off. The customs team tried to ram Steele off the road but he managed to get away from them, crossing the central reservation and driving the wrong way down a dual carriageway at up to 80 miles per hour.

Steele spent weeks in hiding and might have avoided capture forever were it not for his mother having a heart attack. Steele's mother is the archetypal little old lady who goes to church every Sunday and, since the death of his father, the two had grown incredibly close. When the police discovered she was unwell, they suspected that Steele would be willing to risk everything to see her and began staking out the hospital.

They were right. When Steele reached the ward, dozens of policemen were standing around on guard. One came up to him.

'Who are you?' he asked.

Steele didn't miss a beat. 'Oh I'm Jeff, I was just looking for my wife.'

The policeman stood aside. 'Okay son, off you go. We're looking for someone else.'

'I hope you catch him,' said Steele, walking off towards the door.

Steele was in sight of freedom when another officer who had paid more attention to the briefing suddenly went ballistic. 'That's him, you fuckwits. Grab him now.'

In court, Mick was charged with ten counts of smuggling. He pleaded guilty to one – the one he had been arrested for – but denied the other nine and, in a classic display of honour among thieves, swore that Jackie Street, Paul Gwinnett and Peter Corry, who had been captured on film helping Steele unload the goods, had truly believed he was bringing in tobacco. As a result they were all acquitted and Steele was geared up to take the rap for the whole lot. As the case unfolded, customs produced surveillance pictures that they claimed showed Steele at work, but Steele pointed out that they were wrong. The pictures couldn't have been taken where or when customs said they had been. In fact, it looked as if some of the pictures had been taken weeks later than it was claimed. Slowly the evidence against Steele started to collapse, to the point that the only case remaining against him was the one he had pleaded guilty to.

He could never be sure, but Steele could not escape the feeling that if only he had pleaded not guilty to all the changes against him, he might have got away with it.

The judge sentenced him to nine years and ordered that the

courts seize £120,000 cash, half his former marital home, £15,000 from his mum's house, his 33-foot motor cruiser, his £38,000 aircraft and his Toyota Land Cruiser. And as he stood in the dock listening to the judge take away his liberty and everything that he had worked so hard for, he swore to himself that if he ever ended up in court again, he would never go guilty. No matter how strong the case against him seemed to be, he would always deny everything and fight, fight, fight until the bitter end.

5

'If we get stopped by the police, tell them I'm a hitchhiker you just picked up'

NICHOLLS I'd been hinting to Mick that I wanted some kind of active role once he was back in the drug-smuggling business. Selling the stuff had shown me how easy it was to make money at that end and I knew that the profits from smuggling were going to be much higher. Mick seemed to be doing very well out of it and I wanted some of what he had. I told him I wasn't interested in doing anything too heavy, just something to earn some extra money, but to be honest I would have done anything if the price had been right, and Mick knew it. Prison certainly didn't scare me any more, so I felt I had nothing to lose.

But Mick had some doubts. He was worried about the fact that I'd never been abroad before – I'd only got a passport for the first time in my life about a month earlier and had planned to use it on one of those cheap day trips to France, but I hadn't got round to it yet. Mick had pretty much decided that he was going to at least start off with his usual team, but then fate lent me a helping hand. A guy called Paul Gwinnett was under arrest for breaching a warrant banning him from entering Belgium. He had just been caught out by a routine customs check as he was getting off the boat and they discovered he was the subject of a ten-year ban. It all meant that the gang was one man short for the trip. So Mick called on me.

My first job was to pick Mick up from his home in Aingers Green. I arrived in my battered old VW Golf Cabriolet, expecting to head straight for the coast, but he gave me directions to a pub near Clacton. As we pulled up, I saw a bloke standing in the car park wave at Mick and make his way over. He was in his forties around six feet tall, with greying hair.

He actually looked a bit like a slimmer version of Mick, sort of like a younger brother, but without any of the charisma. He sat in the back and was introduced to me as Peter but he didn't really say very much. I remember that he had a bag with him and that he seemed really nervous, but that was about it.

I remembered that Mick used to talk about a Peter Corry that he used to smuggle drugs with, so I assumed this must be the guy, but it didn't seem the time or the place to start asking questions, so I just drove.

As we made our way to Folkestone to catch the ferry, Mick told me that he wanted me to go to Amsterdam with him to meet Dopey Harris, his main contact over there, because with Gwinnett in prison I'd be making the trips over there to complete the first stage in the smuggling process.

All I had to do was to pick up the drugs in Amsterdam, having negotiated a good price, then drive them all the way to Belgium – there was no border between the two countries so I didn't have to worry about being stopped unless I did something really stupid or unless I was just plain unlucky. Once in Belgium, Mick would meet me at the beach in his boat. I'd load the drugs in and he'd set off back to England. After that, I'd be free to make my own way back on the ferry and, even if I did get stopped and searched, there would be nothing to incriminate me.

I have to admit, it sounded like a pretty good plan and the £2,000 a time he promised me for the work sounded even better.

We got to Folkestone and Mick pulled out a bundle of cash from his bag to cover the cost of the tickets. 'How much you got in there anywhere,' I said, as a joke really. Mick looked at me. 'Eighty grand.' He said it so casually; I tried not to sound like I'd never seen that much money before in my life. 'Oh. Right. Drinks are on you then.'

You had to fill in some personal details on the form for the ferry tickets and I went to put his name down but he stopped me. 'My name's too well known among the customs people. Just put your name down.'

We got a cabin on the boat and chatted about nothing in particular until we were bored of each other and got a bit of sleep. We finally got to Ostend in the early hours of the morning and I drove all the way to Amsterdam along the coast road. By the time we pulled into the centre of the city and Mick told me where to park, I was absolutely knackered.

We walked to Stone's Cafe, which is on a road that runs parallel to the Damrak and is nearly opposite a police station. When we arrived Dopey Harris wasn't there and we waited in the bar. Amsterdam is a weird place anyway and all the coffee bars like Stone's where you can legally buy and smoke small amounts of cannabis are weirder still. They're usually full of French and British students stoned out of their brains, even at nine in the morning. This place was just the same with loads of people giggling and the air thick with that funny pong.

But what made Stones different was that it was also full of groups of English blokes just like us. And in every group there would be one bloke holding a bag just a little bit too carefully. And slowly I realised that everyone there was waiting for Dopey Harris – who got his name because of his business interests, not because he was thick – to go off and do a deal. Harris was a friend of the cafe's owner and hung out there when he wasn't dealing so he liked to meet all his contacts there. I don't think the owner had a clue what was going on.

Harris invited us all to a flat close to the cafe. The place was full of masses of video equipment, with loads of cameras trained on the front door and stairway. Apart from that the room was very basic, with a large table, one big corner sofa, a couple of chairs and a ski-machine for exercising. Apart from drug deals, it didn't look like much else went on there.

Behind the smiles and the chirpy conversation, you could see that both Harris and Mick were being cautious, sizing each other up, wondering how much they could trust the other, but slowly the tension eased and they started to get more familiar with each other. We all sat around drinking coffee and chatting about drugs and exchange rates because everything there was brought in guilders. He also explained that he had no drugs to buy and could not say when there might be some as there was currently a shortage across the whole of Amsterdam. He simply didn't know whether it would be soon or not. Mick decided that he couldn't take the money with him back to England so he decided to leave it with Harris – I guess he trusted the guy completely by then. It was left that Harris would contact Mick and then I would go over and do the deal with Harris to ensure the exchange rate was correct.

After we'd finished talking business proper, the conversation dried up so we decided to leave. I was still knackered from driving through the night, so Peter volunteered to take over the wheel. Rather than going back the way we came, Mick was really keen on the idea of coming back through the Channel Tunnel, so we headed off towards Calais.

I was well up for it and neither Mick or Peter had been through the Tunnel before, so it was something we were all looking forward to. I went to the duty-free shop at the terminal and bought some perfume for the wife and a case of lager for myself while Mick and Peter stocked up on cigarettes. When we finally got on the train I was still really tired, so I decided to have a quick kip before we set off. Mick woke me up in Dover – I'd missed the whole thing. I've always believed that bad things happen in threes, so that was number one. As I drove back from Dover to the Dartford Tunnel, it soon became clear what number two would be. The petrol gauge on the Golf was getting pretty close to empty. I suggested we stop off and fill up but Mick was really keen to get home. He insisted that he'd work out what mileage we'd done and there was still loads left, no matter what the guage said. We hit the A12 to Ipswich and passed another petrol station. 'Keep going,' they said, 'keep going.'

Then we passed the Brentwood garage. 'Keep going,' they said, 'keep going.' And we did, for at least a mile until we ran out of petrol and ground to a halt. 'That's two,' I thought to myself.

It was pitch black and freezing cold as I walked along the A12 back to the Brentwood garage. I didn't have a petrol can in the car so I had to buy one, fill it up and trudge back. I kept trying to cadge a lift, but no one stopped, so I just kept on walking. Then my mobile phone went. It was Mick. 'We can see you,' he said. 'You're about half a mile a way. But you're getting closer all the time.' His voice sounded really strange, I'd never heard him quite like it before. Then Mick then burst into a massive laughing fit and put the phone down. About ten minutes later, he phoned again and did the same thing. 'I've got my binoculars and I can see you coming towards us,' he said before collapsing in a fit of giggles again. I didn't find it funny at all and couldn't work out why Mick was behaving in such a strange way; it was really out of character. It's not so much that the guy didn't have a sense of humour, it's just that he was always so serious. It was only when I got back to the car that I found out why they were so happy – they'd got bored of waiting around so they'd broken into my cases of lager and drunk the lot. That was three.

I was pissed off in a major way and really tempted to tell them to fuck off and find their own way back, but I was also only too well aware that, in the next week or so, Mick was offering me the chance to earn £2,000 for eighteen hours' work. So I drove them home. I didn't get back myself until well after ten that morning and had to go straight to bed. In less than thirty hours I had gone from never having been abroad in my life to having been on a ferry, through three European countries and the Channel Tunnel. As far as I was concerned, I was a seasoned traveller. I'd actually really enjoyed it.

A couple of days later, Mick rang to say that the drugs were ready to be picked up. It was time to go abroad again. This time I decided to take my Peugeot 405 because I thought it would be a lot more comfortable. I drove over to Mick's and then followed him in his car to the pub where we had met Pete Corry the last time round. The three of us then went to a cashpoint in Clacton, where Mick took out £250 – money to cover our expenses.

Peter went for a piss – nerves probably – and Mick took the opportunity to take me to one side and explain that, even though he'd given me the marine radio to contact me when we got close to the coast, Peter was in charge. After all, Peter had made the same trip dozens of times and knew exactly what he was doing. If there were any problems, I should do exactly what Peter said. And if there weren't any problems, then I should do what Peter said anyway.

Unfortunately, the only thing that Mick didn't tell me about Peter was that he was a total prat. As we drove down to Folkestone, he kept on going on about what a big man he was and how people across Clacton where he lived were really scared of him. It was like he was really trying to impress me for no reason; after all, I was just there to do a job of work, the same as him. But it was all, 'If you're ever in Clacton, just mention my name and you'll be all right. It's my town, I virtually run the place.'

It was another overnight ferry so we took a cabin, which gave Peter the chance to get on my nerves at right close up. He spent the whole journey saying things like, 'If we get stopped by the police, tell them I'm a hitchhiker you've just picked up.' Basically his attitude was that if we got caught out, I should take the blame for everything so he could go back and explain the situation to Mick.

Peter was so anxious about being able to use the hitchhiker excuse that he refused to drive the whole time. Then, on the way to Amsterdam, the radiator sprung a leak, giving him another chance to panic. We couldn't find a garage anywhere and we were running low on diesel as well. In the end, we parked up on a garage forecourt at around five in the morning and got a couple of hours' sleep while we waited for it to open.

Having sorted out the radiator and filled up, we finally got into Amsterdam proper at 10 a.m. and met Dopey Harris. We agreed a price of £1,150 per kilo, which gave us just under 70 kilos of top-quality cannabis resin. The drugs themselves weren't kept at the cafe so we had to wait them to be brought to us. One of Harris's business partners pulled up outside the cafe in a brand new Merc about three hours later with the drugs in his boot. Rather than just taking them there and then, I asked him to guide me to the main road out of the city so I didn't end up driving round in circles for hours. Once I knew where I was, he pulled over and we swapped the drugs over from the boot of his car to mine and then I set off towards Belgium.

We only made one stop on the way – at a payphone to call Mick and let him know that we were on our way to Blankenberg. He had a four-hour journey across the English Channel and wasn't particularly keen to leave unless he knew we definitely had the goods. I could hear the excitement in his voice as I told him that everything was fine and that we'd meet up with him as planned. It was the first time he had done any proper smuggling since he'd been sent to prison back in 1990. As far as he was concerned, the good old days were back again.

We made really good time and got to the Blankenberg about three hours early. The area had been chosen because it had a perfect ready-made smuggling spot that Mick had taken advantage of many times in the past. If you stand on the pier and look out to sea, on your left is a beautiful, ten-mile-long sandy beach. On your right there are three or four really ugly great concrete pipes, which take sewage or something into the sea. The pipes stick up out of the water a good few feet and Mick was planning to bring the boat up by the second pipe on the right; that way he'd be hidden from the beach and the pier.

Up until now I'd been putting up with Peter, mostly by ignoring him and just going off into my own little world, but once we got to Blankenberg, he became completely impossible to deal with. I said we should just go in the main car park by the beach, like every other person in the area was doing, wait till it got dark and near the rendezvous time, take the drugs from the boot and head for the water. But he wanted to treat the whole thing like some big military operation. Park miles away, walk to the beach to check the coast was clear and then walk back for the drugs. But the problem with that was we'd parked so far away we had no idea if the coast would still be clear by the time we got the drugs. It was stupid, but that's the way we did it because Peter was in charge.

One long walk later, Peter decided that it was time to drive close to the beach and take the drugs out. He changed into his waterproofs – he'd be going back on the boat with Mick – and we took the drugs and hid ourselves in some grassy sand dunes about 200 yards from the waterline. We were sitting there in the dark with these three sports bags stuffed full of cannabis and people were walking right by us, either taking their dogs out or going for a cold swim. None of them seemed to be paying us any attention though.

We had the Marine Band walkie-talkie tuned to Channel 14. The idea was to wait until the allotted time and then switch it on. Once we confirmed that Mick was there, we'd flash a torch to give him a bearing. He was navigating in the dark using this miniature satellite link, but it was only accurate to within about 20 metres, so he still needed guidance for the final approach.

There were a couple of minutes to go and Peter turned on the radio. All we got was some fisherman muttering in French. That sent the big man from Clacton off into a right panic. I was trying to explain that it probably just meant that Mick was still a little far out. Once he got nearer, he'd override the other signal. He'd stressed that we should always wait for him to call first rather than give the game away – until there were drugs in his boat, he'd always be able to bluff his way out of trouble by saying he was fishing or something so, if anything was going to go wrong, it was important that there was no link between the three of us, otherwise we'd all get done for smuggling.

So we waited. And waited. And waited. When it got to fifteen minutes past the meeting time, Peter was practically having kittens. 'I'll tell you what we're going to do,' he said. 'We're going to take the bags and move down to the beach.' I couldn't believe it. 'No way,' I told him. 'No way am I moving from this well-hidden bit of grass to sit on the beach like a fucking idiot with eighty grand's worth of dope on my lap.' But Peter was unstoppable. He grabbed one of the bags and made off.

Just then, the radio crackled into life. 'Sparky, Sparky, are you there?' It was Mick using my call sign. 'Zulu, Tango, X-ray, Tango – receiving you loud and clear,' I replied. Mick then asked me to give him the signal. I shouted for Peter to stay still and flashed the torch a couple of times. The radio crackled into life one last time. 'Gotcha,' Mick said. After a minute or so I could just about hear the boat's engine so I grabbed the bags – it turned out that Peter had left me with the two heavy ones – and headed down to the water.

I met Peter down by the sea and we soon saw the silhouette of the boat come into view. We packed all the drugs in and then Peter climbed on board. Mick turned to me, a big grin on his face. 'Call Jack, tell him that it's all going to plan but we're twenty minutes late.' The boat had come so far into shore that it had virtually been grounded, I had to push it back out to sea and the water was coming up to my chest. I pushed the boat as hard as I could, but it just couldn't seem to break free of the waves that were pushing it back to shore. Then suddenly, the propeller caught and it shot off into the darkness. I was soaking wet and walked slowly back to the car, where I changed into my tracksuit bottoms and trainers. It was absolutely freezing and so was the water, but I was so worked up with the adrenaline that I couldn't feel the cold at all. I was shaking, but it was with excitement.

All my nerves and fear had gone and all I could think was, 'Fuck, I've done it. I've got away with it.' I've got to admit, it was a great feeling.

Blankenberg is just down the road from Ostend, but when I arrived there a little later that evening, I discovered that I'd missed the last ferry. The next one wasn't until 7 a.m. which meant I wouldn't get home until the middle of the afternoon. I didn't fancy that. I knew there was a ferry at 2.30 a.m. from Calais and, looking at the map, it didn't seem to be that far, so I decided to drive there.

When I reached the French–Belgian border, I got pulled over by one of the guards and asked where I was going. They searched my car and found my wet clothes in the boot and asked what I'd been up to. I was feeling confident and cocky; after all, there was nothing at all to link me to any kind of drug smuggling. I had nothing to fear. I told the guard that I'd been playing around in the sea earlier that day and I'd missed the last ferry home from Ostend, so I decided to go back via Calais so that I'd still be home the following morning. He looked a bit suspicious but checked my passport, ran my name through the computer and let me go.

I got to Calais and, on my way to the boat, got pulled over by French customs. 'Fucking hell,' I said. 'I've already been searched once tonight.' The guy's face didn't even break into a grin let alone a smile. 'Not by me, you haven't.' He proceeded to give the car a really good going-over but, of course, couldn't find anything, so he let me get on the boat.

I tried to get to sleep on the ferry but I couldn't because crossing was so rough. Once we got to Dover, the only thing on my mind was getting back home and going to bed as quickly as possible.

I drove the car off through customs and, as sod's law would have it, I got pulled over again. I was so tired, just so totally exhausted, that I just couldn't handle it. I freaked out. I was swearing and shouting and going on about the fact that I must have some kind of guilty sign stamped on my forehead because I'd been pulled over twice already. In the end I think they felt sorry for me. They just photocopied my passport and let me go home.

The next day was even more exciting – pay day. I'd already been planning what I was going to spend the money on and I was really looking forward to seeing all those notes in my greedy little hands.

I got there and told Mick I was there to pick up my wages. He went into the boot of the car and then laid a bar in my hands. 'What the fuck's that?' I said. 'It's a kilo of puff,' he said. 'Over here that's worth £2,200. That's your wages – apart from the £200 which you now owe me.'

Fuck. This was not the way things were supposed to happen. One of the main reasons I wanted to get involved in the actual smuggling operation was so that I wouldn't have to sell drugs anymore because it was such a pain in the arse lugging the stuff around town and then getting the money off people. But thanks to Mick I was right back where I started.

6

'Tell me when we get halfway'

Within two weeks, Nicholls had sold all the cannabis he'd helped to smuggle into the country and was knocking on Steele's door to get some more. He had an extensive customer base, supplying dealers across Braintree and the rest of Essex as well as London and Cambridge, but he kept it restricted to friends and colleagues. Despite steady sales, the new venture failed to be the boost to his income he had hoped.

NICHOLLS I had to be very careful about who I sold to and I never wanted to get out of control. I was only too well aware of the fact that I fitted the profile of a typical drug dealer – I had several cars, albeit it all of them old and tatty, I seemed to live beyond my means and had a large number of visitors each day from my wife's large family, friends and the people I employed. And that was even before I started to actually be one. But selling to people that you knew made it harder to keep it as a proper business. I was giving people credit and discounts. The money was coming in dribs and drabs. I'd expected to have £2,000 in my hand and be able to buy a decent car or something. Instead I just got a few quid here and there and a load of hassle. On paper I was doing well but I had no idea how long I was going to have to wait for the money to come in, so I was pretty stuck.

Nicholls paid off a few bills, bought his kids some clothes and took his wife out to the cinema, but by the end of the month, he was just as broke as ever.

So when Steele called in October and asked him to do another run, he was more than up for it. He got even more keen when Steele explained that, because Corry was on holiday, he wanted Nicholls to be in charge and find someone to go out to Amsterdam with him. A specific amount of money was never mentioned, but Mick implied that, as he was taking on more responsibility, Nicholls would be paid a higher fee.

NICHOLLS As soon as I found out we were off again, I went out and bought a pair of chest waders. I'd got really soaked the last time from trying to push the boat back out to sea and didn't want it to happen again. Over the next few days, I kept asking Mick who would be in the boat with him – the whole scam about coming back into the harbour having dumped the drugs off relies on having at least two people in the boat. You can hardly claim to have been out diving on your own, can you? Mick said he was sorting it out.

The day before we were due to set off, Mick called me up on my mobile and said that he couldn't find anyone to come back in the boat with him, so would I do it. He could tell I wasn't keen so he launched into this big thing to try and convince me. He was going on about how he wanted to expand the business, how he wanted to go back to using two boats and how he needed someone who would be able to get across the Channel on their own. Basically, he was saying he wanted me to experience it so that I could see if I liked it. And, if I did, well, that's where the real money was. 'It'll be worth your while, Darren, promise.' Either I was blinded by greed or just feeling in a generous mood. I said yes.

The next day Mick gave me £70,000 and gave me strict instructions to try and get grass rather than resin, even though it was bulkier and a lot harder to handle. There was, of course, method in his madness. Mick charged £300 per kilo to import drugs; it didn't matter what he was importing, that was the amount he charged. Because grass was a bit cheaper per kilo than resin, it meant that we came back with an extra 30 or so kilos, which meant that Mick earned an extra £9,000 for taking exactly the same risk. Clever boy, old Mick.

I took my mate Christian and we took the overnight ferry from Felixstowe to Zebrugge and then drove to Amsterdam. Mick told me he had phoned Dopey Harris a couple of days earlier to tell him to expect me, so when I got to the bar and he wasn't around, I knew he'd be on his way.

Harris arrived on his pushbike at around 10 a.m. looking a bit mean and serious, guided me up to the flat above the bar and then started tearing into me. He was ranting and raving about the fact that Mick was gonna get us all arrested, that he was not being careful enough on the phone and making it too obvious what he was doing.

'That loud-mouthed fucker is going to get us all arrested one day,' he said. 'For a bloke with his kind of background and experience, he doesn't half run his mouth off. When you get back, you tell him to watch what he says, otherwise he's gonna have to find himself another supplier.'

Once the bollocking was out of the way, we got down to business. We agreed a price for the grass and then Harris asked me what car I was driving and where I'd parked it. I told him, then he asked for the keys. 'Now piss off and enjoy yourself for a couple of hours,' he told me.

When we got back, the car was in the same place. I went to see Harris and he said everything was fine and gave me back my keys. And that was that. We set off for a bit then stopped off down a side street and checked the boot – three nylon laundry bags full of grass – so I called Mick's mobile and told him we were on our way and headed off to Blankenberg.

Mick and the boat arrived at the rendezvous at dusk, sticking out like a sore thumb because it wasn't as dark as it was the time before. But Christian and I loaded the boat and I got in.

I was trying to pretend that I was really cool about it, but the truth was I was really excited about being in the boat at long last. I was a bit pissed off that I'd missed out on the sea trials but I was hoping that this would more than make up for it. I wasn't disappointed. When we sped off it was the most incredible sensation. There was loads of noise and spray flying up all over the place and, because we were so low down, it felt like we were going at a million miles an hour. Mick was in front and I was directly behind him. The sea was really calm, as flat as a pancake, and in the half light you could see for miles. It was like being on some gigantic pond. Absolutely fantastic.

After about ten minutes, when we were well out of sight of Blankenberg Beach, Mick stopped the boat and started fishing around in a bag. 'Here, put this on,' he said, handing me a buoyancy aid. 'The weather's not too clever ahead so you'd better wear it. Unfortunately, I've only got the one life jacket and I'm wearing it.'

As I put the buoyancy aid on, I had a good look at Mick. I saw that as well as the lifejacket he was wearing a full dry suit – proper boating clothing. He also had a safety line attached to the console, so if he fell in, he wouldn't end up separated from the boat. If I fell in, my waders would have filled up with water and I'd have sunk to the bottom in seconds. All I could do was hold on. And pray.

We set off again and Mick told me that, rather than sitting down, I should straddle the seat directly behind him; that way, if the boat left the water for a second and came down with a bang, my legs would act like suspension springs.

After about half an hour, the land behind me was

vanishing fast – and so was my excitement about my first
ever trip in a RIB (a rigid inflatable boat). The waves were
getting quite rough now and we were bouncing up and
down like a trampoline. We'd started out speeding along at
about 33 knots but now we were down to about 12 knots. I
decided the best policy was just to keep my eyes shut and
use my ears instead. I knew that when I heard the engine
note change, the boat had come out of the water and the
whole thing was airborne. That was my signal to hold on
extra tight and brace myself for the landing. I was
concentrating really hard but one time, I don't know, I must
have just lost my focus for a second, because I slipped and
nearly went over the side. That's when I started to get really
scared. I was just about to ask Mick to slow down even more
when I heard the engine roar again.

I braced myself, but this time, when the boat landed it hit
a wave that was travelling sideways and rolled right over to
one side. I fell and just managed to grab the edge to stop
myself going over. I was rolling all over the place and I was
bawling like a baby until Mick stopped to have a look at what
was going on.

I was really shaken. I was convinced that I was going to
die, that I was going to fall out of the boat and that Mick
would be miles away by the time he realised and not be able
to find me before I went under.

We set off again, this time a bit more slowly and with me
holding on tighter than ever, but I'd already decided that
there was no way I was ever going to be making this trip
again.

'How far is it across Mick?' I asked.

'About 70 miles.'

'70 miles! Fucking hell, I always thought the Channel was
about 22 miles wide.'

'Only between Dover and Calais,' Mick explained. 'Not
between Blankenberg and Point Clear.'

'Okay. Well tell me when we're halfway.'

'Why?'

'Just tell me when we're halfway.'

Then, about half an hour later, 'Okay Darren, we're halfway across now. Why the fuck are you so interested anyway?'

'Well if I do fall in, I want to know which way to swim.'

Slowly, the weather started to improve, so I started to play the maritime equivalent of 'Are we there yet, Dad?' I'd see lights and I'd say, 'Hey, look over there, Mick. Is that land?'

'No, it's a boat.'

Five minutes later, 'Hey, how about that, is that land?'

'No, that's a boat too.'

Then I saw a flashing white light. That wasn't land either but some kind of marker buoy, which meant the shore was about 12 miles away. I was starting to feel much better and much braver. The big waves had all gone and we were getting closer to home. We were still going fairly slowly, so I was actually starting to enjoy it when I fell over again. I stood up for a minute, but then I fell again. I just couldn't seem to get a grip properly with my feet. My first thought was that we must have sprung a leak and the boat had started shipping water. I tapped Mick on the shoulder and pointed to the floor.

We stopped, switched on a torch and saw immediately that the main fuel tank had split. We couldn't see the actual hole, but we could see the fuel slowly leaking out. Naturally, I started to panic. After all, I didn't have Mick's experience – this was all new to me. But what really freaked me out was the fact that Mick started to panic as well. He said we'd have to sit on the seats – even though it was more dangerous and made the boat less stable – and that we'd have to go as fast as possible to make sure we hit the shore before we ran out of fuel all together. He reprogrammed the GPS so that we headed for the nearest bit of land rather than Point Clear. If we could get close enough, he explained, then Jack Whomes, his back up man for all his new smuggling ventures, could always come out and get us in his speedboat, but if we ran out of fuel where we were, we'd have to call the coastguard and that would mean dumping £70,000 worth of drugs over the side.

We were flying along and I was absolutely terrified. Mick was trying to work out where we were, but the GPS was playing up. He reset it to read the depth of water rather than location so he could try to work out how close we were, but somehow he fucked it up. The whole screen went blank.

So there we are in the pitch black with no guidance system, totally fucking lost and with a boat that's pissing away fuel going round and round in circles. Then Mick perked up and pointed to some poxy little light he could see in the distance. He said it was definitely Clacton Pier, or maybe Walton Pier, and that he knew where we were, probably. Either way, he reckoned we were only four miles from the coast. I was just gearing myself up to feel a bit more confident when, right on cue, the engine died and we ran out of fuel completely.

We switched to the reserve tank, but that was empty too. We primed the carbs on the engine by hand and it started up, went about 50 yards, and then stopped again. We kept on doing it and I had to rock the boat from side to side – the last thing I wanted to do – to try to get the last remaining splashes of fuel into the pipes.

Then Mick managed to get the GPS working again. I don't know what he did. I don't even think *he* knew what he did. I just heard him say, 'Fuck me, it's working again,' and at last we were going in the right direction. We had to kangaroo hop all the way with the engine firing and dying every few yards, but when we got about half a mile from the spot where Jack was, we realised it was just about shallow enough for me to get out and push the boat to the shore. So I did.

I'd never been so happy to see Jack as I was when I saw him sitting on the beach waiting for us. I could have kissed him. He helped us drag the boat up to his Range Rover and we started unloading the drugs. But the problems were far from over. The plan, as always, had been to unload the boat and then take it back out to sea so we could come in to Felixstowe and pretend we'd been out fishing or something. But with a split tank there was no way that was going to happen and the trailer was back at Jack's workplace so we couldn't even move the boat.

Mick and I were pacing around, telling Jack about our nightmare journey and trying to work out what the best thing to do was. We were so caught up in our own problems that we hardly heard Jack say that there was a problem with the Range Rover. It turned out that Jack had driven it down on the beach and gone over a pole stuck in the ground, which had wedged in his axle. He was totally stuck.

Mick was furious. Only a few minutes earlier we'd radioed him and he told us it was safe to come into shore. 'What exactly is your definition of safe, Jack?' Mick was saying. 'Because I don't think being stuck on a beach with no car and no boat and a load of drugs fits in with my definition of safe.'

We took the drugs out of the Range Rover and hid them a bit further up the beach. Mick then stormed off to his mum's house, which was about a mile away, to borrow her car. While he was gone, Jack and I set about trying to get the pole out of the axle, but didn't have any luck.

Mick came back at about 3 a.m. and took the drugs to go and hide them in his mum's garage – so that was the main worry off our shoulders – and then went off to get a chainsaw to try and cut the pole. In the meantime Jack and I tried a different technique, wedging bricks and stones underneath the wheels as they went into the air. It worked. By the time Mick came back, the Range Rover was free.

Mick had to take his mum's car back and Jack was going to follow him and then take him up to Ipswich where the trailer was and then bring it back so they could get the boat off the beach. In the meantime, they wanted me to sit around and stand guard. Great. Mick had picked up a few sandwiches and a drink from a garage, but I wasn't really in the mood for a picnic.

I was fighting a losing battle to keep my eyes open and terrified that I'd drop off to sleep and the boat would be washed away. I ended up tying the rope from the boat around my ankle, then I curled up on the stones and fell asleep. I woke up a bit later to find my feet in the water and the boat tugging at my leg. The tide was starting to come in. I dragged the boat up the beach and fell asleep again, only to be woken up by the water lapping at my feet once more. I was cold and miserable, I ached all over and I felt like I'd been there for days.

It was just getting light when they finally came back. Mick had a go at me for dragging the boat up on the rocks because I'd scratched the base, but I just didn't care. All I wanted to do was get home.

Jack dropped me at Mick's house and I borrowed his Renault to drive home, nearly falling asleep at the wheel a couple of times. That meant that even though I was freezing cold, I had to drive with the window open.

I was knackered by the time I finally got to bed – I didn't wake up until the middle of the afternoon and I took Mick's car straight back to pick up my money. Once again he paid me in drugs, explaining that he needed his cash to pay to get the boat fixed. And he ripped me off again by only giving me just over two grand's worth of grass. He said the shipment wasn't as big as he planned so he couldn't pay me more, but he'd make it up to me next time. 'And don't forget,' he said. 'you owe me £200 for the drugs.'

I sold it all almost as quickly as I did the time before and was rapidly building up a reputation as a quality supplier. I took a load more orders and went round to Mick's to pick up some more. Only there wasn't any. Pat Tate – along with Tony Tucker and Craig Rolfe – had worked out some deal and bought the whole lot in one go.

7

'I hardly recognised him'

By October 1995, Mick Steele had two successful drug runs under his belt and had earned around £50,000 in smuggling fees alone. It was time to start enjoying the spoils of his life of crime.

He'd spotted a dilapidated bungalow on the outskirts of Clacton called Meadow Cottage, which was in a prime location but in appalling condition, needing rewiring, new plumbing, new ceilings, plastering – the lot. It was perfect. The price was low enough for Steele to get a mortgage based purely on the income from his building business, MJS Trading, without arousing any suspicion. And once there Steele could happily spend as much as he wanted turning it into his dream home.

The total price was £80,000. Steele put down £20,000 in cash and took out a loan for the rest. The bungalow was empty – the previous owner had been shipped off to a nursing home – so once contracts were exchanged he began spending more and more time there, planning the changes he wanted to make and getting quotes from various workmen. Having lost virtually everything just a few years earlier, everything was starting to fall back into place. Michael Steele was back on the rise.

Elsewhere in the county another Essex villain was also celebrating a return to form. Nearly a year after being sent back to prison for smuggling the gun into hospital, Pat Tate was out and lighting up the town with a massive round of wild parties and drug benders. The biggest of the celebrations took place at Tucker's brand new mansion in Fobbing. Going under the name of Brynmount Lodge, the £250,000 luxury hacienda-style bungalow came complete with stunning views of the countryside and stables. In the front garden there was a full-size statue of a naked goddess and 6-feet high Greek urns adorned the wall. In the garage block Tucker kept his Porsche and the brand new Mercedes that he had bought to replace the Jaguar. The property had electronic security gates, a sophisticated video intercom system and was even patrolled by guard dogs at night. And Tucker had bought the lot for cash.

The day of the party started off in the highest of spirits. One of the many pictures taken shows Pat Tate, Mick Steele and Jackie Street altogether. Tate has an enormous smile on his face and looks relaxed in an open-necked denim shirt. Steele is standing with his hand on his hip and is also grinning broadly. Between the two huge men, looking like a little rag doll, is Jackie Street, kicking one of her legs up like a Tiller girl.

Soon after the picture was taken Steele took Tate to one side to discuss business. Steele explained that he was planning another drugs run in a couple of weeks' time and wanted to offer Tate the chance to buy into it. Tate asked how much Steele would charge for importing and then baulked at the £330 per kilo price, saying it was way too much; it would leave him with little profit from selling this drugs over here. Steele calmly explained that with his way of smuggling, there was virtually no risk. The chances of a customs patrol boat coming across his little RIB on the way back from Blankenberg was less than zero. He should know – he'd done it a thousand times. Sure, it might seem cheaper to pay some bozo to pile the stuff in his boot and drive it through customs, but what with the sniffer dogs, X-rays and the like, there was at least a one in ten chance of getting pulled. It would be a false economy. Eventually the pair agreed on a price of £300 per kilo and Tate promised to get some money to Steele in the next few days.

What Tate had failed to let on, however, was that he didn't actually have any money. Having just got out, he needed most of what he had stashed away to buy himself a car, pay a few bills and support the flashy lifestyle he was now living. Tucker had given him control of a couple of clubs, but the profits from those would take time to arrive.

The sensible thing to do was to pull out of the deal and wait. But Tate wasn't about to start being sensible. In fact, since getting out of prison, he had been getting increasingly out of control and paranoid. He began to fear that he was being left behind by Tucker and Rolfe. The two of them had killed Whittaker in his absence and had set up profitable deals of their own. Tucker, in particular, with his house, cars and horses, seemed to be raking it in. Even Rolfe was doing well, having paid £80,000 cash for Tucker's old detached house in Chafford Hundred. And while Tucker had offered Tate a place in his organisation, Tate knew this was more down to friendship than anything else. Tate wanted to prove himself every bit as good as the others and the money he could make out of the deal with Steele could be a great start.

So rather than wait and miss out, Tate decided to take advantage of the friendships he had made in prison, where he had become great pals with the likes of a well-known cop-killer, two brothers from an Essex family known as the Joneses who always had plenty of ready cash knocking about, and Ronnie Knight.

The Joneses are the sort of villains whom even hardened members of the criminal underworld go out of their way to avoid. Totally ruthless, fearless and efficient, the fact that few people have heard of them or their dominance of towns like Romford is testament to the power they wield. When Tate approached them, he made an offer they simply wouldn't be able to resist. Basically, if they lent him £40,000 for two weeks, he'd give them back £50,000. Guaranteed. No one wants to look a gift horse in the mouth – the answer had to be yes. Hands were shaken, the money was duly handed over, and that was that. Tate was back in business.

The parties continued. And so did the drug binges. Everyone goes a bit crazy when they get out of prison – living life to the full and all that – but Tate was taking it to the limit and then some. It got to the stage where Tate himself was no longer calling the tune – the drugs were.

Halfway through his official 'getting out' bash at a snooker hall in Dagenham a few days after the deal with Steele had been struck, Tate ran out of cocaine. He decided that he needed more and, knowing he had plenty stashed near his home, he asked one of the guests to drive him over to his place. The man had been drinking heavily and knew he was in no fit state to be behind the wheel of a car, so he refused. It was the wrong answer. Tate pulled the man to one side and pulled a gun on him. 'Get in your fucking car and drive me back to my fucking house otherwise I'll fucking kill ya.' The man reluctantly agreed. Half an hour or so later, mission accomplished, the pair returned to the party. Tate got out of the car and made his way back to the door before noticing that the man who had just driven him home was following close behind. 'Where the fuck do you think you're going?' said Tate. 'You ain't coming back in here. Fuck off. Go on, fuck off, or I'll shoot ya.'

Sarah Saunders had been Pat Tate's lover for more than six years but, during all that time, the couple were only actually together for a year and a half. 'I saw a side of Pat that nobody else saw. I was really in love with him. He had a terrific personality, but he was always in prison.' Sarah had been there when Tate had robbed the Happy Eater in Basildon. She had been there (along with his then wife) when he jumped the dock at Billericay Magistrates' Court to make his bid for freedom. She had been there when he was captured and sentenced to ten years for robbery and drugs offences. She had even been there when Tate had been shot for the first time. The pair had a son, Joe, conceived while Tate was on day release from Hollesley Bay, but despite Tate doting on his child and providing for Sarah whenever he was 'away' the strain of separation eventually proved too much.

'When he got out of prison for the last time, we would just row a lot. He'd started taking lots more drugs and it was really affecting his personality. He wasn't the same bloke I'd fallen in love with. I hardly recognised him.'

Sarah had been wanting to leave for some time but was too scared and felt she had nowhere to go. The situation continued to deteriorate and finally reached rock bottom soon after the Dagenham party. After a furious argument, Tate stormed out and told her that it was all over. She was no longer welcome in his house and had better not be there when he got back. In desperation, Sarah called the boyfriend of a close friend of hers who lived a few streets away. He turned up in his car and helped Sarah grab a few things and took her to stay with them that night. The following morning, there was only one person Sarah wanted to call. Mick Steele.

While Tate had been in prison, the person he trusted most with his money was Michael Steele. Tate had put him in charge of around £23,000 and given him strict instructions to dish out to Sarah as and when it was needed to pay bills or buy things for Joe. The pair had got to know each other while Steele was in prison and she had also become very pally with Jackie Street. As the months went by, so the friendship between Steele and Saunders developed. As soon as he heard the news about her being kicked out, Steele began to help her to set up a new home.

NICHOLLS I was trying my hand at running a business repairing and selling fridges and freezers. Mick called me up and asked me how much it would be to replace the fridge in Sarah's new house because the one she had wasn't working. Depending on how much it was, he was going to buy it for her, but he told me not to tell Jackie that he was paying for it as she wouldn't like it if she thought he was spending their money on someone else. I told him it was best if I went and had a look at it because I might be able to get it working.

Jackie Street picked me up in her Rav 4 and we met Mick and then went over to Sarah's place. It didn't take long to work out what the problem was. The fridge had been plugged into the cooker socket, so every time Sarah turned off the cooker, she turned off the fridge as well. It was around lunchtime and a couple of friends of Sarah turned up to cheer her up with some bottles of wine so we all sat about in the living room chatting about Pat. The whole conversation revolved around just how bad he was, how out of control he'd become, how much he'd changed.

It turned out that when Pat found out that her friend's boyfriend was helping Sarah to move out, he went completely mad. Even though he'd actually told her to leave, he somehow blamed this bloke for splitting the two of them up. Along with Tucker and Rolfe, they went to track the bloke down.

They basically kidnapped him off the streets and took him back to Pat's house, when they held a knife to his throat and told him to snort six lines of coke. He tried to say no but they made it pretty obvious that if he didn't do as they said, they would hurt him really badly. So he started snorting. And they made him snort more and more and more until, basically, the guy passed out. Once he was unconscious, they stripped all his clothes off and started putting out cigarettes all over his body until he came round. Then they made him snort more coke until he passed out then burned him until he came round again.

After a while Tucker and Rolfe were getting bored and said they thought the bloke had had enough, but Tate wasn't having it. He was like a man possessed. He just kept waking the bloke up and making him snort more and more until they eventually ran out of drugs. Then Tate chucked the bloke in the boot of his car and dumped him in the front garden of his house.

When the bloke's girlfriend came home, she found him rolling around naked in the living room, covered in burns and gasping for air. He had so much powder up his nostrils that he couldn't breathe through them. He had no idea what was going on or who he was. He was in a total state, just crying constantly. They had really broken him. He ended up in a psychiatric unit for three days. When he got out, surprise, surprise, he decided not to press charges.

Sarah was upset by the whole thing, but I was surprised to see that Mick was almost in tears himself. He kept saying that he just couldn't believe how someone he had once considered such a good friend had changed so much. He'd get more and more angry every time Sarah mentioned something new thing that Pat had done to her. He seemed to be taking it really personally. Eventually he walked over to Sarah and gave her a big hug. It was a whole new side of him.

Over the next few weeks Steele busied himself working on making his new house into a home. Having discovered what seemed like fifty years' worth of rubbish in the barn, Steele enlisted the help of a few of his friends to help clear the place out. The pile of old boxes, pallets and bamboo canes that emerged was nearly twenty feet high and just crying out to be turned into a bonfire. Guy Fawkes Night was just around the corner, so Steele planned a big party to coincide with him becoming the legal owner of the house.

It was soon after the work on Meadow Cottage started that Tate called Steele at home and told him he'd speak to him again in ten minutes. Both men were paranoid about their home phones being tapped so they had taken the numbers of the two public call boxes nearest their houses. Whenever they needed to talk 'business', they would make a quick call and then rush over to the payphone. More than once, Tate would cut off whoever was using the payphone and tell them to fuck off. No one ever tried to argue.

Ten minutes after they first spoke, the pair were talking again. 'I've got that money here,' said Tate, excitedly. 'How soon can you go?'

8

'Who the fuck do you think you are? Secret Squirrel?

NICHOLLS I'd just got in from cleaning the car when the phone rang. It was Mick being all weird and casual. He said he was having a few friends around for a drink that afternoon at Aingers Green, and why didn't I pop over? Oh, and could I bring my fishing gear with me because he wanted to borrow it. So I gathered up my waders, a change of clothes and my passport and said goodbye to the wife. I knew we were on for another run.

I drove over in my Sirocco, parked in the driveway and then walked up the path. Mick met me at the door and ushered me into the living room, where I saw Jack Whomes and Peter Corry, already sitting down chatting. The other thing that caught my eye was this enormous pile of money on the coffee table, a pile so big that, depending on where you sat, you couldn't actually see some of the other people around the table. But no one mentioned it.

The others nodded hello and Mick told me to get myself a drink. I walked over to the fridge and got myself some beer then came and sat with the others so the pile was blocking out Corry. Then we all start talking about this and that until the conversation died down and suddenly Mick grabbed a

pile of money off the table and started flicking through it.
And then Jack and Peter start doing the same. Then Mick said
to me, 'Don't just sit there like a prat Darren, grab some
money and start counting.'

It turned out it wasn't one big pile after all – it was several
smaller piles all gathered together. There was supposed to be
£76,000 from Pat Tate and friends, £28,000 from some
friend of Mick's from Down South, £14,000 from Jack
Whomes, and Mick had put in a little bit himself to make up
a total of £124,000. But nothing was taken on trust. We each
had to count each person's money and then hand it on to
someone else for checking.

I don't think anyone was particularly surprised when Pat's
bundle turned out to be £200 short. Mick wrote a note to
himself so he'd remember to subtract the difference from the
amount of drugs he gave to Pat. Then we bundled all the
cash into a bag so that Corry and I could get on our way.

Although Corry hadn't put any money into the deal, Mick
once again insisted on giving me the big speech about how,
if there were any decisions to be made, Corry should make
them because he was the experienced one. Then, just like
before, he gave me rather than Corry the radio.

'What do you reckon the weather will be like for the
crossing this time, Mick?' I asked. He shrugged. 'All right I
suppose, certainly not as bad as the last time we came over.'
That wasn't what I wanted to hear. I wanted to hear that it
was going to be the worst crossing ever, that Corry was
going to hate every minute of it. 'Well,' I said, 'I'll keep my
fingers crossed for the two of you.'

The plan this time was for Corry and I to take the ferry as a
couple of foot passengers and then hire a car once we got to
Amsterdam. Although there's no real border between
Amsterdam and Belgium, Mick was always concerned that a
British car driving between the two was far more likely to be
stopped than a local one. As far as he was concerned, we'd
been lucky up until then, but now he didn't want to take any

more chances, especially as he'd gone over the magic
£100,000 mark for the first time.

On the way down to Harwich, in the light of what Mick
had said, I made the decision to make a real effort to get on
with Corry, but somehow, he managed to start pissing me off
almost straightaway. When we got to the docks, he refused
to buy the tickets because he didn't want to get seen by the
cameras, then he refused to carry the money through
customs and insisted on walking through on his own ten
minutes after I'd gone through, just to be sure he could say
he wasn't with me if it all came on top.

I suppose the thing that really got to me was the way he
spent so much of the time bragging about what a big man
he was and how so many people were scared of him. The
truth was he was a spineless twat with no bottle. And I was
lumbered with him.

We got a cabin on the boat and I left Corry there to look
after the money while I went off and had a few drinks in the
bar then went to the casino. I lost a fair bit of money, but I
didn't care. I stayed there for the rest of the trip just so I
could avoid Corry.

The next morning, Paranoid Peter was living up to his
name in full. He made sure that I carried the money through
Dutch customs when we got off the ferry and he stayed a
little way behind me. Then he insisted that I booked the train
tickets in my name and, when the ticket inspector came
along, he made sure it was me who had the money, just in
case. But when we got within spitting distance of Stone's
Cafe, he had a sudden change of heart.

'Give me the bag,' he said.

'Eh? What for?'

'Look, don't fuck about. You know I'm in charge here. Just
give me the fucking bag.'

I didn't have the energy to argue. I thought fuck it, if he
wants to look like the big man, as if he's been the one in
charge of the money the whole time, let him.

This time Harris was waiting for us along with one of his Dutch partners when we got to the cafe. I'd seen this other guy hanging around before – he was the one who led me out of the city the first time I brought drugs from there – but this was the first time he had actually been there while we were striking the deal. He didn't say anything the whole time; he just sat in the background making me nervous.

We wanted grass but Harris checked with his partner then said there wasn't any around. That seemed fair enough – after all the first time we'd gone over he didn't have anything at all – so we settled for resin. We fixed the price and I checked the exchange rate on Teletext. It worked out that we were getting the stuff for £1,125 per kilo, roughly half what it would be worth once we got it back to Britain.

It was pretty much then that the problems began. Corry started getting the money out, emptying his gear including his dry suit on to the floor and Harris looked over and said, 'Oh, what's that?' So as quick as a flash, I said it was a flying suit for the helicopter. Corry looked at me as if I was totally mad, like I'd lost the plot. 'Don't be soft,' he said, 'it's my waterproof for the boat.' He then looked at Harris and raised his eyes to the ceiling like I was some kind of moron. I was still trying to think on my feet, trying to save the day. 'Yeah,' I said, 'but they only use the boat if they're having a problem with the helicopter, but it's fine today.' I'm no expert in the drug business but one thing I do know is that you don't trust anybody and you don't tell anybody any more than they need to know. It's just too big a risk. And telling your supplier just how you're going to get the stuff out of the country is pretty fucking high up on the list on things not to do. But that's just what Corry had done, and to make it worse, Corry didn't even realise how daft he'd been.

That was just the first hiccup. The deal was done and the next step was to hire a car to drive to Belgium. Me, Dopey Harris and Corry took a cab over to Eurocar, where I'd pre-booked a Toledo. I filled in the form, smiled at the man behind the counter and handed over my credit card. He ran it through the machine, frowned and handed it back. It had been declined. The car company asked if I knew how much I had left on my limit and I told them – about £250. That turned out to be the problem. They used to charge only £200 deposit but they'd had a spate of people hiring cars then sodding off to Germany and selling them for a huge profit. Since then they had upped the amount of deposit they took to £500.

Harris was not impressed and wasn't about to let me use his card, while Corry didn't have one so we were buggered. In the end we went back to the bar and I used Harris's payphone to call the TSB back in Braintree and ask if there was anything I could do. They said if I could get someone to pay cash in at my local branch, they would credit it on my card immediately. I got straight on the phone to Sandra, who then had to go rushing about like a blue-arsed fly trying to borrow money off people. Within about an hour she'd got £300 together and paid it in and the three of us got another cab back over to Eurocar. This time, Corry realised that he'd left all the bags in the boot and ended up chasing this cab about half a mile down the road until it stopped at some traffic lights. I don't think Harris was particularly impressed at that either. He must have thought we were some kind of slapstick comedy duo trying out for Dutch television rather than a pair of serious drug smugglers, but I guess our money was as good as anyone else's.

We finally got the car, drove back to Harris's and parked in a road around the corner from the bar to wait for the drugs to arrive. About ten minutes later Harris and two cronies turned up carrying five cardboard boxes between them. I'd expected the drugs to have been packed in bags or wrapped in plastic – that's the way they had come the last couple of times – but Harris just mumbled something about not having any bags in stock and proceeded to dump the boxes in the boot. We didn't have time to argue – all the problems with hiring the car had put us well behind schedule and I only had a couple of hours to get to Belgium. Once we got on the motorway, I just followed whichever car was going the fastest and hoped that if anyone got stopped, it would be them not me. The last thing I needed was a speeding ticket.

We got to Blankenberg with a few minutes to spare so I bought some bags from this supermarket across the harbour and Corry and I started transferring the drugs over. In our rush to leave Amsterdam, I hadn't realised just how badly packed the drugs were. Even the individual blocks hadn't been wrapped up properly – the whole lot had just been thrown together. There was no way any of it was going to be waterproof. Then Corry and I realised that we'd run out of bags and the shop we'd bought them from had shut for the evening. We ended up having to leave one load in the box – not the best place to store something for a 70-mile trip across the sea, but we just didn't have any choice.

By the time we finished it was almost the rendezvous time and Corry started taking charge again. He insisted on doing things by the book: parking about 2 miles away and walking down to the beach to check the coast was clear, walking back to the car and then bringing it a little closer. I just looked at him and shook my head. I'd already spent twenty-four hours too long in his company and it was really starting to get to me. Whether he was in charge or not, I wasn't going to behave like a prat unless it was absolutely necessary.

'Who the fuck do you think you are,' I said to him. 'Secret Squirrel? Look we're parking here and that's it. If the coast isn't clear, we'll see it from the car and we can drive away. If you don't like it, you can just fuck right off.'

That pissed him off something rotten, so after we'd put our waterproofs on and started taking the bags down to the beach, he stormed off in a huff. And in the wrong direction. I pointed out that he was at the first concrete pipe and that the meeting place was at the second one.

He looked at me with daggers in his eyes. Basically he was

so pissed off with me he didn't want to agree about anything. If I had told him his name was Peter he'd have wanted to have a row about it. 'No it ain't. It's always the first one.'

I shook my head. 'No it isn't. The reason it isn't, moron, is because if it was the first one you'd be too close to the fucking pier.'

'Darren, I think you're forgetting who is in charge here.'

So I left it.

By now Mick was five minutes late and Corry was in quarter panic mode. We were sitting in a sand dune on this little mound of grass surrounded by bags of puff, looking out over the water and listening to the radio for Mick to come in. But he didn't. And there was nothing we could do apart from wait. And wait.

Fifteen minutes later and Corry was in half panic mode. I was starting to feel a bit uncomfortable myself. There were all these people taking their dogs out for walks on the beach, passing within just a few yards of us each time. And as they passed us, their dogs were going absolutely fucking mad for the drugs. I mean these dogs were going crazy for the stuff, tearing at their leashes and barking like crazy. And all we could do was sit there in our waterproofs with these dodgy-looking bags and pretend we didn't know what was going on. And wait. And wait.

Mick was now twenty-five minutes late and Corry had missed out the interim stage and had gone into full panic mode. He grabbed one of the bags (the lightest one, surprise, surprise) and ran down to the water, desperately scanning the sea for any sign of Mick. Just then the radio crackled to life. 'Sparkey, come in Sparkey.'

'Yeah I'm here.'

'Okay,' said Mick, 'flash your torch.' I did and he told me that he couldn't see it. I flashed it again, but he still couldn't see it. 'Where the fuck are you? I'm at the beach,' he yelled. 'I'm actually on the fucking sand, where are you?' I grabbed the other bags and dragged them down the beach but still couldn't see Mick, let alone hear the boat. Corry was literally running around in circles and generally being useless so I flashed the torch again.

'I see you,' said Mick. 'You're in the wrong fucking place. You're fucking miles away. What are you doing there?'

Mick had, quite rightly, parked at the second concrete pipe, so Corry and I had to drag all the drugs about a quarter of a mile to where he was. There was no point in explaining. I knew that whatever I said, Corry had a good four hours to convince him that it was my fault so I just pushed the boat back out to sea and waved them goodbye. And good riddance.

I thought I'd had more than enough excitement for one night but unfortunately it wasn't quite over yet. I'd parked the Toledo right next to this karate club and when they saw some bloke in waders struggling to get into a car – my hands were freezing from the water and I couldn't work the lock properly – they thought I was a car thief. The next thing I know, there were twenty-five massive blokes in judo suits running towards me shouting out in French. I didn't have a clue what they were saying but decided I wasn't going to hang about to find out. I got in the car and watched them grow small in the rear-view mirror. What a night.

I drove back to Amsterdam and got totally lost trying to find the car hire place so in the end I flagged down a cab and got him to drive there so I could follow him. After that, I got the cab to take me to the Delta Hotel. It was too late to get a ferry back to England and I fancied a few beers anyway so I spent the night in Stone's bar talking bollocks and drinking myself into a stupor. By the time I got back to the hotel I was shattered. I slept like a baby. It might have been a bit of a nightmare, but at least nothing else could go wrong.

9

'Surely you know your own brother?'

Just after 2.30 a.m. on 8 November 1995, Essex Police Constables Crick and Cohen were called to Felixstowe Ferry car park to investigate a report of three men landing a boat in suspicious circumstances.

The pair arrived to find a blue D-reg Range Rover attached to a trailer with a large inflatable boat on it in the car park close to the sailing club. The side lights of the Range Rover were on and the doors were open but there was no one was around. PC Cohen was examining the vehicle and making a note of the large iron bar that had been placed between the front seats when a someone came running over from the direction of the sea defences.

'Oh,' said the man, slowing down when he realised that he was dealing with two policemen. 'I thought someone was trying to steal my motor.'

'So all these items belong to you, do they, sir?' asked PC Crick.

'Well the boat is, but the Range Rover belongs to my brother. We've just been out diving, me, my brother and Gordon Stevens. You've just missed my brother. He drove off about ten minutes ago. He's got all the wetsuits and diving gear with him.'

'Diving? In the middle of the night? What's the point, you can see anything.'

The man scratched his head for a second. 'Well the thing is, the water's not that clear anyway so it's just as good at night as it is during the day. But anyway, we didn't get much diving in, we had a bit of trouble with the boat, that's why we've been out so late.'

'I see. And what would your name be, sir?' asked PC Crick.

'Whomes,' came the reply. 'Jack Whomes.'

Just then a second man appeared by the slope over the embankment but vanished again as soon as he saw what was going on. PC Cohen rushed over to try to find him.

At the top of the slope he looked to his left and saw lights on in a wooden beach cabin called Feronia. He could see a man standing by the window looking at him and walked to have a word. The man identified himself as Gordon Stevens and, according to Cohen, behaved in a way that looked evasive and uncomfortable.

He said he had helped a couple of people who had had difficulty with their boat on a sandbank but didn't know their names. PC Cohen asked if he could look inside the house to see if anyone else was there. Stevens refused.

By now other police officers were starting to arrive and they escorted two men who had been hovering around the nearby sand dunes to PC Cohen just outside Feronia. Both men refused to give their names. One of them was in a furious mood. 'Why the hell have you surrounded this bloke's house with police officers? He hasn't done anything wrong. This is his home, for fuck's sake. Don't you people have any respect?'

Eventually the man calmed down and reluctantly gave his name. Michael Steele. When no one reacted, no one instantly reached for the handcuffs, he seemed almost surprised. As far as the police were concerned, he wasn't one of the men who had been in the boat with Jack Whomes. He clearly knew Gordon Stevens but that was the only connection they could come up with. He was pretty much free to do what he wanted.

Once Steele had relented and given his name, the man with him finally agreed to do the same. He was Peter Corry.

The police now concentrated their efforts on Whomes. It was his boat after all, and they needed his permission in order to search it. Nothing was found so Whomes was told to wait until the customs officers arrived while Steele and Corry simply wandered in and out of Stevens' house, chatting quietly to one another.

With hindsight it might have seemed a little naive, but at the time the officers at the scene felt they were doing the right thing. There didn't appear to be anything in the boat and, although the men were acting a little suspiciously, there really didn't seem to be anything going on. When Steele asked if he could start cleaning the boat to prevent the salt deposits from building up on it, they saw no reason to say no to him.

And so it was that customs officers arrived some twenty minutes later and saw their sworn enemy – the man they had vowed would never make them look stupid again – washing down his flashy new boat with a bucket of hot soapy water that Steele got the treatment he'd been expecting all night long. There was a chorus of screams – 'Get that man the fuck away from that boat' – and Steele and the others were dragged away in handcuffs.

At 4.25 a.m., Steele, Whomes and Corry were all arrested for being concerned in the importation of drugs. The process of gathering evidence against them began.

Back in Basildon, Tony Tucker was having a sleepless night. He wasn't worried about Steele and the drugs. As far as he was concerned at that time, everything was going according to plan and his little £15,000 investment was about to double in value. Tucker was nervous because the previous evening, he had performed the ultimate act of friendship: he had given Pat

Tate the keys to his black Porsche so he and his new girlfriend Lizzie could go for a spin down to Southend.

Tucker was in a difficult position. Tate was his best friend and a fully grown man. You couldn't treat him like a child. But then again, Tate had only been out of prison for a couple of weeks and was smack bang in the middle of this hedonistic bender where he was burning the candle at both ends and living life to the limit, rather like an irresponsible teenager. So irresponsible, in fact, that despite the fact he was driving his best friend's valuable and cherished sports car, Tate had spent most of the day indulging in his favourite cocktail – Special K and cocaine. The result was inevitable: as he sped across a mini-roundabout on the edge of the A127, he lost control and smashed headfirst into a set of railings, instantly converting Tucker's pride and joy into a twisted heap of scrap metal.

By then, Tucker had heard that Steele had been arrested, but he had no idea what was going on. When Tate phoned to tell him about his car, he just started ranting and raving, screaming out abuse, 'That fucking bastard, all he was trying to do was impress some silly young tart.' Tucker was even more pissed off because Tate, still high on his drugs cocktail, couldn't stop giggling. Even when he explained that he'd been arrested on suspicion of having stolen the car, driving without insurance and driving under the influence, he'd break into a big belly laugh every few sentences. Then, to rub salt in the wounds, a still giggling Tate asked whether Tucker would mind getting into one of his other cars, driving down to Southend police station and giving him a lift home.

Under the circumstances it was almost a pleasure for Tucker, on his arrival, to tell Tate that Steele had been arrested. Although Tucker stood to lose some cash, Tate had put more than £55,000 in the deal, most of it borrowed from the notorious Jones brothers. If the deal had gone belly up, Tate was going to have to find the cash to repay the debt. Right away. Tate went very quiet. Revenge. Tucker then said he'd arrange for someone to come and get him before slamming down the phone and calling Craig Rolfe.

'By the time we got there it was obvious that Tate knew all about Steele being arrested,' Rolfe's girlfriend Diane Evans told the police later. 'He had the most money in the deal and he was anxious to find out what was going on. He couldn't make the call while he was banged up, so as soon as he got in the car he grabbed Craig's mobile and called Jackie Street. She told him everything was "safe" and immediately he seemed to calm down a lot.'

But it only lasted a few minutes. Once he was sure his investment was safe, Tate soon began to get hyped up once more. He demanded to know if Rolfe had any cocaine or ecstasy on him and they insist they make a detour to find some. When Evans protested that she and Craig had plans for that evening, Tate suddenly exploded in a fit of rage. He started smashing his fists up and down on the dashboard, screaming at the top of his lungs that all he wanted was a good time and that they shouldn't be so uptight. It was like watching a kid having a tantrum. Then Tate started bragging about all the deals he had in place, about how rich he was going to be in just a few days' time. How he was going to set up his own smuggling ring with his brother and hire a new, cheaper pilot than Steele to bring the stuff over. How he was going to get a bigger house, a brand new Merc. How he'd even buy Tucker a new Porsche to make up for the one he trashed.

Whatever planet Tate was living on, it certainly wasn't Earth.

Just after 6 p.m., more than twelve hours after being arrested, Jack Whomes found himself sitting opposite customs officer Rodney Sales. Having been friendly and talkative earlier that morning when he thought he might be able to bluff his way out of trouble, Whomes now resorted to a classic criminal technique – the 'No comment' interview.

'Right, Mr Whomes. Well, I want to ask you about events at about three o'clock, half past two this morning, but really I want to start yesterday afternoon, and I want to start with the other people if I may. Do you know Michael John Steele?'

Silence.

'Is that no reply? If it's going to be no reply, can you say no reply or it will be all me.'

Jack cleared his throat. 'No comment.'

'No comment, all right. Do you know Gordon Edward Stevens?'

'No comment.'

'Do you know Peter Corry?'

'No comment.'

'I feel bloody stupid asking you this, but do you know your brother John?'

'Whomes? No comment.'

'Now come on, Jack, surely you know your own brother?'

'No comment.'

And so it went on for the remainder of the seven-minute interview.

Michael Steele had little short of a lifetime's experience of interview rooms behind him. He knew his rights, and he knew the law only too well. And, as customs officer Richard Hills was about to find out, with a villain of that calibre, unless you've got a cast-iron case on the table in front of them, they'll never admit anything and they'll make your life hell for even daring to try.

'Right, Mr Steele,' Hills began. 'You were arrested at Felixstowe ferry this morning. What were you doing there?'

'Let me explain something to you before you go any further. Yesterday morning I think I was asked my name and address six times by different officers. Now, that one little bit of information has led to me being arrested and charged with a serious offence. I was brought to this police station, strip searched, put into a cell – no ventilation, no urinal, no drinking water, no bedding. Furthermore, I would like to explain to you this moment right now that I've nothing whatsoever to say to you for this simple reason. You've arrested me on what I call a trumped-up charge and anything I say now in answer to your questions will be no comment, no comment, no comment and to save yourself and me any further time wasting, I'll explain to you now that I don't intend to answer any questions. I've done nothing wrong and the reason I'm not answering any questions is because the way I've been treated.'

'Yes . . . but.'

'Now therefore I'm going to answer no more questions as of now and for anybody who reads or listens to this tape later orally or in a transcript, I don't want to sound unreasonable by sitting here being quiet while you put question after question to me. I'll tell you now, I'm not answering any of your questions, I've no intention of doing so, I've no need to answer the questions, I've done nothing wrong and, like I say, so far all I've done is give six people my name and address that's landed me up in here. Nothing further, nothing more to say to you as of now.'

And that was that. Steele refused to utter another word throughout the remainder of the eight-minute interview.

Finally it was the turn of Peter Corry, with Richard Hills doing the honours once again. At first, it seemed that Corry might be the weak link with the loose tongue. He was offered a solicitor but declined, wrongly assuming that the customs officials would believe he had nothing to hide if he didn't want one. But, not having had an opportunity to speak to the others and find out what stories they were giving out, he soon realised he was painting himself into a corner.

'Okay,' began Hills. 'You were arrested this morning at Felixtowe ferry in the early hours of the morning. What were you doing there?'

'I was coming in on a boat.'

'What sort of boat was that?'

'Diving boats, I don't know the names, I just went out in them.'

'Right. I take it that the boat is not your property then.'

'It's definitely not mine, no.'

'Whose is it?'

'As far as I know, it's Mr Steele's.'

And what was the purpose of the trip in the boat?'

'He put a lot of work into it and he wanted to go out and test the computer on board, whatever it is, I think and he said, "Do you want to come out?" and I said yes.'

'I see. Did you launch the boat from Felixstowe ferry?'

'Where's Felixstowe ferry?

'It's where you were arrested last night.'

'Oh yes, yes, yes, yes, yeah, yeah.'

After that, Corry's answers to Hills's questions became more and more vague until he finally realised that he was making the situation far worse and requested a solicitor. Forty minutes later, Corry was back in the hot seat with a new attitude and confident response to the questions. 'I've said all I'm going to say,' he told Hills, bringing the proceedings to an unexpectedly premature end.

Later that evening, the news came back from the customs forensic lab that cannabis resin had been found on the deck of the boat. But it was no cause for celebration. The total weight was 262 micrograms. It wasn't enough to charge someone with personal possession, let alone with smuggling. It wasn't even enough to roll a decent joint. The Range Rover had been examined and it was clean. Customs had no choice but to let the trio go.

Darren Nicholls had left the Delta Hotel early in the morning to catch the train that would take him to the ferry terminal. Totally oblivious to the events back home, he booked a cabin and spent most of the journey losing even more money on the roulette wheel then drowned his sorrows in the bar.

Back in Harwich, he bought some duty-free lager for himself and a pile of cigarettes for Sandra then made his way to his car for the drive home.

NICHOLLS I switched on my mobile phone as I thought I'd probably have a message from Mick or Jack. But there was nothing. I tried calling them on their mobiles but couldn't get through, so I called Sandra and told her I was on my way back. I kept trying Jack and Mick all the way back to Braintree with no luck so finally I tried Mick at home.

Jackie Street answered. 'Hi Darren,' she went, 'Mick's not here at the moment. There's been a bit of a misunderstanding. He was out fishing in his boat and customs thought he was up to something so they arrested him coming into Brightlingsea marina. Everything's going to be okay though.'

Mick was a clever git. He knew only too well that someone might be listening in on the phone and he wasn't going to give anything away. By telling Jackie that everything was going to be okay, he was giving me a clear signal that the drugs had already been unloaded and that customs hadn't found anything.

Mick didn't get home until really late that night so I didn't get to see until him the next day. Customs had held on to the Range Rover and the boat for further forensic examination and I wanted to get the full story.

With a big grin on his face, he explained that once they'd unloaded the drugs and stashed them safely in Mick's mum's garage, they decided to get the boat out at Brightlingsea where they had been spotted by the harbour master who, unbeknown to them, had called the police. Mick's friend, Gordon Stevens, lived right on the beach so once the boat was on the trailer, they all stopped off for a cup of tea. Jack remembered he'd left the lights on in the Range Rover and went to turn them off. But he never came back. When Mick went to find him, he poked his head over the embankment and saw Jack being interviewed by the two coppers and dashed back to the house.

He and Peter took all the incriminating evidence they could find – receipts from abroad, foreign money, maps, back-up co-ordinates for the GPS, everything – and burned them in the toilet. Mick had been trying to avoid giving his name because he knew that with his track record, they'd clap him in irons as soon as he did. Only they didn't. So he decided to call their bluff. While they were waiting for customs to arrive he made an excuse about needing to get on the boat and deprogrammed the GPS. That was pretty crucial, because the system stores all the co-ordinates of the last journey. If anyone had looked at it, they would have seen that Mick had left early the previous day, made a brief stop in Blankenberg, a brief stop in Point Clear and then come back to the marina. Mick wouldn't have a leg to stand on. But as it was, he was able to get rid of the evidence. He still had time to kill and the police didn't seem bothered, so he gave them a story about needing to get the salt water off the boat and began washing down the insides, hoping to get any loose traces of cannabis out. And he'd virtually succeeded.

Mick was totally relaxed about the whole thing. In fact he thought it was really funny that they'd blown it and kept right on laughing about it as he took me to his mum's garage in his Hi-Lux and gave me a couple of kilos to sell. It was another story he could add to his list of narrow escapes. He was also totally convinced that it was just bad luck that they'd been spotted by the harbour master, but I wasn't so convinced.

Now, I've got no way of proving it, but I'm pretty sure I'm right about what really happened that morning. Everyone knows that customs don't find fuck all by pure chance; most of the time they're acting on tip-offs. And when they swooped on Mick and Jack, I think they were acting on a tip-off that they should be on the look-out for a certain small boat coming back in from the sea in the early hours. And who did the tipping? I think it was Dopey Harris. Why him? Well for one thing, that was the trip that he found out that we took the stuff back to England by boat. None of us knew about the second reason at the time, but once we did it became blindingly obvious that Harris had absolutely nothing to lose and £124,000 worth of everything to gain.

10

'This is bang out of order, this is gonna fuck things up for all of us'

At the start, everything seemed perfect. The new outfit that she'd bought fitted like a glove and everyone said she looked stunning; the cake she'd begged her stepmum to bake had come out brilliantly. And, as promised, a friend had come up with the drugs to make her special day just that little bit more special.

It was early in the evening of Saturday 11 November and Leah Betts and her best friend Sarah Cargill were in her bedroom at her parents' house in Latchingdon, Essex, getting ready for her eighteenth birthday party.

Originally Leah's parents had planned to go out for the evening and leave the teenagers to it, but earlier that day they changed their minds and decided to keep an eye on things. As a former policeman, Paul Betts was addicted to order and only too well aware of how easily such parties could get out of control. He wanted to be completely sure that the toilet didn't end up wrecked, the carpets weren't covered in sick and that no one tried to sneak in any alcohol. Or drugs. Which was why, as Paul and his wife Janet prepared snacks for the party, Leah and Sarah were in hidden away upstairs, each staring at a fingernail-sized white tablet, embossed with an apple motif, in the palms of their hands.

Leah was no newcomer to drugs. Since leaving home to study at Basildon College, she had experimented several times. She and Sarah had smoked dope, snorted speed, tripped out on LSD and dropped E at least four times. But as Leah went to take her latest tablet, Sarah stopped her. The ecstasy they had taken before had been embossed with a dove logo. Apples were reputed to be far stronger and Sarah thought it might be best if they took only half a tablet. Leah thought for a moment then popped the whole pill into her mouth. 'We've done it before,' she said. 'Don't worry, we'll be fine.'

Within a few hours, Leah's other friends had arrived and the party moved into full swing, her parents keeping their distance to spare their daughter's blushes. 'Once everyone arrived we kept out of the way,' says Paul, 'but we thought we knew what was going on. The wrinklies were supposed to be banished to the kitchen for the evening but I told Leah that I would have my one dance. And we did, to "When a Man Loves A Woman".' Paul went back to the kitchen leaving a laughing, smiling Leah to blow out the candles on her birthday cake.

Seconds later, Leah's younger brother, William, burst into the kitchen. 'Leah's being sick in the toilet upstairs. She's calling for Mum.'

The scene that greeted Janet Betts was like something out of a horror movie. Leah was on the floor throwing up violently and screaming that she'd gone blind, that her head felt like to was going to explode. Leah turned round and Janet saw that her eyeballs were so bloated that they were literally bulging out of her head and her pupils were enormous.

'I said, "Oh my God, what the hell have you done?' and she said, "I've taken ecstasy". Then she started clawing at me, screaming, "Help me, Mum, help me, please help me." Those words will haunt me for the rest of my life.'

By then, Paul Betts was also in the bathroom and fell back on his instincts, switching into detective mode in a flash. 'Where did you get it from, who gave it to you?' he asked. Leah, in between spasms, gasped the name 'Steven' a couple of times, then collapsed and stopped breathing. Paul and Jan took it in turns to give her mouth-to-mouth, but by the time an ambulance had arrived Leah was in a deep coma.

Earlier that same afternoon, Craig Rolfe had made his way from Essex to Golders Green to meet Black Gary, one of north London's top drug dealers. Having picked up his share of Steele's cannabis, Rolfe was anxious to turn it into hard cash as quickly as possible and Gary was the man for the job. The deal was as straightforward as could be – the price per kilo worked out to an even £10,000 for the lot, with Rolfe's personal profit coming in around £6,000. It would have been more but Steele, insisting that the risks were greater since his brush with customs, had pushed up the price for his importation service, something that had pissed off Tucker and particularly Tate no end.

No money was changing hands between Rolfe and Black Gary that day. Instead, the cannabis was being 'laid on' and Gary would pass over the money as soon as he'd sold the drugs. It meant that Rolfe would have to wait a little longer to get paid, but the drugs were out of his hands in one fell swoop and he didn't have to run the risk of being done for possession. All he had to do now was sit back and wait.

Elsewhere in Essex, Darren Nicholls was also waiting for the money to start rolling in. He had dozens of buyers waiting for the latest consignment of cannabis to arrive and the 3 kilos he'd taken from Steele – 1 as his wages, 2 more to satisfy demand among his regulars – had all gone in a couple of hours.

Pleased with himself for having done a good day's work, Nicholls was preparing himself for a long, hard Saturday night down the pub when the first phone call came.

NICHOLLS I wasn't worried, just a bit pissed off. You always get someone who wants to try it on – they buy some puff on credit, have a few joints and then try to pull one over on you by saying that it isn't any good and asking you to cut the price. You just have to be firm and aggressive. But this time was different. It wasn't just one or two calls – everyone I'd sold to was coming back and complaining. And it wasn't like they were saying that the stuff wasn't as strong as they expected or that I'd sold them short; they were saying the stuff was shit, complete unsmokable cack. A couple of them were going totally mad. They thought I was trying to have them over. They were screaming down the phone at me, 'What the fuck are you playing at? What is this stuff you've sold us 'cos it sure as shit ain't puff. You're having a laugh, ain't ya?'

Darren Nicholls was not alone. A furious Black Gary had got on the phone to Craig Rolfe less than an hour after their meeting to tell him that he wouldn't be getting a penny as the cannabis was totally unsellable. Pat Tate, Tony Tucker and Peter Corry had also received complaints. And as with Nicholls, the situation was quickly getting out of hand.

NICHOLLS I called up Mick and told him that Harris had ripped us off. It turned out that he'd been getting complaints all night long as well but couldn't get hold of Harris. We arranged to meet in a pub near his house and he handed me a 5-kilo pack of drugs wrapped differently to the rest. He asked me to test them to see if they were any good. I took them home and Sandra tried a bit and immediately felt sick. It was all rubbish, every last gram.

Nicholls phoned Steele again and tried to break the bad news as gently as possible. He slowly explained that the biggest drugs shipment Steele had been involved in since getting back into smuggling – the one he'd almost got caught bringing into the country by customs – had been a complete waste of time. Steele went ballistic.

By Sunday afternoon, there had been no improvement in Leah Betts's condition. Paul and Janet, who had been at their daughter's bedside since she had been admitted, fought back the tears as doctors at the Broomfield Hospital in Chelmsford explained that the longer she stayed in the coma and failed to respond, the less chance there was that she would ever recover.

It was then that Janet made the decision to have a photograph taken of Leah – eyes closed to the world with a horrific tangle of tubes erupting from her mouth and nose and monitors plastered across her chest – as a warning to others who might be thinking of taking ecstasy. 'You can tell them, but they don't listen,' Paul said at a press conference shortly afterwards. 'The message that I have for other parents is that you have only got to see my daughter. If you want to take drugs or sell them, look at her. Look at my pretty daughter, lying there dying. She looks so peaceful. We just keep expecting her to wake up at any moment.'

The release of the picture was a marketing master stroke. It transformed what would have been the latest in a line of tragic ecstasy-related deaths into the launchpad for a massive drugs awareness campaign. Virtually all of Monday's newspapers ran the photograph, most of the tabloids featuring it on their front pages with huge banner headlines. '*Look what drugs do,*' screamed *Today*. '*The picture her parents want Britain to remember,*' said the *Daily Mail*. You simply couldn't move without being confronted by Leah Betts. Swarms of journalists had descended on Basildon, asking questions about who ran the clubs, who sold drugs, who the local villains were. The photograph featured on every TV news broadcast, the story was at the top of every radio bulletin. And soon the names of the members of the Firm were at the top of every police agenda.

Emotions were running particularly high because, in those first few days, it was believed that Leah had been sold a

contaminated pill. The race was on to find the men the
tabloids had dubbed the 'evil dealers' who were 'peddling in
death' before there were any more tragedies. It was one of
those situations where the man in charge of the police investigation, Detective Chief Inspector Brian Storey, needed to be
seen to be doing something. And quickly. By Monday afternoon it was becoming increasingly obvious that Leah was not
going to make it and that her death would only provoke a
greater outcry.

Within hours of her being admitted to hospital, Storey had
established from Leah's friends that the tablet had been
brought on the Friday evening from Raquels nightclub after
Louise Yexley, another friend of Leah, had failed to obtain any
drugs herself. 'Steven' was either Stephen Smith or Steve
Packham, both of whom were friendly with Louise and both of
whom had been to Raquels that night. One of the two was definitely responsible for buying the pills that later found their
way to Leah's house but, with the allegations of poison tablets
firmly in his mind, Storey was also after the person ultimately
responsible for supplying pills to the club. The name of Tony
Tucker had come up repeatedly during police inquiries and a
quick background check soon revealed that he had been
linked to a club drug death before.

Some eighteen months earlier, in March 1994, twenty-year-
old Kevin Jones died at Club UK in south London after taking
ecstasy. In a bid to track the source, police put two of the club's
suspected dealers under surveillance and discovered they had
been paying Tony Tucker, the man responsible for security at
the club, £1,000 per weekend for the exclusive rights to sell
ecstasy and cocaine.

Though the connection was clearly there, Storey knew that
Tucker was much too clever to have anything incriminating
on his person or even back at his home in Fobbing. There was
no point in arresting him – he wouldn't even begin to crack.
Instead, Storey needed to find another tactic, a weaker link in
the chain where, if he applied enough pressure, the whole

drugs ring behind the Leah tragedy would come tumbling down.

Even before DCI Storey had made his first move, Pat Tate was starting to feel the pinch. The business with the bad cannabis was really starting to hurt: contacts that he'd spent years nurturing were now thinking twice about dealing with him, just in case they too ended up with a duff load. In his twisted, drug-addled mind there was only one possible explanation for the whole mess: Michael Steele, the man he had once considered a friend and whom he had trusted with his money, was trying to rip him off.

Tate was also worried by the fact that he'd passed on some of the duff puff to the Jones brothers, the men who had lent him the money to get into the deal in the first place. They, not surprisingly, had been furious when the goods turned out to be unsellable, and they had sent some of their heavies round with orders to bring Tate before them so he could explain himself, or face the consequences. As he stood before the impromptu kangaroo court, Tate explained that the bad cannabis had been entirely down to Michael Steele. In order to prove that he was telling the truth, he made the brothers a solemn promise. 'I will bring Steele here and I will make him get down on his knees and beg forgiveness for trying to rip you off,' Tate explained. 'And then, when you've heard enough, I will put a gun to his head and blow his fucking brains out.'

The explanation was accepted, but it still left the small matter of the money that Tate owed. So far as the Joneses were concerned, a deal was a deal. They had given him £40,000 and he had promised them £50,000 back. Tate promised he would get the money just as soon as he could. The Joneses gave him one month.

Even the most laid-back member of the Firm was feeling distinctly uncomfortable. Normally Tony Tucker was so distanced from any actual drugs sold in his clubs that it wouldn't have been a problem, but Raquels was different. The main dealer there, Mark Murray, had suffered a string of police raids on his employees, losing more than 2,500 pills worth more than £40,000 in just a few of weeks. It meant that he hadn't been able to pay Tucker his usual rent and had gone into the red. A compromise was reached: Tucker would supply Murray with his ecstasy direct, with Murray buying the pills at twice the usual rate in order to make up the debt.

Murray reluctantly agreed. He had long realised that it made good business sense to sell tablets that were as weak as possible. They cost the same but it meant that punters would buy two or three Es during the course of an evening and his profits would be far higher. Tucker's pills were much stronger, so strong that one would let you rave all night long. It would take forever for Murray to repay his debt, but Tucker was determined to get his money back, so he had no choice. The problem Tucker was facing was that everyone knew that his pills were the 'apples' that Leah had taken and that everyone was now talking about. And it was only a matter of time before the police found out too. Tucker was certain that he was going to be betrayed. Everyone around him became a potential grass. Every knock on the door was a potential raid. Tucker, very much the brains behind the organisation, was starting to let it all get to him.

The paranoia was highly infectious. By the time Darren Nicholls arrived at Steele's house early on Monday evening, the master smuggler's mood had gone from bad to worse.

NICHOLLS Mick was pacing up and down and showing me the pictures of this girl on the front of the local paper. He was really angry, stamping around, swearing, ranting and raving. He was saying, 'This is bang out of order, this is going to fuck things up for the rest of us.' Mick was particularly upset because of Leah's dad being an ex-copper. He was convinced that the bloke would pull in all sorts of favours and, thanks to the wall-to-wall publicity the whole case was getting, make sure the gang behind the pills was caught. And as far as Mick was concerned, if one of them got done and the police started looking into their associates, then he'd be in the frame too.

It wasn't like the police would have far to look either. Tate was on the phone to Steele virtually every night, complaining about the dodgy cannabis shipment and demanding his money back. Normally, Steele would have told him where to get off, that picking up a bad shipment is just one of those things and that he'd lost money on the deal too. But that would only have made Tate more angry and he was desperate to get him out of his hair – the last thing he wanted was to be dragged into the Leah thing.

Tate, in the meantime, was shooting his mouth off to anyone who would listen about how Steele had tried to stitch him up and how he wasn't a man that anyone should ever cross. I think some of it was just bravado to make him look good in front of Tucker and Rolfe, and some of it was just the drugs talking. I don't think Tate would ever have said any of it directly to Mick but he did the next best thing – he told Sarah Saunders. Since she'd broken up with Pat, Mick had started spending more and more time with her and was helping her out in all sorts of ways. Mick thought of himself as something of a ladies' man and I'd started to think the two of them might even be having an affair.

Mick wasn't scared of what Pat was saying. He was just pissed off that he was going to fuck up the operation. At the end of the day, Mick had a good, clean, neat little set-up, which no one knew anything about. It had gone completely unnoticed several times before they had got accidentally spotted, but even then everyone had been released.

But Pat was spoiling it because he was telling too many people. He thought the bit that we did was easy when it fact it was the most difficult bit of all. Pat was always trying to set up other people to smuggle for him. A week or so before the bad shipment he'd even had the cheek to bring some bloke who'd only just got his pilot's licence round to Mick's house and insist that Mick tell him all about flying the drugs over the Channel. But Mick wasn't worried about losing business as much as about Pat letting too many people about how he operated. Pat thought he was out of reach. That everyone was sacred of him. But he reckoned without Mick.

As Steele and Nicholls chatted, Steele's mobile phone rang. It was Dopey Harris who proceeded to explain that there had been a terrible accident – that the wrong boxes had been put in the car. Harris insisted, however, that at least one of the boxes, around a third of the total drug consignment, had been good stuff. Steele told him in no uncertain terms that unless things got sorted and quickly, he was going to pass on Harris's address to Tate, Tucker and Rolfe, who would come over and sort it out in person, probably by smashing the fuck out of his bar and then smashing the fuck out of him. Harris quickly agreed that, if Steele returned all the drugs, he would get all his money back. Steele passed the message on and over the next few hours the cannabis started to filter back. Most of his customers were a little annoyed but willing to forget and forgive, especially with the promise of a full refund. Tate, however, was still in a fit of temper about the whole affair and massively frustrated about the Leah Betts thing. He smashed each and every slab with a hammer before delivering it back to Steele. He also held back some of the drugs, telling Steele that he'd only return them when he had the money in his hand. It didn't take Steele long to work out that Tate was holding back roughly a third of the whole shipment, the same amount that Stone had insisted was good. There could be only one conclusion: Tate was trying to rip him off.

NICHOLLS Later that night Steele called me up and asked if I wanted to go to Amsterdam with him. Apparently everyone else that he'd tried had said no. They all suspected that Harris had deliberately ripped us off and that going back over there to try and get the money back was suicide. But Mick didn't seem worried and that made me more confident. There was also the fact that, although I'd already spent it, I hadn't earned any money from the last deal because I'd had to give it all back. I was desperate for cash and Mick promised to pay me for the trip. Also, Mick only planned to be in Amsterdam for a couple of hours – just enough time to pick up the money and have a drink, he said. He'd done enough to convince me. 'Okay Mick, count me in.'

I picked Mick up from Aingers Green and we drove down to Harwich in my old Land Rover, freezing our bollocks off all the way because the Rover's got a window missing. We were travelling overnight so I had a change of clothing with me and, when we got to the ferry terminal, I booked the tickets in my name and got some guilders from the bureau de change.

We were trying to make a holiday of it, keep the mood light. We had a meal in the restaurant at the departure lounge then got a cabin on the boat. We had a few drinks in the bar where they had some live singers, then went to the boat's cinema and watched a film, then went to our cabin to get a few hours' sleep before we arrived in Amsterdam.

Early on Tuesday morning, DCI Storey put his plan into action and raided Pat Tate's flat in Swanstead, where Tucker's mistress, Donna Garwood, was living. A small quantity of amphetamine was found and Garwood spent a few hours in the cells before a fuming Tucker arrived to bail her out. There had been other raids across Basildon that morning too, most of them friends of Leah's or bag men some way down the drug supply chain. But for Tucker the message was clear. They were on to him.

He had an emergency meeting with Tate and Rolfe about what they were going to do. Then the firm had its first lucky break. Steve Packham and Stephen Smith had been arrested and charged with supplying the tablets. The police had their result and the public had their scapegoat. All the Firm had to do now was wait for Steele to sort out their cannabis deal and everything would be sweet as a nut once more.

NICHOLLS We met Dopey Harris in the bar. He said he was happy to give us the money back there and then, but he only had it in guilders. Harris wanted the drugs back – God knows why as they were all crap – but Mick told him they were safe back in England and that as soon as we had the money he'd set up a collection. It was just after 10 a.m. so Mick said we'd go back in the afternoon to give him some time to get some money together. No one was going to want to have to change their money over back in England, especially as banks and bureau de changes have to report transactions of more than £10,000.

We spent the day sightseeing and went back to the bar at around 5 p.m. Harris took us upstairs and handed over £30,000 sterling. He apologised but said basically there hadn't been many Brits making sales that day so there wasn't a lot of sterling around. Again he said we could have the rest in guilders but Mick decided to stay overnight and see what he could raise the next day.

For the rest of the afternoon we were either sightseeing, or having a giggle in the red light district, or in some bar drinking loads of beer, or in some restaurant stuffing our faces. I was having the time of my life. It was the closest thing to a holiday that I'd had in years and Mick and I were getting on really well.

That night we booked into the Delta Hotel and I booked a twin room in my name – Mick didn't want anything to link him there, but gave me the money to pay for it. We put the cash that Harris had given us into the hotel safe and spent the rest of the night out on the piss.

It was nearly lunchtime when we got round to Harris's the next day, but he said we still hadn't left it long enough. We'd have to come back. That afternoon, Mick and I went to

Madame Tussauds and had our photograph taken with Tina Turner.

Around 5 p.m., we went back to the bar again and Harris gave us another £50,000 in sterling. He said that he might have more tomorrow so we decided to spend yet another night in the Delta. By now the novelty was really starting to wear off. I'd enjoyed it at first, but I was still wearing the only set of clothes that I had and all the endless drinking and eating was starting to get really boring. We could never relax properly because we were anxious to get going, but every plan we made to catch a particular train or something ended up being postponed. Most of the Brits who go to Amsterdam just spend their whole time off their faces on super skunk, but neither Mick nor I smoked the stuff. We just smuggled it.

We went to Harris's yet again the next day and he told us that he wouldn't have any sterling at all that day. At first Mick decided to stay another night and we booked the Delta again but at around 5 p.m. Mick was getting so bored and restless with Amsterdam that we decided to accept the rest – about £40,000 – in guilders. We went back to Harris's and told him and he said we could have the rest of the money in one hour. In that time, Mick bought some phone cards – the batteries on both our mobiles were dead by now – and called up Jack Whomes, Pat Tate and the others to tell them to come over and meet him in Ostend to pick up their money. Mick didn't want to risk being found with too much on him at one time, so the idea was for lots of people to come over and take a few thousand back each.

Harris told Mick that, with the way the exchange rate was, he had given us more than enough to cover the debt. He seemed very keen to make amends, and never stopped apologising for having sold us the dodgy puff in the first place. Having hated the guy's guts a few days earlier, we ended up thinking as he waved us goodbye and wished us well that perhaps he wasn't such a bad bloke after all.

We collected our bags from the hotel and were just

making our way down to the train station when I thought I saw a familiar face. Now Amsterdam's a fairly small place and if you hang out in the centre long enough you do tend to see the same faces doing the usual circuit of bars and clubs. But this bloke didn't look like he was actually going anywhere. He looked like he was following us. I couldn't be sure. The bloke was quite far behind and he may or may not have been with a couple of other people, but I thought I might as well mention it to Mick. It turned out he had already spotted him and was equally concerned. Instead of heading straight for the station, we took a slightly longer, odder route. The bloke was still there. So we walked along a canal and popped into a bar for a quick drink. When we came out, the bloke was still there.

The fact that we'd spotted him meant the guy wasn't good enough to be a professional so the most likely explanation was that Harris had decided to arrange a nasty little surprise mugging in an attempt to get his money back. With that in mind, neither of us liked the idea of being trapped on a speeding train if it all kicked off so we decided to take drastic action. When we got to the station, we nipped over the road and jumped into a taxi.

'Hi,' said Mick. 'Can you take us to Ostend?' The driver's jaw nearly hit the floor. It was a bit like getting into a black cab outside Charing Cross station and asking to be taken to Manchester.

At first the driver wanted 1,000 guilders but we offered him 600. Eventually we settled on 800 – around £400 – and we set off. We told him to take a scenic route out of the city, going round roundabouts several times, that sort of thing, until we were sure that no one was following us any more.

Back in England, the members of the London firm were preparing to go to Ostend to collect their money. Tony Tucker had decided to drop out at the last minute. It was the day before his birthday and as a treat his live-in lover Anna had arranged a surprise night at a London hotel. Tucker had no interest in cancelling it, and besides, it wasn't as if the job was so difficult that Rolfe and Tucker couldn't handle it on their own.

The firm needed as many people as possible to help bring back the cash. That way each person would be carrying a relatively small amount so that if they were stopped by customs they wouldn't look too suspicious. Rolfe had asked his girlfriend Diane Evans, but she didn't like the sound of it and turned him down. It was not so much the trip to collect the money that she objected to, it was another 'bigger job' that Rolfe had started to mention that was simply getting much too serious for her liking. 'Craig told me that Steele had approached Tate and asked him to nick someone else's gear from them. Steele had been asked by a London gang to import 30 kilos of cocaine and was going to fly it over from Holland. He told Pat he was going to be given £50,000 up front and bring the cocaine back with a member of the London gang in the passenger seat.

'The idea was that Tate and Tucker would rob the firm of the cocaine once it arrived over here. Steele suggested they share it between them and had told the firm he planned to land in a field near Clacton. In fact, Steele was actually going to land in a south Essex field where Tate and the others would be waiting.

'A week or so earlier, Craig, Tony and Pat had obtained a machine gun from a man called Mad Mick. It had been handed over in a meeting at the Granada motorway services in Essex for £300. They were planning to use the gun on the man from the London firm in order to take the cocaine. I didn't know how far they were planning to go when they robbed the firm but I knew they had made sure that the gun worked.'

(Rolfe and Tucker had already used the gun to spray bullets into the car of a man threatening to give evidence against Tucker in a forthcoming assault case. After putting some extra ventilation holes in the doors and windows they knocked on the man's door. 'Next time, you'll be inside it,' they said, then left.)

By now Evans was getting increasingly nervous herself and terrified that she and Rolfe were going to be arrested at any time. She hoped that if she refused to go to Amsterdam, that Rolfe might pull out. Instead she found her boyfriend was really excited at the prospect of a night on the tiles in a foreign country with no one to tie him down and he looked forward to going even more. Rolfe took his Range Rover and picked up Tucker's other girlfriend Donna Garwood, Tate, Tate's girlfriend Liz Fletcher and her friend Gaynor. To make up the numbers, Tate also asked his car dealer friend Barry Doorman to come along, and he agreed to follow in a separate car, bringing his girlfriend Annette to keep him company.

The Range Rover was the first car in the convoy to arrive in Ostend. Tate left the others in the pub while he went to the entrance of the train station where he'd had agreed to meet Steele. Garwood and the others watched from a distance as Tate and Steele returned to the pub and made their way to a quiet table in the corner, where they talked for around twenty minutes. When Steele got up to go, he had passed over the bulging carrier bag he had been holding to Tate. The transaction was complete.

In the meantime, Darren Nicholls was standing across the road from the pub, trying to shelter from the rain and waiting for Steele to reappear. When the pair had arrived in Ostend, Steele had booked into a hotel and sent Nicholls off to the ferry terminal to buy a ticket. The idea was that he would take £20,000 back with him on the overnight ferry and that Steele would travel back to England the following morning, once he'd dished the rest of the money out to the others.

As always, Steele had told Nicholls to make himself scarce – he didn't want anyone knowing who was on his team just in case they tried to poach them or use his drug contacts. After twenty minutes of getting wet and watching the gang laughing and joking in the warm, dry pub, Steele eventually came out and Nicholls called him over.

NICHOLLS It had all looked really jolly from where I was but Mick was actually really pissed off. Tate was saying it was too late for them to get the ferry back and that they'd have to stay overnight. But they wanted Mick to pay for it because they didn't have any Belgian money and, besides, he owed them for making them wait all week for their cash.

I think by then Mick just wanted the whole thing to be over as quickly as possible. He was saying how out of control Tate seemed, how he was really hyped up about everything and behaving like a five-year-old. It was getting quite late and he said that I might as well stay as well, as Jack would be there soon, so I used my credit card to book into the same hotel as him.

About ten minutes later, Jack arrived in his Transit van and, as Mick wanted something to eat, we all wandered up the road to this Greek restaurant for a snack.

Jack had been so paranoid that he had worked up an elaborate excuse to explain why he was leaving the country. He was pretty freaked out by what had happened with customs at Felixstowe ferry and wanted to make sure he had a cast-iron alibi in case it all came on top. He had travelled over in his Transit and had even put a spare wheel and brake drum in the back so he could say he was on his way to repair a vehicle. He even booked a commercial ticket, which cost him around £220, just so it was all legit. And as is Sod's Law, he didn't get stopped by customs once. Jack had two glasses of orange juice and then left, taking half the guilders with him.

After that, Mick and I stayed in the restaurant and had a chat about what to do with the dodgy cannabis that Harris had sold us. After the experience of being followed, Mick didn't trust the guy at all and didn't want to risk handing it over to someone in Britain, just in case it turned out to be a set-up. 'Just get rid of them, Darren, the whole lot,' he told me. 'I don't care what you do. I just never want to see any of it ever again.'

It was just after that that Mick first asked me if I could help him out.

I don't remember anything about what I was doing, who I was with, where I was or even the time of day. The only thing I remember was the question, 'Can you get me a gun?'

We'd only been back from Amsterdam a few days and Mick was saying that any sort would do, a handgun or a shotgun. Anything. I had a friend, Roy, who used to have an illegal shotgun, which he used for shooting rabbits, so I told Mick I'd ask him. Roy had sold his gun but he told me he'd ask a couple of people and see what he could come up with.

Over the next week, Mick called me virtually every single day to find out how I was getting on. I told him I wasn't having much luck but he just told me to keep on trying. I know it sounds stupid but I didn't bother to ask Mick what he wanted it for. I knew he had a bit of a rat problem at Meadow Cottage and I guess I just assumed that he was going to use it for that.

Then, as quickly as they started, the calls just stopped and I forgot all about it.

On 4 December, Pat was planning a quiet night in with Liz. She called up the London Pizza Company in Basildon and asked the twenty-one-year-old manager, Roger Ryall, for a pizza with different toppings on each quarter. Ryall told her that would not be possible.

Suddenly Tate grabbed the phone. 'You will deliver the pizza I fucking want or I'll come round and get it.'

'I wasn't going to take that,' Ryall said later. 'So I said to him, "Get rid of the attitude and I will send you a pizza."'

'What's your fucking name?' screamed Tate. That made him worse and he slammed the phone down.

Half an hour later, Tate turned up. Who's Roger? When

Ryall put his hand up, Tate picked up the till and threw it at him. Ryall quickly backed out of the office and pushed the panic button as Tate vaulted the counter and rushed towards him.

'He punched me in the face then smashed my head up and down on the glass plate on the draining board.' Blood streamed out of a wound in his head. Tate warned him not to call the police or he would return and smash the place up and beat up all the staff. But it was too late, The panic button brought officers and Tate was traced to his home in Basildon.

At first Ryall, who had concussion, was determined to have the man who assaulted him brought to justice. But as friends and colleagues told him more about Pat Tate's reputation and that of the Firm that he belonged to, Ryall's resolve softened. By the following morning, he had withdrawn his statement and decided not to press charges.

Within the space of a few hours, the incident had become legend across south-east Essex. For some, it was a testimony to Pat's increasing arrogance and influence that he could commit such a public crime and get away with it. There was a time when his strength, his wit and charm made him a valuable asset to any now. But that was in the past. Now there was only one way to describe Pat Tate: a liability.

11
'Come and get us'

NICHOLLS All day long I'd been dying for a beer.

I'd got this new contract working on a site down by Heathrow Airport, which was paying good money but meant getting up at five in the morning and driving more than 100 miles. We finished quite early and I'd normally be home by six, but the days were still pretty exhausting. After a long, hard day, the only way I can unwind is to go down the pub for a few pints. Most of the time that was okay, but every now and then Sandra would kick up a fuss and have a go at me for not spending enough time with her and the kids. When that happened I'd stay in for a couple of nights and make sure I got in the way, then she'd practically be begging me to go down the pub so she could have some peace and quiet.

I'd been a good boy for the past two nights, even helping out with housework and stuff like that, and now I was going to get my reward. I was going to go down the local, have a couple of games of pool and get completely and utterly plastered.

At around 2 p.m., just as I was finishing up for the day,

Mick called my mobile and asked me to meet him at Marks Tey as soon as possible. It was a place we'd met a few times before because it's roughly halfway between our two houses, but it meant a detour on the way home and therefore a delay in getting the beers in. Mick didn't say why he wanted to meet so I assumed it was something to do with drugs – either another run he wanted me to go on or some new stock he wanted me to sell. I was really tempted to say I couldn't make it but I didn't want to let him down. I'd been doing a lot of work on his house during the evening and at weekends and I didn't want to risk losing the extra income. At first I said I'd meet him at 4 p.m. but then I changed it to 5 p.m. because that way I knew I'd have time for a couple of quick beers on the way.

At that exact time, in a quiet corner of the TGI Friday's at the Lakeside Shopping Centre in Thurrock, Tate, Tucker and Rolfe were deep in discussion.

The initial plan could not have been more straightforward. They had agreed with Steele that they would be hiding in some bushes when the plane landed, leap out, fire a few shots in the air to scare the pilot and then take away the 30 kilos of pure, unadulterated Charlie. To make it look good and ensure that no one suspected it was an inside job, they'd have to threaten Steele as well, maybe even tie him up for a while, but it would all be play-acting. The Firm would leave with all the drugs and meet up with Steele a couple of days later to divide it all up.

But now the plan had changed.

As far as Tate was concerned, he explained to the others, Mickey Steele was guilty of having tried to rip the Firm off with the dodgy cannabis. Okay, so he'd eventually paid the money back, but he had still caused them a huge amount of grief. And now it was payback time. Rather than handing over 10 kilos of pure cocaine, they would give Steele just 3 kilos of the good stuff mixed with a load of impurities such as caffeine or chalk dust to make it up to the full weight.

That would leave the Firm with 27 kilos of premium-quality Bolivian marching powder between them. Tate had already discussed a price with a certain John McCarthy, a man well used to dealing in large amounts of the white stuff and the quote that came back was one of those magical numbers that, whether you're a pop star, a merchant banker or just a gangster, announces to the world that you have definitely arrived: McCarthy was going to pay the Firm a cool £1 million.

Steele had apparently already been paid his fee for flying the plane and the drugs were packed up and standing by to be collected in Holland. The only delay to the deal was the snow on the ground, which Steele explained made landing in such a small space too hazardous, even for a pilot as skilled as he was. But the Firm regarded the money as good as theirs. To celebrate they had booked a table for that same evening at the Global Net Cafe in Romford where, along with their girlfriends, they would toast their soon-to-be-stinking-rich status.

Diane Evans was also just finishing work for the day when Craig Rolfe called her. 'It was around 3 p.m. and I was just about to leave when he phoned to say that Mickey the Pilot had been in touch earlier in the day and wanted to meet Tucker and Tate that evening to show them where he was going to land the plane.

'Craig was really excited that the deal was getting so imminent. He wanted me to wear something new at the meal that evening, so he said he'd take me to the Lakeside Shopping Centre, go off to see the airstrip and then come back and pick me up.

'I met him at home an hour or so later and he told me for the first time about the change in the plans and how they were going to rip Mickey off. As Craig explained what was going on, I was getting more and more worried and told him I didn't want him to have any part of it. He told me that they were only going to look at a field, that Mickey didn't know he was going to be driving and that he wasn't nearly as heavily involved in what was going on as the other two were. But mostly he told me about the money. He said that for once he would have enough money to enable us to go ahead with whatever plans we wanted. We would be able to live anywhere and do nothing all day, visit anywhere in the world. It would be the life we always dreamed of.

'I realised there was just no way I was going to be able to talk him out of it. Even though I didn't want him to go through with it, it was obvious he was just in too deep.'

As Rolfe dropped her off at the shopping centre, Evans tried one last time to talk him out of going to the rendezvous, but his mind was made up. 'He said to me, "If I don't go, then Tony can turn around later when the drugs come in and say I didn't have anything to do with the arrangements so my cut will be smaller. I don't want that to happen. I've got to do my bit. I've got to play my part." And then he left.'

As he approached the outskirts of Marks Tey, Darren Nicholls was beginning to realise that stopping off for a beer on the way had been a terrible mistake.

NICHOLLS It had really gave me a taste for it, but I hadn't had anywhere near enough – I'd only teased my taste buds. As I parked up, I started hoping that, whatever it was that Mick wanted, it wouldn't take too long so that I could get home and get on with some serious drinking.

After a few minutes I saw a familiar red Hi-Lux pull up and went over and got in on the passenger side. Mick started telling me that he and Pat had finally sorted their differences out and that he was planning to meet him that evening. Apparently a plane with a mother load of cocaine was going to be landing in some field and they were going to meet it for some kind of deal.

'Sounds good,' I said. 'So what do you want me to do?' Mick explained that my role was to drive Jack down to the meeting place and then pick the two of them up afterwards.

'I want Pat to think that I'm meeting him on my own,' he told me.

Now this is the point in the story where people start saying to me, 'Didn't you think it was all a bit odd? Weren't there alarm bells ringing in your head?' The answer, I'm afraid to say, is no. As far as I was concerned, there was some kind of cocaine deal going on between Pat and Mick. I knew by then that Pat was a bit of a loose cannon, especially after the pizza incident, and was not adverse to ripping people off. Even his friends. Now it was unlikely he'd try anything with Mick, but if it was me I would have played it the same way. Rather than going down to the meet with all the money, I'd have someone else holding it nearby to make sure it wasn't a trap. It was exactly the same deal that I'd pulled when I was trying to sell that counterfeit money at that hotel. It was standard underworld practice. I didn't see anything wrong with it at all.

As Mick and I were talking, Jack pulled up behind in this tatty old B-reg VW Passat that I'd actually sold to Mick a couple of weeks earlier. Jack came up to say a quick hello and then we set off towards the Halfway House pub, me and Mick in the Hi-Lux and Jack following behind. On the way Mick explained that, when we got a bit nearer, we would pull over so I could get in the Passat with Jack. Mick didn't want us to be seen, otherwise Tate would realise he had company. Once I was in the other car, Jack would tell me exactly what to do.

Just before we got to the pub, we stopped in the entrance to the country park and Mick told me to get into the Passat with Jack, who turned the car around then produced a set of false number plates with double-sided sticky-tape on them. He tried to stick them over the existing plates but it was too damp and wet, so he eventually gave up. I got into the driver's seat and he told me to head to the Halfway House and wait close to the exit of the car park. From where we were, we had a clear view of the car park entrance and could see all the cars coming in. We could also see Mick's Hi-Lux parked on the other side of the pub, but no sign of Mick.

'What are we waiting for?' I asked Jack.

There was no reply.

It was pretty cold so I kept the engine running to stop the windows steaming up and to stop us freezing. But I knew a much better way of staying warm.

'Hey,' I said, 'While we're waiting, let's go in the pub and have a couple of beers.'

Jack slowly turned his head and looked at me. 'No,' he said firmly. I suppose I wasn't all that surprised: Jack wasn't just teetotal, he was some kind of freak. All he ever drank was water and orange juice. He didn't touch anything fizzy and wouldn't go near tea or coffee. His only vice was chocolate – he ate Galaxy bars like they were going out of fashion.

All of a sudden Jack said, 'Right, off we go.' As I pulled away, I looked over towards the car park entrance and saw a dark-blue Range Rover coming in. I couldn't see who was inside, but I assumed it was Pat's car.

We set off down the A130 and Jack said he was going to show me where to drop him off and pick him up and that I was to leave him there and come back when he rang me as soon as they had completed the deal. I drove over the Rettendon Turnpike, still on the A130 towards Chelmsford. I went up the hill through Rettendon village and was bombing down the other side when Jack told me to slow down as we would soon be doing a right turn. He pointed out this tiny little lane up ahead and told me to turn into it and turn the car round immediately. I did as I was told and watched as Jack got out of the car and took some stuff off the back seat. He took a coat – a prison donkey jacket with the plastic bit on the back cut off – and a big canvas sausage bag.

As Jack was walking away, I asked him if I had time for a quick beer while he was gone. 'What are you, some kind of alcoholic? We won't be long. Just fuck off and wait. And

when you come back, turn around straightaway again so we
can head off straightaway.'

Then he vanished in the darkness and I drove off.

Sitting alone at home, Sarah Saunders was starting to feel a
little sorry for herself. Earlier that day she'd phoned Pat Tate
hoping to have a civilised discussion about how much main-
tenance he planned to pay her. She might just as well have
hoped for world peace. Tate had been almost impossible to talk
to. He was in a really excited, hyped-up state and had obviously been taking drugs. There was no point in trying to
reason with him like that. It had ended up in a furious row and
he had slammed the phone down.

But despite everything that had happened, Saunders still
cared for Tate deeply and was anxious that their son would
have a proper relationship with his father. She glanced at her
watch. It had been more than five hours since they had last
spoken. With any luck he might have calmed down. She took
a deep breath and reached for the phone.

It may have been close to freezing outside but the atmosphere
inside the Range Rover was warm and jolly. Tate, Tucker and
Rolfe were preoccupied with the vast amount of money they
were soon to be collecting and the pre-celebration meal they
had planned for later that evening. They were firing questions
at Steele, who was sitting in the back beside Tate, asking
exactly when he'd be leaving for Holland and when he'd be
landing.

In between giving directions to Craig Rolfe, Steele reassured
the gang that they were at most a couple of days away from
their nice little earner.

Just as the Range Rover turned into Workhouse Lane, Tate's
mobile came to life.

'Hello . . . oh hello darling . . . really . . . ahh, you sweet-
heart. Well maybe I can come by tomorrow . . . Listen I can't
talk now, I'm with some people. We'll talk later . . . okay . . . I

miss you too. Bye.' Steele bit his lip and tried to stop his anger mounting. Up until that point, everything that Sarah Saunders had told him indicated that she and Tate could hardly stand one another. Yet here they were having this loving, caring conversation. But Steele didn't have time to dwell on it for long. A split second later, the Range Rover reached the bottom of the lane.

'Hey, there's a gate down here,' said Rolfe. 'What d'ya wanna do?'

Steele had to think quickly. When he and Jack had checked the lane out before, the gate had been open. Had Jack shut it for some reason? Perhaps there were some other people in the field. Perhaps Jack wasn't there at all. The only thing to do was play it by ear. 'I'll get it,' he said. 'You lot stay in the warm.'

Craig Rolfe was the first to die. As soon as the rear passenger door had opened and Steele was clear, Jack Whomes had leaned in with a pump-action. He pressed the barrel against the back of the driver's headrest and pulled the trigger. The pellets ripped through the fabric and straight through Rolfe's skull, leaving a gaping hole right between his eyes. Both his hands were still on the steering wheel, his foot was on the brake. He looked like he had just pulled up at some traffic lights.

Tony Tucker was next. With the blast ringing in his ears from just a split second before, he had no time to react. Whomes moved the gun and shot him in the back of the head. He died with his legs crossed and his mobile phone sitting in his lap.

Tate, sitting in the back seat, was the only one who would have known he was about to die. By the time Whomes trained the gun on him, less than two seconds after firing the first shot, Tate was wailing and pushing himself back into the corner of the car, making a futile escape.

Whomes paused for a second as Tate began begging for his life, wailing and whining. This time Steele fired first, both barrels ripping through Tate's belly. 'Wait. Stop. What ya doing? No.' Tate's voice was getting higher and higher as his pleas got more desperate. Then Steele appeared beside Whomes, holding a gun, and Tate knew it was all over. He raised his hands to protect himself with such ferocity that his knuckles smashed through the rear window and he screamed for his life. At that same instant, one shot tore off the left side of his face while another split open his chest, ripping his liver apart.

There was no doubt that the three were dead but this was more than just an execution. Whomes pumped his shotgun and opened the front door of the car. He put the barrel up against what was left of Tucker's head and fired again. The pressure inside Tucker's skull was more than it could bear. His head literally exploded as the bones broke through the skin.

Then Whomes went round to Rolfe and did the same. This time the shots were fired from such close range that they singed the fur collar on his anorak and pushed his jawbone across to where his ear would normally be.

In the meantime Steele was getting excited and reached out to Whomes. 'Gimme more cartridges, gimme more cartridges.' He reloaded and fired again, only to have his gun fall apart. Both men burst out laughing and Steele scrambled around on the floor in the pitch black looking for his barrel.

Darren Nicholls had driven down the road, past several tempting pubs, and parked on the side of the road to wait for Jack to call him.

NICHOLLS I checked my phone and saw that it wasn't picking up much of a signal so I decided to move. I ended up driving back past the lane and then took the first turning on the left. I went down a little way and turned around so I ended up parked on a bit of a hill. I looked at the phone again to check the signal and at that very moment it started ringing. It was Jack.

'Come and get us,' he said.

'That was quick,' I replied, but the line had already gone dead. He'd hung up.

I retraced my steps, pulled into the lane and immediately turned the car around.

Almost straightaway, Jack was at the back door of the car and got in, sitting down in the darkness.

'Where's Mick?' I asked.

'He won't be long. He's dropped something. Doesn't want to leave it there,' said Jack. And then he made this really weird sound, a bit like a series of quiet little snorts. I could just about make out his silhouette in the rear-view mirror and his big shoulders were bobbing up and down. It took me a while to work out what was going on. Jack was giggling.

I was still looking at Jack in the rear-view mirror when Mick appeared and opened the front passenger door. As soon as he did, the interior light came on. And that's when I saw Jack's hands. He was wearing surgical gloves. And they had been splashed with streaks of blood. And on the back of one hand was a lump of greyish slime surrounded by lumps of hair and skin and more blood.

'Turn that fucking light out,' screamed Mick. I didn't think, I went into autopilot and started scrabbling about on the roof of the car trying to find the light switch. But as Mick sat down he shut the door and the light went off anyway.

And suddenly it was pitch black again. But I could still see Jack's hands. And I could still see the blood and the bits of brain. And I felt like someone had sucked all the air out of me because I wanted to speak. I desperately wanted to say something, but no matter how I tried, I just couldn't get any words out.

Mick told me to get going and though my mind was elsewhere, my body somehow obeyed, putting the car into gear and moving off towards the main road.

From then on everything happened in slow motion. I saw the headlights, heard the screech of tyres and braced myself for the impact. But it never came. Mick had grabbed the steering wheel at the last moment and wrenched it to one side, avoiding a crash by just a few inches. The other driver flashed his lights and swore at me out of his half-open window. I'd just pulled out on to a main road without looking, but I honestly didn't know where I was or what I was doing. I just sat there like a zombie.

'For fuck's sake Darren, drive carefully,' said Mick. 'What ya trying to do, kill us all?'

Jack, sitting behind, thumped the back of my seat with his fist. 'Fucking arsehole,' he growled. I was still in shock but I felt myself slowly coming back down to earth. I mumbled a half-hearted apology and carried on driving back towards the Rettendon Turnpike.

All at once I felt like I was going to be sick, that I had a splitting headache, that I was freezing cold and boiling hot. My mind was racing but it kept coming back to the fact that I'd only been away for a couple of minutes. Surely they didn't have time to do anything. I desperately wanted to know exactly what had happened back there. But at the same time I desperately didn't want to know anything about it. I just couldn't take it in. I wanted to pretend that I hadn't seen anything or heard anything. But it wasn't going to happen.

Mick turned to Jack and broke the silence. 'Those cunts won't be threatening us again,' he said. 'Too right,' came the reply.

I was trying to concentrate on the road when a glint of metal caught my eye. I chanced a sideways glance and saw that Mick was passing Jack the barrels of a sawn-off shotgun, followed by the stock and the trigger mechanism. And then it got worse.

Jack moved forward so he was sitting with his head between the two front seats, just the way that naughty kids do when they're little and he and Mick started going over all the details of what they'd done. 'I tell you Darren, it was well funny,' he said with a grin. ''Cos Mick shot one of them and his gun fell apart. Bits all over the place. That's what he was looking for, the thing he dropped. I couldn't believe it. There we were trying to do a job and he spends half the time on the floor trying to find his fucking barrel.'

By now Mick was smiling too. 'Did you shoot the back window by mistake?' he asked.

Jack shook his head. 'Nah, I think Pat must have done it with his hand. I never miss. Not from that distance anyway.' Then Jack turned to me. 'You should have seen him, Darren. It was pathetic. Hard man? Pah. Squealing like a baby, he was.'

I had absolutely no idea what to say or what to do. How do you respond to something like that? I felt as if I was no longer in the car, just a spectator looking on and listening in. All I could think was: What the fuck am I doing here? What's going to happen now?

Mick spoke again. 'Hey, you'll never believe it Jack – that soppy cow Sarah, she only phoned Pat's mobile just as we were going down the fucking lane. All that talk about how she hates him and wants him out of her life and how pleased she'd be if something bad happened to him and then there they are having this lovey-dovey chat. Made me want to throw up. Actually I was shitting myself. I was just waiting for him to say, "I'm here with Mick and some of the lads," and that would have been it. We'd have had to call the whole thing off. But he never did, thank fuck. I bet she'd kick herself if she knew how close she'd come to saving him.'

Jack grunted in agreement and Mick continued, 'Mind you, don't know how I'd have stopped you. When we got to the bottom of the lane and the gate was locked, I didn't have a clue where the fuck you were until you handed me the gun and started shooting. I thought we'd blown it.'

I heard myself speak, my voice soft and low, 'I hope I never upset the two of you.' For some reason, Mick and Jack thought this was hilarious. The two of them fell about, absolutely pissing themselves.

'Nah,' chuckled Mick, wiping away tears of laughter. 'You're not like them. It wouldn't happen to you.'

Although I knew the roads reasonably well, the state I was in meant Mick and Jack had to give me instructions for every turn like I was some learner driver – left at the swimming pool shop, left at the first set of traffic lights, down to the bottom, second on the right, into the car park of the Hungry Horse pub. I spotted Mick's Toyota Hi-Lux pick-up in a corner and pulled the Passat alongside. It was only when I tried to stand up that I realised how much I was shaking.

Jack and Mick jumped out and started changing their clothes. They were still really animated and talking quickly, but I was no longer listening to what they were saying. It was then that I had noticed for the first time that they were wearing identical outfits: dark green boiler suits, Wellington boots and surgical rubber gloves, all of which were stuffed into a couple of bin liners and placed in the back of the truck. And as I stood watching them, I tried to throw up. But nothing came out.

Jack took the Passat and drove off while Mick got into the Hi-Lux and waved me into the passenger seat, then we set off for Marks Tey where my own car was waiting. As soon as Jack had gone, Mick's mood changed. He was quieter, more thoughtful. He was obviously going over the evening's events in his mind. Then, after a few minutes of silence, he suddenly said, 'Jack's a cold-hearted bastard.'

'What do you mean?' I asked.

'The second I got out of the Range Rover, he leaned in with the pump action and shot the three of them, boom, boom, boom, just like that, like it was nothing to worry about. He was just so detached, so emotionless. It was like he was serving up chips or something. I mean, he could have been doing anything. But we had to do it together you see. That way one of us could never give evidence against the other. We'd both be equally guilty. That was the deal.'

I said nothing.

All day long I'd been dying for a beer, but now all I could think about was drinking half a bottle of whisky to blot everything out. I suggested we both went for a drink or three. At first Mick agreed, but by the time we got back to Marks Tey he had changed his mind and said it would be best if he went straight home. I knew my wife and kids were expecting me, but I just couldn't face them. I pulled out my mobile and phoned my mate Rick, told him I'd had a really shitty day and asked him to meet me down the pub. He stayed for a couple and we talked about any old bollocks, but then he had to go home to his girlfriend. In the end I just stayed there on my own, sitting in a corner and drinking myself into an absolute stupor.

12

'Why are you wasting your time on scum?'

Had the frost not been quite so severe that morning, so severe as to render it impossible to mix mortar, then Ken Jiggins would simply have gone to work. As it was, the amiable brick-layer decided to start the day helping his friend, Peter Theobald, feed the 800 pheasants he kept at Whitehouse Farm in Rettendon.

Jiggins arrived just after 8 a.m. and, eager to get the job done, the pair decided to skip tea and headed straight for Theobald's Land Rover. It had snowed during the night; there was a thick layer of ice on the car's windscreen and windows which the two men diligently scraped off before driving across the field and then turning left into Workhouse Lane. As they neared the bottom, they found their path blocked by a metal-lic blue Range Rover, parked in front of the locked gate that leads to the fishing pond. Inside Jiggins and Theobald could clearly see the silhouettes of two men slumped in the front seats. Their first thought was that they must be asleep so Jiggins jumped out to ask them to move out of the way.

'I tapped on the driver's window, looked in and saw the driver lying with his head on one side. There was blood coming from his nose, mouth and on his chest,' says Jiggins. 'The passenger sat with his head slumped forward and blood on his chest.'

Theobald was still in the car, worrying that the men might be poachers and turn nasty when Jiggins called out to him, 'There's two dead men here.' As the pair nervously dialled for the police on Theobald's mobile phone, they noticed the third body in the back with more blood and gore spilling out from its head and from a gaping wound in its belly.

Detective Superintendent Ivan Dibley had been with Essex police for thirty-one years since the tender age of seventeen. He was just four months away from retirement and getting ready to enjoy a rare day off when, just after 8.30 a.m., the call came asking him if he'd like to come in and take charge of what would undoubtedly be the biggest case of his entire career. Although he was officially on leave that day, the killing had occurred on his designated patch, so through polite protocol a colleague phoned to offer him first bite of the cherry. Dibley had a first-class record when it came to murder: of the twenty-five homicides he had investigated, only two had remained unsolved. He also took any gangland murder on his patch as a personal challenge, as if someone was throwing down a gauntlet saying, 'I bet you can't catch me.'

'I said yes but on one condition – I'd promised my daughter that I'd change an electrical fitting at her house and I wanted to do that first. The only information I had was that there were three men dead in a Range Rover, so I knew a pathologist would have to be called to the scene and that the inquiry wasn't going to take any real steps for several hours at least.'

His chores done, Dibley made his way to the scene of the crime and was immediately disturbed by what he saw around him. 'The first thing you do when you're investigating a murder scene is look around for things that may help you. As I was walking down the lane, I looked around and there was nothing. Absolutely nothing. No houses overlooking the scene, not even any houses close enough to consider house-to-house enquiries. There was a slight covering of snow on the ground but that was melting before my very eyes and taking any footprint evidence with it. The further I got down the lane, the more isolated I realised it was. There was no chance of a live witness having seen anything or even having heard anything. My first thought was, "Christ. Where do we start?"'

At that stage, Dibley didn't even know who the men were. Despite the dinner arrangements that had been put in place the previous evening, the girlfriends of Tate, Tucker and Rolfe saw no cause for alarm. They were well used to their men vanishing at short notice, sometimes for days at a time. Besides, phoning the police to report them missing so quickly would have done nothing to ingratiate themselves had they turned up later on. The car gave no clues either. The man in whose name the vehicle was registered was found to be alive and well but could throw little light on the occupants, having sold it on some months before. However, the police records did show that a local officer had run a check on the same vehicle the previous day. When he was tracked down, he explained that he'd seen the vehicle being driven by a well-known 'face' and had pulled him over to check whose vehicle it was. The 'face' was Craig Rolfe and Dibley had his first name.

But it was only when local news bulletins about three men being executed in a Range Rover started airing around the middle of the day that Diane Evans and the other relatives sensed that something might be wrong and reached for the phone.

About this time that Tony Tucker's mobile phone began to ring. 'We have just heard that there are three men have been found dead in a Range Rover,' said the voice of a worried friend. 'We think one of them is you.'

As the names slowly started to filter in, so the manner of the execution began to make more sense. Especially when it came to one of the dead men in particular.

'I'd actually met Tate before,' says Dibley. 'I was working as a DI in Brentwood at the time and there had been a number of armed robberies that Tate was rumoured to be involved in. Before we could do anything, he'd escaped from the Magistrates' Court, run off to Spain, been brought back and banged up on some other charges. But I was still keen to try to clear these crimes up so I went on a cold visit to Swaleside prison to see if I could persuade him to admit to some of the unsolved cases.

'So I'm waiting in this interview room and the prison officers have gone to call him over. As it's a cold visit, he has no idea who I am or why I'm there. And I'm looking at this 6-foot 6-inch doorway, waiting for him to turn up, and when he does, he fills the doorway completely. I have never seen such a big man in the whole of my life. He actually took all the light away from the room, that's how big he was. His arms, chest – everything was just enormous. He sat down and I said, "Hello, Mr Tate, you don't know me, but I'm investigating some armed robberies . . ." and for the next twenty minutes I talked and talked and talked. I was going on about what I suspected that he had done and saying that the only way he'd get parole for his current sentence would be if he came clean about everything. The whole time he just sat and stared at me. He didn't say a word. Then, after twenty minutes, he just got up and walked out of the room. The next time I saw him he was dead.'

By the end of the first day, the identities of all three men had been firmly established and the grim task of informing the next of kin was well underway. For some the news was simply too much to bear. Tony Tucker's sixty-three-year-old father, Ronald, was at home in Folkestone, Kent, when he found out. Ronald had half seen the news bulletins about the brutal killing but had never believed even for a second that his precious son could have been involved. Within seconds of finding out, he had a massive heart attack and dropped dead on the spot.

The following morning, local and national newspapers started running stories about the backgrounds of the three dead men and speculating about what was going on. The Essex police press office was besieged with calls from hacks who wanted to know if this was going to be the start of a massive gangland war in the county, if the dead men had been armed, how many shots had been fired and, most of all, if anyone had been arrested.

The police were saying nothing, but there was so much background to write about they didn't need to. There was the link to Leah Betts, the attack on the pizza parlour man, the previous attempt on Tate's life and even a celebrity angle, thanks to Tucker's friendship with Nigel Benn.

That afternoon, Dibley held a press conference where he answered a few questions, then produced Diane Evans to make a direct, emotional appeal – an attempt to humanise the three men, who were already being typecast as mindless thugs. Weeping uncontrollably, Evans proved that at least someone cared about them. 'I would just like anyone who was with them, who knows anything about what happened to them or if they saw anything to just come forward. We need all the help we can get.'

Dibley couldn't have put it better himself. Earlier in the day he had received a report from his forensics team. Dozens of fingerprints had been lifted from the interior of the Range Rover but they had all turned out to belong to Tate, Tucker or Rolfe. A few fibres had been recovered, but with no control samples for comparison they were worthless. There were a few unexplained footprints scattered around the scene, but as the lane was regularly used by local anglers, it didn't seem worth getting excited about. For a while, everyone thought the best lead would come from the seven spent cartridges found on the ground by the car, but even that had come to nothing. Not only were all the cases clean of fingerprints but they also turned out to be just about the most common brand of cartridge available. The chances of finding out where they were bought and therefore who had bought them was nil. As far as background information or details about the recent activities of the dead men were concerned, none of Tate or Tucker's relatives were willing even to have an informal chat.

Then Dibley got his first break.

It took a while for it to dawn on Diane Evans that she might hold a clue to tracking down Rolfe's killers. Her first instinct had been to protect herself and their child, to ensure she said as little as possible for fear of implicating herself. She had, after all, been there when Kevin Whittaker was killed, she had been present at many of Rolfe's drug deals and she had witnessed first hand the increasing tension between members of the gang in the weeks leading up to the killing. Most of all, she knew that Rolfe and the others had been on their way to meet the man she knew only as 'Mickey the Pilot' on the night they died.

Soon after the press conference, she made a new statement explaining everything she knew.

It was less than thirty-six hours after the murder and Dibley now had the name of his prime suspect. All he had to do now was find out who 'Mickey the Pilot' actually was. 'I didn't know who or what I was dealing with, so I wanted to keep things pretty close to my chest. I was in the canteen at police headquarters when I saw a friend who worked in criminal intelligence. "You don't happen to know a pilot called Mickey?" I asked him. He said that he did. "Oh right. Listen, at some stage do you think you could let me have whatever you've got on him?" He said he was just on his way to the office and that he'd get it for me then and there. That was just what I wanted. I didn't want to have to wait a week or even a weekend but I had to make it look as casual as possible.'

As soon as Dibley saw the details of Steele's previous convictions, a possible motive for the killings – a drugs-related double-cross – became clear. But for the theory to work there had to be some firm connection between Steele and the dead men. Did they live near each other? Did they ever work together? Did they socialise together? Did their girlfriends know each other? 'It's like working on a thousand-piece jigsaw when you only have fifty pieces. Even if the stuff you have is all in the right place, it's still not making a picture at all. It's easy looking back with hindsight – you just think, well, they were all in prison together, it's obvious. But at the time that's just one of dozens of possibilities. Everything you do in those early stages is pure guesswork.'

Even having an idea of where to look is no guarantee of success. Checking whether prisoners have served time together is no easy task, even for the police. Chelmsford prison, for example, has forty movements per day. Records are not always kept and even if you find two prisoners in the same jail at the same time, you still need confirmation from staff or other prisoners before you can say for sure that they actually knew each other, particularly if they were serving on different wings.

With neither Tucker or Rolfe having served much time, the connection with Steele had to be through Tate. And once it was established that the pair had been banged up together at Swaleside prison throughout most of 1992, another clue was on the table. If Steele knew Tate best, then it might well have been Tate's behaviour that led to his death.

Two days after the murder, just as Ivan Dibley was beginning the task of identifying Mickey Steele's associates, a jumpy Darren Nicholls received an unexpected visitor.

NICHOLLS I was just about to get in the bath when I heard the bell go. I almost jumped out of my skin. Since the murders, I'd been convinced the Old Bill were going to be around at any time. When I opened up and saw it was Mally, this young gypsy bloke who I'd seen around town it was a real relief. But not for long.

   'Someone told me you were looking to buy a shotgun,' he said. 'I've got one in my van.'

This was fucking tricky. You have to remember that at the time every single newspaper, every magazine, every TV bulletin and radio broadcast is about these three local blokes who have been brutally murdered, blasted in their car by some bloke with a shotgun. And then you have to remember that up until the day before that, I'd been asking everyone I knew, I mean everyone, to get me a gun. I was really desperate for it.

And now that gun had arrived. What I wanted to say was, 'No thanks mate, I don't need it any more,' but that would have been a bit of a giveaway.

'Okay,' I said. 'Great. I'll have a look.'

I went to the bloke's van and he opened up the back to show me this nine-shot single-barrel pump-action shotgun with three cartridges, all in a brown plastic case. He wanted £350 for it so I told him I'd just have to call a mate to check if the price was right.

I slipped back indoors and phoned Mick. He agreed that the best way to avoid suspicion was to go ahead and buy it and he promised he'd pay me back right away.

As soon as Matty was out of sight, I drove straight over to Meadow Cottage. Mick wasn't around so I took the gun and hid it in the barn behind some bamboo poles. Eventually Mick turned up and I told him what I'd done and followed him into the barn.

What happened next I will never forget. Mick took the gun out of the case, took out the three cartridges and slowly pushed them, one by one, into the magazine of the gun. The he started playing around with it, tossing it from one hand to another to test its weight and balance. The gun was spinning all over the place, but every now and then it ended up pointing directly at my head. And all the time I was standing there thinking, 'Fuck, how did I let myself get into such a stupid situation?' Eventually Mick unloaded the gun and put it back in its case. It was only when I got back into my van to drive home and couldn't get the key in the ignition because

my hands were shaking so much that I realised just how
scared I'd been.

Bill Davidson knew Michael Steele of old. A long serving
member of the National Investigations Service of Customs and
Excise, he had been one of the leading lights behind Operation
Waterski, the large-scale customs investigation that had
resulted in Steele being sent to prison in 1989.

After hearing of his release on parole in 1994, Davidson
knew it was only a matter of time before Steele tried to get
back into the game. It was nothing more than a hunch based
on Steele's love of smuggling for the adrenaline kick as much
for as the money, so there was nothing to justify a surveillance operation there and then, but Davidson carefully
ensured that any odd bits of information that related to Steele,
his activities and associates, were compiled and co-ordinated
on a regular basis.

Davidson's hunch was proved right when Steele was
arrested, along with Whomes and Corry, at Felixtowe ferry in
November 1995. Although there hadn't been enough evidence
to press charges, it was blindingly obvious what the trio had
been up to: a boatload of cannabis had been brought over
from Belgium, landed somewhere on the Essex or Suffolk coast
and then Steele had gone back out to sea and brought his boat
back in at the marina.

When the boat was finally returned to Jack Whomes – it
was, after all, he who said he owned it – Davidson learned it
was being stored in a garage at G & T Commercials, the dock-
side haulage firm in Ipswich where Whomes worked as a
freelance mechanic, looking after the company's vehicles. The
boat was clearly the key to Steele's smuggling activities so
Davidson decided to assign a team to keep the premises under
watch and issue an alert to ports and airports to look out for
any new trips abroad.

The first few weeks yielded little of interest as far as the
boat was concerned, though a report from Harwich showed

that Steele had made a ferry trip to the Hook of Holland along with a Darren Nicholls around 15 November.

A few days after the Rettendon murders, Davidson was preparing to submit plans to his superiors asking for the operation to be stepped up when a call came in from Essex police explaining that Michael Steele was the number one suspect in the triple killings. An urgent meeting was arranged and it was quickly agreed that the police investigation should take priority and that they would put Steele and some of his associates under round-the-clock surveillance. If the police came across anything that indicated that the target was planning another smuggling trip, customs would immediately be brought in. By the same token, customs agreed to pass on all their information about Steele and his associates and keep the police informed of any movements through ports and airports. Less than two weeks after Steele had committed what he considered to be a near perfect murder, the net was starting to close in.

For a man accused of a gruesome triple murder and said to be involved in drug smuggling on a massive scale, Michael Steele seemed to be living a life that would bore a hermit. Dibley's men watched him going to the shops, pottering about in the grounds of his home, going out for the odd meal with Jackie Street, visiting his ex-wife or sister-in-law, visiting Sarah Saunders and then pottering about once again.

Yet despite finding nothing out of the ordinary, Dibley found himself under enormous pressure to arrest Steele there and then. 'A lot of people in my team were saying that the gun that had been used for the murders would be in a case above the mantelpiece in his house. They reckoned it would be a real trophy and that he'd definitely hang on to it. All we had to do was raid him and the case would be solved. I didn't agree. From what I knew of Steele, he was much too clever to have anything like that lying around. The clothes, the shoes, the guns – anything that could link him to the murder would have been destroyed almost immediately. If we had picked him up he would have sat on his hands and said, "I don't know what you're talking about." No comment all the way. It was too risky to even contemplate. The one possible advantage we had was that Steele had no idea we were on to him. An arrest would spoil all that. My bosses would have loved to have brought him in, the press would have loved it, the families of the dead men would have loved it, but the time just wasn't right.'

Instead Dibley decided to let the job run long-term, doing nothing more proactive than watching, waiting and building up a picture of Steele's gang. Whomes and Corry had already been identified as key members of Steele's smuggling team by customs but that didn't mean they were involved in the murder. Dibley, however, was convinced that Steele had not acted alone.

'The way I saw it, Steele couldn't have been on his own because there was no way that he would have risked getting into the Range Rover with a gun. Even if it was a sawn-off, then it would still be bulging out under his raincoat or trouser leg – it would have been really obvious. And even if he did find a way of concealing it, he'd never be able to get it out quickly enough to take all three men by surprise.

'There had to be at least two killers, Steele in the car itself and another man hiding in the bushes down the lane with two guns. That way, as Steele got out of the car, the other man could hand him a gun and then lean in and start shooting.

'I also felt there was at least one more person involved because of the question of transportation to and from the murder scene. Steele was easy – he'd arrived in the Range Rover – but what about the other man. He must have been hiding down the lane for a while, at least half an hour. Would he risk parking his own car somewhere nearby or down the lane itself? Unlikely. It was only a small risk, but if a member of the public or worse still a policeman saw it, thought it was suspicious and made a note of the number, then it would all be over. There's also the question of your state of mind after you've done something like that. No matter how cold and unemotional you are, you wouldn't want to do anything to draw attention to yourself as you're driving away from the scene. The only possible solution was to have a third member of the gang parked up somewhere and have them pick Steele and the other killer up once the deed was done.'

Dibley took his theory one step further. He predicted that when an arrest was eventually made it would be the getaway driver who would prove to be the weak link. Whether he knew the killings had been about to take place or not, he would have taken no actual part in it – he would have had to be away from the scene – and would therefore do everything he could to distance himself from the actual crime. If anyone was going to talk, it would be him.

It was less than ten days after the murder and Dibley, in an astonishing bit of classic detective work, had managed to work out exactly what had happened and pretty much who was responsible.

And he didn't have a single scrap of evidence to prove it.

Just before Christmas, a member of Dibley's team pulled him to one side and asked how much he knew about the way that mobile phones work. Dibley admitted he didn't know that much and asked why. The man explained that whenever a mobile phone is switched on it automatically sends a signal to the nearest radio beacon so that the network knows where the phone is. The information is instantly transferred to a central computer. When a call comes in for that particular phone, it is sent out via the same beacon. If a phone moves out of a particular area, it continues sending out signals until it is picked up by the next nearest beacon.

The man could see his boss's eyes were starting to glaze over so he quickly got to the point. If Steele and his accomplices had their mobile phones with them on the day of the murder, then they would have logged on to the beacon nearest

Workhouse Lane at some point that evening. They'd be able to see what time Steele got there, what time he left and who was with him. They'd be able to check his movements earlier in the day – as well as see who he was in contact with – and compare that to the movements of Tate, Tucker and Rolfe. 'It sounded brilliant. Almost too good to be true. I asked him what he'd need to compile the information and he scratched his chin for a second then said just a couple of computer terminals and a corner of the incident room. I told him to go for it and keep me informed on a daily basis.'

It took a few weeks to track down all the different sources of information and work out the best way of putting it together, but when the first print-outs emerged, they were beyond Dibley's wildest expectations. 'You couldn't see the people and you couldn't hear what was being said, but you could follow everyone's movements – or to be more exact, the movements of their phones – throughout the day and see all the different sides slowly coming together and ending up at Workhouse Lane. It was incredible.'

It all started around 2 p.m. with a call from Steele's land line to Nicholls's mobile, which at the time was out in Sunbury on the site close to Heathrow. Eleven minutes later, Steele called Whomes at G&T in Ipswich. Soon after that there were calls from a payphone at the Sorrel House Inn, a pub just down the road from G&T, to Tucker's mobile and then Tate's mobile as Whomes set about arranging the meeting for that evening. The call to Tate's mobile was brief and followed, a few minutes later, by a much longer call to a payphone close to Tate's house – an attempt to get around any bugging devices that may have been planted.

After that there were a series of calls between Steele and Nicholls, with the latter getting ever closer to Essex until both his phone and Steele's connected with the beacon nearest to Marks Tey.

At 6.44 p.m., Tate's mobile received a call from the land line belonging to Sarah Saunders. At one minute to seven,

Whomes's mobile connected to the beacon nearest Workhouse Lane for a three-second call to the mobile of Darren Nicholls as he asked to be picked up from the murder scene. Although no calls had been made or received by Steele's phone during the time the murders were believed to have taken place, the print-outs showed that it too had logged itself on to the beacon nearest Workhouse Lane around the crucial time.

The phone records not only fingered Steele and Whomes as the killers and Nicholls as the getaway driver but also put Corry in the clear. 'When you sat down and looked at it all, it seemed to be pretty damning evidence, but as far as I was concerned it didn't change a thing,' says Dibley. 'The pressure to arrest Steele was on again but all he would have said was that he didn't have his phone with him that day, his wife borrowed it and went on a drive around Essex. It wasn't enough to prove any different so all we could do was add it to the pot and continue with the long-term plan. It was another piece of the jigsaw, but the picture was still far from complete. In fact, short of getting Steele to throw his hands up and shout out, "I did it! It was me all along!" there didn't seem to be any way to close the case.

'But we had to keep going. The alternative is you pack up your bags and say we think he's done it but can't prove it so let's just leave it. And that would have suited a lot of people. All the time I was being asked, "What are you worried about? Why are you wasting your time on scum? Whoever did this has done the whole population a favour."'

It was on the evening of Thursday 15 February 1996, shortly after the nine o'clock news had come on air, that a relaxed and confident Michael Steele received the first telephone call.

The voice was not one that he recognised but Steele listened patiently as the softly spoken Irishman on the other end of the line explained that he had been trying to track him down for several weeks. Along with his brother, John, the caller, Billy, had been part of an organisation working closely with Pat Tate. Unbeknown to Steele, all the merchandise that he had been shipping into the country and passing to Tate had eventually made its way to the Emerald Isle. When the enterprise started up, Billy and John had been led to believe that fresh supplies would be reaching them on a regular basis and, with that in mind, they had invested a good deal of their own money into the venture to ensure its smooth operation. But now with Tate dead, the brothers had suddenly found themselves out of pocket and out of stock.

Everyone had assumed that Tate was working with the Joneses. Perhaps Billy and John were linked to them.

The initial request was simple enough. Would Steele be willing to supply the same goods at the same bargain price Tate had offered to them directly? If that wasn't possible, then how about delivering the goods, at a reduced rate, to a local third party whom they would nominate? Or if Steele himself had a suggestion for the best way to do business, they would be more than happy to listen. Up until that point, Steele had said nothing more than 'hello'. He held his silence for a moment longer and when he finally chose to speak again, he chose his words carefully. 'I haven't got the faintest idea what you're talking about mate,' he said, and promptly put the phone down.

The second call came two days later and the first threat followed almost immediately. 'Pat owed us £40,000,' said Billy, the voice having suddenly developed a much harder edge. 'We want our fucking money. Where is it? This isn't some game.' Even under pressure, Steele remained the epitome of cool. 'I think the police have got it. Why don't you talk to them?' he said, and promptly put the phone down.

After that it all started to fall apart. 'Don't fuck with us, Mickey,' hissed John the following evening. 'We want our money or you'll be sorted out just like Pat was.' Steele had to stifle a giggle. The idea of someone threatening him with the same fate as Pat was, under the circumstances, so ludicrous it almost brought tears to his eyes. Over the next week or so, the calls became more and more frequent and Billy and John made more and more references to the end of the IRA ceasefire and the bombing of Canary Wharf. The implication was obvious, but Steele wasn't going to be pushed around by anyone.

The threats became ever more direct. 'You're going to have to emigrate,' Billy told him one day. 'That's the only way. I'm going to have to follow these matters up. And watch your car, I have A-Levels in whacking people.' Steele's response was curt and to the point. 'I've told you, I don't know what you're talking about. Why don't the pair of you just fuck off and bother someone else.' Billy just laughed. 'You'd better watch your back. The ceasefire's gone Mickey, and your ceasefire's gone.'

A few days later, a tearful Sarah Saunders called Steele. Billy and John had taken him at his word and called her up to make similar threats. Saunders, unaware at first that Steele had also been contacted by the brothers, had gone straight to Basildon police with the phone number they had given her. Their response did little to comfort her: not only had the number traced to a well-known Republican bar in Belfast, but Billy and John – both identified as known members of a major terrorist cell – had recently travelled to the mainland. They had been tracked entering the port but the special agents tailing them had now lost track. No one knew where they were.

Saunders was terrified but Steele was full of doubts. Would terrorists really hold him responsible for the £40,000? Could they really have been dealing with someone as unreliable and unpredictable as Tate? Would they really be phoning him up and threatening him so openly on the phone? None of it made sense. He took a gamble and did nothing. And almost as soon as they had started, the phone calls stopped. 'It's bollocks,' he told Darren Nicholls. 'I reckon it's probably the Old Bill or someone.'

13

'I know you, you're a drug dealer'

NICHOLLS I'm sitting alone on the sofa in my living room watching some crappy TV show when I hear a car pull up outside. At first I think it's my neighbours getting back from work, but as I listen I realise that the footsteps on the gravel are making their way towards *my* front door. I sit there, waiting for the sound of the bell, but it never comes. Instead there's this horrible racket, this crashing, tearing sound of wood splitting and glass shattering. They're kicking the door down, smashing their way in. Before I've had chance to react, I hear them running through the house, knocking stuff over, throwing things against the walls and screaming out my name over and over again.

I want to run away, to hide, anything, but I'm frozen to the spot with fear. And the noise and the stamping and the screaming goes on and on and gets louder and louder until finally the door to the front room bursts open and Mick and Jack are standing there. And their faces are both covered in streaks of blood and they have shotguns in their hands. And as they see me, they start laughing, harder and harder, then they raise the guns so they are level with my head and I see their fingers tighten on the triggers. And then there's this blinding flash.

And then I wake up.

It was more than a month after the murders but the nightmares were still as vivid as ever, so bad that I was almost afraid to go to sleep at night. Christmas had been the worst time: for obvious reasons I'd been doing my level best to avoid Mick and Jack. I'd stopped selling drugs, I'd been working all hours to keep myself occupied and basically stayed away from places where I knew they might go. But after a couple of weeks Mick, clever git, sent over some really expensive Christmas presents for my kids and invited me and the wife over for lunch. Short of telling Sandra the truth – something I just couldn't do – there was just no way to explain to her why I didn't want to go. She was always into being polite and proper: if someone did something nice to you, it was only right to go and thank them. So off we went.

I'll never forget that day: the kids were running around in Mickey's garden chasing after rabbits and having the time of their lives, Sandra was having a good old smoking and drinking session with Jackie Street, Mick was pissing about with his new toy – a radio-controlled plane – and I was standing about like a prat, stone cold sober, desperate to be anywhere but there.

After that I didn't see Mick again until the New Year. He'd ring me up every now and then and ask me to do some electrical or other building work at his house, and like some spineless dog I'd always say yes. I felt pretty shit every time but the truth is I just didn't know what else to do. In my mind I was as guilty of the murder as anyone else. If it ever came on top, all it would take would be for one of them to say that I knew all about it and agreed to drop them off and pick them up afterwards and that would be it. I'd be doing life right along side them.

But the more I saw of Mick after the murders, the less I believed that he would ever stitch me up like that. He wasn't the same person anymore. Whenever we were alone together, he'd start trying to justify the killings to me. He'd start off by saying how all three of them were scum and no one was missing them, that he'd done the world a favour. Then he'd talk about the fact that even Sarah Saunders, even though she'd lost the father of her kid, was much happier now that Pat was dead. He told me that when the police had questioned Sarah, they'd asked her if she knew anyone who might want Pat dead. She said she didn't. Then they said, well do you know anyone who might want Pat dead because they found out that he was informing on them. Mick was always convinced that Pat was a grass and finally, through Sarah, he'd got confirmation. 'You see Darren,' he told me. 'That's another reason to have killed the cunt.'

Another time he started talking about how the police were saying they had no idea who was behind the murder. 'I'll tell you what Darren, you could look in the phone book and just pick a name at random and I bet you'd find someone who wanted one of them three dead. No one is going to miss them at all.'

But it was all talk. Deep down, Mick was really bothered by what he'd done. Before the murder, when I was working at his house, I'd always suggest going for a couple of pints at lunchtime but he'd always refuse, saying it was better to work through and get everything done. After the murder, we'd do a couple of hours' work and then he'd literally drag me to the nearest pub as soon as it opened and we'd spend the rest of the day there getting pissed. And it didn't just happen once or twice. It happened every single time I saw him.

Jack, on the other hand, didn't seem to have changed at all. I found that really scary. It wasn't just what Mick had said about the cold-hearted way he carried out the murders – though I couldn't get that image of Jack as a robotic killing machine out of my mind – there was just something about him that gave me the creeps. Although we never really admitted it, the two of us had never really got on from the time we first met at Hollesley Bay. Jack loved Mick to bits and would do absolutely anything for him, but me he didn't seem to have any time for. And the feeling was completely mutual. We'd had a few laughs over the years and we were always pretty nice to each other whenever we met, but the truth was I trusted Jack exactly about as far as I could throw him.

Around the middle of February, on one of those days when we should have been working but went to the pub instead, Mick and I started talking about flying. I don't remember how it started but we ended up having this friendly argument about how easy it was to navigate from the air. I was saying that it couldn't be that hard because you'd be able to recognise fields and roads and buildings. Mick was saying it was really difficult and that I probably couldn't even recognise my own house from the air. I'd never been in any kind of plane in my life so when Mick started saying, 'Let's put it to the test – why don't you come flying with me next week?' I started to get really excited and told him I'd love to. 'That's agreed then,' Mick said. 'You and me up in a plane next weekend and we'll see how well you do.'

I thought it was just the beer talking but the following weekend Mick phoned up and said he'd be round for my flying lesson in half an hour. I was at the door within seconds of the bell ringing and when I tugged it open there was Mick. And there was Jack standing right beside him. 'Ready for your flying lesson?' asked Mick. I looked at the two of them again. 'Is Jack coming as well then?' I said. Mick looked over at Jack then back at me. 'Don't worry,' he said, 'he can sit in the back.' Silence. Then I took a deep breath. 'Actually, I can't today after all. I forgot that I'd promised Sandra I'd take the kids to the pictures. They're almost ready to leave. Maybe some other time.'

As they walked away I don't mind telling that I was

absolutely shitting myself. Maybe I was just being paranoid. Maybe it would have been fine. When I told Sandra about it she said I was stupid, knowing how much I've always wanted to go flying. But the fact that Jack had turned up really scared me. Up until then Mick and Jack had only really used me because of my skill as an electrician or to move drugs for them. Going flying would have been the first time ever that they wanted to do something with me purely for pleasure. And that just didn't feel right. I was pretty sure the only lesson I'd have got was in freefall parachute jumping without the parachute.

After that my relationship with Mick started to get more and more strained and by the beginning of March any change in his personality seemed to have faded away completely. I was still working for him, doing up his house and stuff, but he never had time to take me to the pub any more. Sometimes he'd even forget to pay me.

I knew he was planning to start smuggling again, having hooked up with some bloke called Russell, and I was getting more and more tense waiting for him to call and ask me to join in. I'd already made up my mind that I was never, ever, going to do it again and now I had the perfect excuse – my one-year passport had run out – but I was still worried about how he'd react.

The day I told him about it there was this long, awkward silence on the other end of the phone. Eventually Mick just said, 'Okay,' and put the phone down. Instantly I felt like this huge weight had been lifted off my shoulders. The work on the bungalow was finished and I wasn't able to go abroad and I no longer had any real use as far as Mick was concerned. He dropped me like a stone and I was more than happy for him to let me go.

I thought that was going to be the end of it. Then, out of the blue, something happened which completely turned my life around. Suddenly, I was desperate to spend as much time with Mick as possible. Not only that, but I also wanted to

return to the drug business. I wanted Mick to sell me all the
puff he could get his hands on.

The first time he spoke to me I almost cacked my pants. I was
in the Sailing Oak pub having a quick drink when I thought I
felt someone tap me on the shoulder. I was going to ignore it
when I heard a voice say, 'I know you, you're a drug dealer.'
Fuck. In the instant it took before I turned round, all kinds of
things were going through my head. I was wondering if the
person was definitely talking to me, whether anyone else had
heard. Most of all though, I was wondering who the fuck it
might be. I was really, really hoping that it would be one of
my old customers or some friend of a friend with a big
mouth. Someone stupid. Someone I could just tell to piss off.
And then I turned round. And I saw Detective Constable Jim*
standing next to me with a big smirk on his face. Fuck. Fuck.
Fuck. There and then I wanted the ground to open up and
swallow me whole. Anywhere but there was where I wanted
to be. This was bad news. Really, really bad news.
   I'd never spoken to Jim but I knew who he was because
our paths had crossed twice before. The first time was the
same pub about a month or so before the murders when
someone pointed him out as the copper who had lent his car,
an XR3i, to three of his mates who were going out on a pub
crawl. They'd written if off, naturally, and one of them ended
up in intensive care. We were all talking about it in the pub
and I said something like: 'Fucking hell, not much of a
detective if he couldn't see that one coming is he?' Jim was
standing right next to me at the time but he never said
anything. He just looked really pissed off and a bit
embarrassed.
   The second time was outside the Sailing Oak just after

---

*For legal reasons, the true name of the detective concerned cannot be
used. Jim is a pseudonym and any resemblance to other current or
former officers in the Essex police force is purely coincidental.

Christmas when I saw him unloading a load of bottles of spirits from the back of his car and taking them into the pub. I remember asking someone later what he was up to and they said that the landlord was a mate of his and Jim had managed to sort him out with some cheap booze from one of those police auctions.

So there I was in the pub with this copper and he was looking me straight in the eye and accusing me of being a drug dealer. And I was desperately trying to think of something to say when he started up again. 'I suppose you're going to deny it,' he said. 'Everyone always denies it.'

Double fuck. He'd taken the words right out of my mouth, but I thought I might as well say it anyway. 'I don't know what you're talking about,' I said. 'All that was a long time ago. You're out of date, mate.' And then I walked off.

Two days later, Jim phoned me up on my mobile having got the number from my boss, who it turned out was a mate of his. 'I'm only telling you this because you're a friend of Dave,' he said. 'You're about to get spun. The drugs squad is planning a raid on your place because they reckon you've got a load of gear stashed there.' I just laughed. 'I didn't think the drugs squad were that slow. I've told you mate, that was all in the past.'

He didn't care. 'I'm telling you Darren, you're gonna get spun this week, any day now. There's a note here on the office wall. I'm looking at it right now. I'll tell you what though, if you're telling me the truth and you're not at it any more, well I might be able to stop it. I'll have a word with some people, see what I can do.'

A few days after that, Jim phoned me up again. 'See, I stopped it from happening. You didn't get spun after all. I think we should meet up because you owe me a beer.'

Even I could see right through this one. It had to be just about the oldest trick in the book. Okay, the bloke was a copper and he obviously knew a fair bit about me, but I was pretty certain that I was never about to get spun. He had

just made the whole thing up to get me to believe I owed
him and now he wanted to meet up so he could call in the
favour.

It crossed my mind that it might be some kind of ploy the
police were using to try to find out about the Rettendon
killings, but the more I thought about it, the less likely it
seemed. I'd been reading the papers and watching stuff on
TV and it seemed pretty clear from what the police were
saying that they didn't have a clue who was responsible for
the killings. The list of suspects who might have had a
grudge against Tate and the others seemed to stretch all the
way to the west coast. They'd even interviewed the parents
of Leah Betts. The only way they would get on to me would
be through Mick or Jack and I knew neither of them had
been picked up so I had to be in the clear. In the end I was so
intrigued by the whole thing I decided to let my curiosity get
the better of me and meet up with Jim after all.

As it happens, he wasn't at all what I expected a cop to be
like. But then again, I'd never been friends with a policeman
in my entire life. We had a few drinks and a bit of a laugh and
I found I was really enjoying myself. In a funny sort of a way,
we had quite a lot in common. It turned out that Jim was a
bit of a maverick who was always getting into trouble with
his bosses for not doing things quite by the book. But, as he
told me more than once as the beers started to disappear, he
had an excellent arrest rate and was basically one of the most
successful detectives in the whole of Essex.

As Nicholls would soon discover, the key to Jim's success was
an extensive network of well-placed informants. He would
befriend dozens of low-ranking villains and play them off
against one another or sometimes against themselves. After
manoeuvring himself into a position where the person
believed they were in his debt, he would ensure his informant
knew that their future was in his hands. He'd promise people
impossible favours – wiping out parking fines, getting them

moved to a bigger council house, anything to keep in with them – and then he'd play mind games.

One of his favourite tricks was to get a couple of his informants together without them realising. He'd choose crooks who knew about each other's underworld dealings but didn't realise they were both providing information to the police and then invite them to a pub at the same time. He would spend some of his time talking to one and then talk separately to the other. It worked like a charm. Each crook would start thinking that the other was giving information against the other and then, at the earliest opportunity, give even more information in order to make the other person seem like a much better target.

Working reams of unpaid overtime and regularly spending considerable amounts of his own money in order to keep his informants sweet, Jim was considered to be completely mad by most of his colleagues back at the station. He also frustrated them because of his unwillingness to share information. He always worked alone and such was the spread of his informant network that he would often come across intelligence that would be of great use to other squads. As far as Jim was concerned, though, if it wasn't a collar that he could make personally, then it wasn't something he had any time for. It was only the fact that he got results, often very good results, that kept him away from the disciplinary committees. But it also held back his career. What Jim craved the most was promotion; however it was anathema to think of an officer like him ever rising in the ranks. His only hope would be to come up with bigger and better collars so that eventually his bosses had no choice but to move him up. And that really would be a victory.

As for Nicholls, Jim knew that he had sold a few bits of cannabis in the past, sometimes in quite large amounts. It was a good bet that he was connected to someone fairly high up the chain and, with a little friendly persuasion and a lot of alcohol, Jim might just be able to find out whom.

But the ball was actually in Nicholls's court. As Jim had

yapped away about this and that and how much the pair could help each other out, Nicholls had come up with a way to use Jim to his own advantage.

NICHOLLS It suddenly occurred to me that if I played my cards right I might be able to find a way out of this situation I was in. There was no way I was ever going to go to the police and tell them about the murders, but if Mick and Jack just happened to get arrested while smuggling drugs, they'd be out of my hair for years. I needed to make sure there would be no comeback on me but Jim was going on about how good he was at protecting his contacts. I still wanted to put it to the test though.

After a few more meetings – including one where Jim had invited me round to his house – I started to feel more comfortable with him. It was almost like he was a friend who just happened to work for the police rather than anything else. But he was never completely off duty. His priority was always getting information from me. Every now and then he'd mention the name of some local toe-rag and ask if I knew anything about what they were up to. Sometimes I told him, sometimes I didn't. It usually depended on how drunk I was.

I was starting to trust him more and more and basically confessed that during my drug-smuggling days (which were long over) I had been involved with a sizeable load of duff cannabis which I'd ended up chucking away. He got really excited and we jumped in his car and drove over to the fishing lake at Sand Pit Lane and I pointed out where the drugs were. I was saying to him, 'It's about 50 kilos of puff and I'm sure it would looking blinding on your record that you've had this astounding find because of your initiative,' and he was like, 'Yeah, yeah.' He was getting really excited. He said if the cannabis was really there, I'd get a reward. And if there was any information I had on other people, I could get more rewards for that as well. I made it clear that there was plenty more I could say about other stuff going on, but he had to do his bit by making sure my name wasn't linked to the find in the lake. If he did that, then I'd lead him to some bigger fish.

Not surprisingly, Jim got really excited and promised there would be no come-back. Within a day or two, he'd arranged for a diving team to go down an have a look at the place. I had to laugh when I saw the headlines in the local paper. To protect me they announced that the Essex diving team were on a routine training mission at the lake when they just happened to find all this cannabis. Jim also told me that, as each and every bar was pulled out of the water, he wiped it down to ensure that my fingerprints would never be found. The papers put the street value at something like £100,000, which was a bit mad considering it was all cack and the reason we'd chucked it away was because we couldn't even give it away.

When the news about the find broke Mick was straight on the phone. I hadn't actually told him what I'd done with the cannabis. After all, he'd just told me to get rid of it. I don't think he cared as long as he didn't have to look after it any more. But he called up and said, 'Is that ours? Did you dump it in the sandpit?' Mick was most worried about whether they might find his fingerprints on the puff. I calmly told him not to worry, that I'd wiped every bar before I chucked it all in. 'Great, nice one Darren,' he said, and then he was gone again.

Jim seemed to be keeping up his end of the bargain. I began to realise there was a pretty good chance of the rest of my plan working out. The very next day Mick called me again and asked if I could pop round as he might have something for me. He was talking about drugs, of course. It was all going like clockwork. The future was looking rosy.

When it came to collecting the reward, Jim told me I'd have to become a registered informant and meet his guvnor. If I wanted to stay anonymous it would also mean coming up with a plausible story about how I knew the cannabis was in the lake. Jim suggested I say I'd overheard a conversation in a pub with a couple of dealers talking about having hidden some dope there. The final step was to come up with a code, one that didn't relate to any other villain or any other real person that either of us knew. It's not as easy as you think and after what seemed like hours of stupid or useless suggestions, we settled on Ken Rugby, because Jim's son was in the school rugby team and Ken was the name of his instructor.

Using a false name was another way of protecting me. Along with our cover story, it meant that the top cop brass didn't need to know anything about me or my personal drug connections. I met Jim's guvnor in the car park of the Dolphin pub and told him the made-up story. He said, 'Brilliant,' and counted me out £400 in £10 notes. I signed for the money (as K. Rugby) and waved goodbye as he left. As soon as he was out of sight, Jim held out his hand and said, 'Bottle of scotch.' I paused for a second then counted him out £50 from the money I'd just been given.

It should have been another one of those times when warning bells were ringing in my head, but I just didn't see it. I mean, we'd just spent ages making up this totally false story so that I could get the money in the first place. I wouldn't have got any of it without him so sharing the wealth seemed the decent thing to do.

I'd been teasing Jim something rotten about all the other stuff I knew and he was so keen to find out about it that he started making all sorts of promises to get me on side. I'd mentioned to him that I was really interested in getting a burger van in the area, 'cos you can make good money from them. My bank had already agreed to give me a loan but the hard part was getting a licence. Without it, you'd just get moved on every couple of hours and spend all your time paying fines.

Jim said he had a friend at the council and that, if I helped him out, he'd make sure I got my licence. It was almost too good to be true. I was going to get rid of Mick and Jack, I wasn't going to get into trouble myself and I was going to be able to set up my own business. There was no room for doubt: meeting Jim had to be the best thing that had ever happened to me.

It had happened more than two years earlier but I still hadn't forgiven Alan Richards. It was one of those Christmas parties where everyone was drinking too much and I wasn't going to be left behind. But after a couple of hours I started to feel really ill and decided to go home early. Maybe it was something I ate.

Sandra was having a good time and Richards, who I knew fairly well because he used to go out with one of Sandra's sisters, said he'd drop her home for me. When the time came, Sandra got in Richards's car and off they went. Only he didn't take her to our place; he took her to his place, which was out in the middle of nowhere. And once they got there he started going on about how he was too drunk to drive and how she'd have to stay the night. She tried calling me but I was too far gone to hear the phone, so she had to sleep fully clothed on his sofa. Richards tried it on a couple of times but obviously didn't get anywhere. Even though nothing happened, Sandra knew I'd be really pissed off about the whole thing. And she was right.

Although we'd sort of been friends, I didn't have a lot of time for Richards even before the thing with Sandra. He worked as a car sprayer and he used to hire someone to go out and put key scratches down the side of every nice car in his neighbourhood just to generate business for himself, so I always thought he was a bit of a scumbag.

I finally ran into him a couple of days later and I wanted to tear his head off, but as soon as he clapped eyes on me he started crying like a little baby and saying, 'Please don't hit me,' and all that. His excuse for that night was a classic – he was so drunk that he forgot she was in the car with him and had just driven home.

I walked away. Ever since then, whenever our paths have crossed, he would try to clear the air and offer to buy me endless drinks. Me, being the well-adjusted sensible adult that I am, would mercilessly rip the piss out of him at every opportunity, winding him up and showing him up in front of everyone.

Richards happened to be a friend of Jim. In fact, he was the man who had borrowed the XR3i and written it off. On this particular night, Jim was in the pub actually sitting next to Richards while I took the piss out of him. Richards was getting more and more upset, not just because of what I was saying but also because he considered Jim to be a really good friend of his. But rather than standing up for him, Jim was just giggling to himself.

Richards finally had enough and stood up and said that the two of us should go and talk outside. I was really getting into it by then, really enjoying the wind-up, so I pretended I'd misunderstood what he'd said. I was going, 'Fucking great idea. You and me outside right now. Let's go. Let's get it on.'

Richards was horrified and sat back down immediately, saying, 'No, not like that,' but as he sat down his chair collapsed and he ended up rolling around on the floor.

Everyone in the pub started laughing at that point and Richards skulked off with some excuse about needing to use the toilet while I started trying to put his chair back together. It was like a jigsaw puzzle and I was bashing bits with my hand and all sorts when the landlord saw me, came over and accused me of trying to smash the place up. He went mad. His first words were 'People like you' and then he started going on about how thugs were putting him out of business and how important it was to respect people's property. I was on my feet straightaway.

'What do you mean, people like me?' I shouted back. The guy was a little fucker and I was towering above him. I threw the bits of chair back on the floor and told him to poke it up his arse 'cos I hadn't done anything wrong.

As I walked away, Jim and the others explained to the landlord what had happened and he came running over to apologise and promised me drinks on the house for the rest of the night. But I was still fuming so I went out into the car park to calm down. Jim came with me and we started chatting about various dealers around the town and how to catch them at it.

He was telling me that I could trust him completely because nothing I said would ever be official unless I wanted it to be. So I basically told him that Mick was a big-time drugs smuggler. In an instant, Jim started to get excited. He was saying, 'You've got to get back in with him. Yeah, yeah, yeah. Get in with him.' I was asking how? The only time he ever spoke to me was when I was buying drugs off him.

Jim told me to buy drugs off him to find out when the next big shipment was coming in.

'But what should I do with the puff that I buy from Mick?' I asked him.

'Sell it, of course.'

'Fair enough.'

'In fact, if you let me know who you sell it to, I can go around and nick them.'

'That's a bit strong, isn't it? You are kidding ain't you?'

There was a pause. We'd both been drinking heavily. I was a bit fuzzy headed but even then, it was obvious that he was being completely serious. 'Of course I am,' he said at last. 'Of course I am.'

Somewhere in my head alarm bells were ringing but I was so swept up in the idea of Mick being arrested that I just ignored them. The thing is I had no idea what it actually means to be an informant, how it actually works. On TV it seems to involve nothing but wearing a really bad suit and hanging about in dodgy pubs and then sitting next to cops in their cars and telling them 'the word on the street'. The reality is probably very different, but Jim never sat me down and gave me a lesson or handed over some police pamphlet called *How To Be A Grass* so I just made it up as I went along. The unwritten rule so far as I saw it was that I was allowed to buy drugs from Mick, sell them on in the usual way and keep any profit that I made for myself, just so long as I always kept Jim informed about what I was doing. No problem.

The idea of me stitching up my friends – proper friends that is, not people like Mick – just to make Jim look good was really bothering me – right out of order – but then the conversation drifted off into some other area, I really can't remember what. By the time we went back inside, Richards had vanished.

It didn't matter how many different ways he tried looking at it, the conclusion was always the same. Alan Richards hardly got any sleep that night. Instead he went over the events of the evening again and again in his mind.

It started when Nicholls had been taking the piss out of him and Jim hadn't said anything. That just wasn't fair. After all, Richards had been giving Jim information on the Essex criminal underworld for months now and he thought they'd established a good friendship. Richards had been involved in a wide range of petty criminal activities and Jim had encouraged him to maintain his contacts so that he'd have more information to pass on to him. What disturbed him most though was what he had witnessed when he came back from the toilet after his chair had collapsed. Through the pub window he had seen Nicholls and Jim talking in the car park. There was something about the way their lips were moving, the way their eyes were shifting as they spoke. Richards knew, he just knew that they were talking about him. Not just talking about him; he felt convinced they were planning to set him up.

Early the next morning, sweating profusely and shivering with fear, Alan Richards walked into police headquarters in Chelmsford. 'I'd like to speak to a senior officer,' he told the desk clerk. 'I have some information about one of your officers who has been involved in numerous criminal activities. And I can prove it.'

Skimming money off the payouts to his informants and falsifying his records was just the tip of the iceberg. Jim was into much worse than that. He took bribes to lose bits of evidence; he lied to those he worked with and, when it suited him, turned a blind eye to serious criminal offences. Jim was playing a dangerous game. He was burning the candle at both ends and then, for good measure, setting light to the middle as well. He may have been the one with the warrant card but in the eyes of his informants he was more of a crook than some of the people he arrested.

Of all the people in the whole of Essex that Darren Nicholls could have chosen to confess all to, Detective Constable Jim had to be just about the worst.

14

'It's his brother'

At first Sandra Nicholls put it down to a series of coincidences. Then, after a week or so, she thought she must be going mad, and after that, just for a little while, she was convinced that Darren suspected she was being unfaithful and was having her checked out. It was only after she had exhausted a host of other possibilities that she reluctantly faced the truth: that the periodically familiar faces, the oddly parked cars with silent occupants and the men and women talking into the buttons on their collars that she saw on every street corner could mean only one thing. She was being followed by the police.

'Our relationship was going through an all-time low. Darren was doing his level best to try to keep the fact that he was selling cannabis quiet, but his level best was pretty useless. The thing is, he was selling most of it to people that I knew so it didn't stay secret for long. When he'd gone away over the counterfeit money, I came so close to breaking down. I hated every single minute of it. I really didn't think I'd be able to handle it again and I wanted out. To this day I don't think Darren knows how close I came to leaving him. I really didn't want him to be arrested but at the same time I just knew it would come as a huge relief because at least then he wouldn't be able to do it any more. I was saying to him, "Look, we're being watched. I know that you're going to be arrested, I know it's going to happen. You're gonna go away." He'd just tell me not to be silly, that I was imagining things. I was begging him to stop. "Look Darren, you're working, you're earning more than enough money to have a pretty good life. You just don't need to do it any more." But he just didn't want to listen.

'Mick seemed to have some sort of incredible power over him. Whenever he phoned, Darren would jump. He would be there, dash off to be by his side, no matter what. If he was in the middle of something else, it didn't matter how important it was, he'd drop it to go and see Mick. He'd cancel absolutely anything. If we'd managed to arrange a babysitter and I'd convinced him to take me out for the night, he'd think nothing of cancelling the whole thing if Mick called him up.

'And I got really sick of the fact that he'd always promise that he wasn't doing anything illegal when it was blatantly obvious that he was. In fact, because he was so hopeless at keeping all his other criminal activity from me, I was stunned that he'd never let anything slip about the murder. But he hadn't. Not at all. At that time I had no idea that he'd been involved at any level. It was on the news and in the papers all the time, but we only ever talked about it once. It was a couple of days afterwards when the police first announced the names of the dead men. We were watching TV when Pat Tate's picture came up on the screen and I said, "Hey, look, that's the bloke you were in prison with." At first Darren didn't say anything, he just nodded. But then he said something which has always stuck in my mind. He said that Mick wouldn't be going to the funeral. Then after that he never mentioned it again.'

Central Detective Unit, Essex Police
Surveillance Log, 26 March 1996
Mobile Surveillance Unit
0537hrs. Black Mercedes, index E532 NMU seen entering car park of McDonald's, Chelmsford.

0840hrs. Black Mercedes at the Mobil services at the Boreham interchange. Driver: black leather jacket with white shirt beneath and short cropped hair.

0855hrs. Black Mercedes in McDonald's car park next to red Toyota pick-up index N551 BOO. Both vehicles unattended.

0902hrs. Driver of Mercedes walking from McDonald's in company of MICHAEL STEELE, wearing a burgundy jacket. STEELE and other man have conversation before both returning to their own vehicles and driving off.

End of Log

Blissfully unaware of the massive surveillance operation that was in place against him, Michael Steele was gearing up for a big return to the drug-smuggling business. It was pretty obvious to those watching that the driver of the black Mercedes was somehow involved, but it took Dibley and his team a little while to work out exactly who he was. When the positive ID came through they were surprised to say the least. Darren Nicholls could hardly believe it either.

NICHOLLS Mick had asked me to meet him outside this parade of shops in Southend, and when I arrived his car was already there with Paul Gwinnett in the passenger seat. Mick was in a bit of a funny mood and started telling me about this big row he was having with his new smuggling partner. He said he'd just brought over 80 kilos of cannabis and given the bloke a right good price of just £200 per kilo for importing. The reason he'd given him such a discount was because the guy had said that, once it was in this country, he'd be able to buy loads of it at a discount price of £1,600 per kilo, sell it on for £2,200 per kilo and make his money that way. But once they had got back the bloke had sold all the dope straightaway, leaving nothing for Mick. 'That's what you get for dealing with a Tate,' he said bitterly.

'A Tate? What do you mean?'

'Oh, didn't I tell you? My new business partner – it's Russell Tate. Pat's brother.'

I wasn't sure which I found more shocking: that Mick was now dealing with the brother of a man he'd watched squealing like a baby before emptying both barrels of his shotgun into his belly, or the fact that I'd missed out on a smuggling run. If only I'd known about it a bit sooner, I could have told Jim, the whole gang would have been arrested and all my worries would have vanished overnight.

Either way, I was just coming out of shock a few seconds later when I heard Mick saying that he had something for me, which was what he always said to me when he had drugs for me to sell. He pulled a plastic bag out from the space behind the cab in the truck and walked over to my car. On the way I asked him if the thing with Russell was going to be regular and reliable – if I was going to get him arrested, I needed as much information as possible. Mick told me they had a totally new way of doing it, which was much better and far more profitable than the one I'd been involved in. Basically, three cars would drive down to Spain where, using his contacts, Russell was able to buy puff for just £750 per kilo. The three cars would then head back north in convoy. The drugs would be in the middle car and the other two vehicles would be spaced out, one a mile or so ahead and the other a mile or so behind. That way if either car thought they saw anything suspicious or thought they were being followed they could radio the middle car and give them a chance to change the route or dump the drugs. The really clever part was that Tate's gang included a couple of women. Rather than a bunch of single blokes travelling on their own, which always looks suspicious, each car in the convoy looked like a couple off on their holidays. The cars would come up through France and then Belgium, where the drugs would be driven up to the beach at Blankenberg and Mick would meet them on his boat.

As far as the argument with Russell was concerned, Mick

said that had all been sorted out. From now on Mick would be putting his own money into each deal in addition to whatever cash Russell was carrying. Once in Spain, Russell would buy as much cannabis as Mick could afford, all at the cost price of £750 per kilo, and bring it up with the rest of the convoy free of charge. In return Mick would continue to charge Tate £200 per kilo for his smuggling services.

Under the new arrangement, Mick was more than trebling every pound he invested so he was desperately trying to pull in all the money he possibly could for the next run. Jack Whomes and Paul Gwinnett had each put in a good few thousand and Mick had also invested the money he made from selling his mum's house in Point Clear. He asked me if I could let him have the money from the two kilos as soon as possible because he wanted to put that back in as well. I was doing my best to get as much information as possible. I said I'd try to sell the drugs but it was difficult because all my customers wanted regular supplies – could he guarantee that I'd get some from the next load as it was going to be huge, more than 150 kilos?

That same afternoon I sold all the drugs I'd been given in one go for just £250 over the cost price of £4,400. Mick was waiting on the money and I wanted to make sure that nothing delayed the deal. Seeing Mick and Jack behind bars was, after all, far more important than making a few quid. When I handed over the cash the following morning, Mick was getting really hyped up, like a little kid about to go to the fair or something. He told me that Tate and the others were planning to leave for Spain that very evening. As soon as I got back home I rang Jim and told him all about it. I could hear him making notes in the background and started to feel sick and dizzy with excitement. This was it. Soon it would all be over. Now the only thing left to do was sit back and wait.

I knew it was roughly a two-week trip for Tate and Co to get down to Spain and back so I wasn't surprised when, ten days later, a week before my birthday, Mick asked if I could rent a car for him. He insisted that he wasn't planning to do anything illegal with it, just that he needed the car to go down to Portsmouth for a meeting and didn't want to be seen with his own car. He had a few endorsements on his licence so it was difficult for him to hire cars himself. I knew he was probably lying to me but I didn't care because I knew the next shipment was getting really close. His days were numbered. And as long as I told Jim everything that was happening, I'd always be in the clear.

But when I phoned Jim, I discovered he'd buggered off to Spain to sort out some problem on a villa he owned out there. This was not good news. What with him being a bit of a maverick and not particularly keen on paperwork, I felt incredibly unsafe knowing that he wasn't around in person to defend me. But by then I'd already agreed to get the car for Mick. No one seemed to know how long Jim was going to be away for so all I could do was hope he would be back in time to catch the shipment coming in before I found myself in any more trouble.

I arranged to hire a Mondeo from Budget Rent-a-Car of Chelmsford and Mick picked me up at around 5 p.m. to take me down to their offices. On the way, he said he only needed the car that evening and that he would pay all the charges and let me keep the car for a week to make up for any inconvenience. He'd also lend me his Hi-Lux to drive home in and would drop the Mondeo back at my place at 5 a.m. on the dot, the time I normally got up to get ready for work. On the outside I was smiling and nodding but inside I was shaking my head and saying, 'You're a fucking liar mate.' If what Mick was saying was true, it would be the first time in the four years that I had known him that he had ever given me something for nothing.

I went to bed early that night and got up just before 5 a.m. to call Mick. I didn't want him calling the house in case he woke Sandra and the kids up. I dialled his mobile and he

answered straightaway, saying he'd be with me in about
fifteen minutes and that I should get the kettle on. I was
watching by the window when I saw Jack's Transit van pull
up and Mick and Jack step out. There was no sign of the
Mondeo.

They both came in and we all sat around the kitchen
table. Mick had some tea, Jack had some orange squash and
we all talked about bits of bollocks until I got fed up of
ignoring the obvious and asked what the hell had happened
to the hired car.

Mick took a deep breath then started to explain. Tate and
the others had got the drugs and had arrived in Blankenberg
a couple of days earlier. The problem was, the weather was
too bad for Mick to set sail. The sea was so rough it made the
storm the two of us had been in the year before seem like a
night in the bath. The car with the drugs had been parked up
near the port for three days now and Tate was getting
increasingly worried that the police would get suspicious.
Mick and Jack had driven the Mondeo over so the drugs
could be transferred to its boot and buy them all a bit more
time. He'd also taken Tate's gang some cash because none of
them had expected to be in Belgium for that long and they
were starting to run a bit short.

As Mick spoke, I just sat there listening. None of it came as
a surprise; it was all pretty much as I expected. I didn't care
about the car, I just wanted to know when he was setting off
on the boat and hoped to God that Jim would be back in
time to do his stuff.

'When do you think you'll be going over then?' I asked.

'Well, the weather is starting to get a bit better. I think
tomorrow but if not then Sunday night at the latest. You
could then get the Mondeo back on Monday afternoon.'

'Okay. Fine. Just let me know when you leave.'

Sandra and I have always had pretty good sex, even after the
kids and all that, but I have to say that the biggest orgasm of

my life had nothing to do with her. It came late on Saturday night soon after I answer the telephone and heard Jim's voice telling me that he was back in the country. Yeeeeeeeessssssss! Oh God Yeeessss! I couldn't get all the words out fast enough. I was speaking so fast that no one could have had a clue what I was talking about and it took a while and several attempts before Jim understood what was happening.

I'd spoken to Steele earlier in the day and knew he was planning on setting off that afternoon. He'd be back in the early hours of Monday morning. This was it. This was really it.

But then something incredible happened.

Jim said he wasn't going to do anything about it.

'The thing is Darren, each time they go they are bringing back bigger and bigger shipments,' he told me. 'They invest all the profits they make back into the business. If we let it run, then we'll be able to catch them with a really massive load. And in the meantime we'll be able to do lots of good work with the drugs that you buy as well.'

I didn't really hear the last bit. I was focusing on the idea of Mick being caught with hundreds of kilos, enough to make sure he went away for a very long time.

Central Detective Unit, Essex Police
Surveillance Log, 14 April 1996
Mobile Surveillance Unit

At 1342 hours I saw a blue Transit van, index number L98YDX leave the entrance to the premises known as G&T Commercials, Barham, Suffolk. The vehicle was towing a trailer on which was an orange and black rigid hulled inflatable boat (RHIB). The vehicle and trailer headed westbound on the A14. At 1350 hours the vehicle and trailer left the A14 at the Stowmarket exit and proceeded to the roundabout at the bottom of the slip road. It then circled the roundabout twice before taking the exit towards the Tesco petrol station. At approximately 1351, the vehicle went to the fuelling area. From a position in the supermarket car park, I saw a white male wearing a maroon top (STEELE) standing on top of the trailer, filling the RHIB with fuel. At 1356 hours I saw a second male whom I would describe as white, well built with short dark hair, balding on top (WHOMES). He was wearing a brown leather jacket and dark trousers and was looking up at the male fuelling the RHIB. At 1401 hours, Whomes went into the petrol payment kiosk. At 1402 hours Steele climbed down from the RHIB. At 1408 hours the vehicle and trailer departed heading towards Felixstowe on the A14. At 1425 the vehicle left at the A12 exit. It then circled the roundabout twice before taking the first road towards Levington marina. At 1458 I saw the vehicle with just one occupant – Whomes – heading away from the marina. At this point the vehicle was still towing the trailer which had water dripping from it but the RHIB was no longer there.

End of Log

Steele and Whomes had no idea they were being watched but years of smuggling experience meant that, whenever he was 'on a job', Steele would ensure that everyone practised basic anti surveillance techniques. Every roundabout had to be driven around at least twice, and every now and then you should pull over and wait for twenty cars to go past you. So far as the police and customs teams were concerned, Steele's antics were a bit of a pain in the arse but caused them no real problems. They had now established that the boat had been launched and was on its way to Blankenberg. All they had to do was wait for it to return and they would be able to catch Steele red-handed.

The only fly in the ointment was that although customs knew the exact methods that Steele used to get his drugs into the country, they had no idea where he actually landed them before heading back out to sea and working on his 'fishing trip' cover story.

The speed at which events were now moving had taken the police team by surprise. By the time they called customs in, it was too late for any air support to be brought in to follow the boat. Instead, all that Bill Davidson and his team could do was stake out a few likely landing points.

But at 11 p.m. a report came in that the boat was being landed at Brightlingsea harbour. There were two people on board who looked as though they had been fishing. Wherever the drugs landing had been, the team had missed it.

'There was a lot of pressure to arrest Steele anyway,' said Davidson. 'But there was no point. We had no drugs and only the most circumstantial evidence of any involvement in smuggling. It would have been the November bust all over again. It might have kept him out of the game for a couple of weeks, but he'd just go right back at it. And the worst thing would be that he'd then be aware he was being watched. We decided to leave it but make sure we were far better prepared the second time around.'

Every customs officer has a system. George Stephens had several but his favourite was to add together all the figures in that day's date and then count off the passing cars until he reached that number. And so it was that by pure chance on 14 April 1996, car number 34 – a white Mondeo passing through Dover at just after 9.45 p.m. – got pulled over for a random inspection.

At training school, front-line inspectors spend hours learning how to read the subtle affectations of speech and body language that can help to indicate that a person is lying. It might be a brief loss of eye contact, a minor shudder in the voice, even an idle hand gesture. Mastering and fine tuning such a skill can take many years of dedicated service. But, as any customs officer will tell you, many of those who pass through make it so obvious that they are hiding something that even a trained monkey could tell.

As the white Mondeo pulled over to one side, George Stephens walked over to the driver's window and waited for him to wind it down.

'Good evening, sir,' said Stephens. 'Would you mind telling me your name and where you've been?'

The driver was a small-time crook hired by Tate's gang at short notice. He was nervous and turned out to be hopeless at hiding it.

'Er, sure. My name's Androliakos. Craig Androliakos. Er, I've just come back from Paris. I was over there seeing, er, this bird that I met a couple of weeks ago. Yeah.'

'I see. And is this your car, sir?'

'No.' There was a pause. 'It's hired. Er, a friend of mine hired it.'

'Who was that then?'

There was another pause. This time slightly longer. The customs officer spoke again. 'I need to know the name of your friend who hired the car, sir.'

Tiny beads of sweat formed on Craig's forehead as he struggled to remember, struggled to stay cool. And then, in a flash, the name came to him. 'Er. Nic . . . Nic . . . Nick Reynolds.'

It was not the most convincing performance he could have hoped for so Androliakos was hardly surprised when he was asked to get out of the car so that it could be searched. His situation quickly went from bad to worse. The obvious place to start was the glove box, where Stephens found the agreement from Budget-Rent-A-Car. 'This car's been hired by someone called Darren Nicholls.'

Androlaikos could have kicked himself. 'Oh yeah, that's him. That's my friend. Silly me.'

In the boot Stephens found a pair of fisherman's waders. They were still damp with sea water and had sand sticking to them. In his hand luggage, Stephens found maps of the Netherlands and Belgium. In his pockets were scraps of paper with names and mobile phone numbers. It was all pretty suspicious but there was nothing illegal, nothing to warrant an arrest. And Adroliakos knew it. So, having gone through everything once with a fine toothcomb, Stephens decided to search the car all over again before finally letting the man go and then rushing back to the office to run a few names through the computer.

NICHOLLS Mick called me the following Monday morning and told me the Mondeo was at his house and that I could collect it. I got my wife to drop me off at his house and then we got in Mick's car to drive down to the Robin Hood pub because he'd left the Mondeo in the car park. My heart sank. Why had he parked it there? Mick almost looked embarrassed as he explained that the car had been pulled up and searched twice over. The reason they pulled it was because the driver couldn't remember my name – the name the car had been hired in.

'Who the hell was driving it?'

'Some silly fucking South African. I told them your name. All they had to do was say they had borrowed it off you when you were drunk to come over on a day trip.'

Mick told me to expect police or customs to come round and ask about the car and just to make up an excuse if they did. While he was saying all this, I sat in the Mondeo and switched the engine on. It was empty. I complained to Mick and eventually he gave me thirty quid.

When I took the car home, I had a closer look at it and found loads of small scratches. I spent a couple of hours cleaning and polishing it up. I was more worried about the £150 excess that I might lose than the fact that someone else had driven the car, because I knew getting any more money out of Mick would be like getting blood out of a stone.

I took the car back early.

And I spent the night dreaming of the day that he would get caught.

Around 30 April 1996, Detective Superintendent Ivan Dibley retired after more than thirty years in the police force. The celebrations were only slightly marred by the fact that there had been no arrests in the Rettendon case – after all, Dibley knew exactly who had done it and how. As he handed over the investigation to Detective Superintendent Brian Storey, the man who had pursued the drug dealers behind the death of Leah Betts, he knew that it was at most only a matter of weeks before arrests were made.

With so much ground work having already been done, Storey's task, though by no means easy, was greatly simplified. He organised a mass briefing between the police and customs teams to discuss tactics. It didn't take long. It was clear that the boat was the key factor and a decision was taken to place G&T Commercials under twenty-four-hour surveillance. Customs spotter planes were also put on standby and dozens of undercover officers were earmarked for duty. Intelligence reports showed that Tate & Co. had just left for Spain. As soon as the transmissions from their mobile phones showed they were on their way back north, the whole shooting match would swing into action. This time, there would be no mistake.

NICHOLLS I'd got my fingers burned with the Mondeo but this was different. I had an E-reg Jaguar for sale which had been in the paper for a couple of weeks with not much interest when Mick phoned me up and said he was interested in buying it.

He and Peter Corry turned up at my house at around 5 p.m. and Corry took the car for a drive around the block. Once he got back, Mick said he'd give me £3,000 and we shook hands on it. We never talked about it in detail but I know Mick was hoping to use it to tow the boat and trailer rather than always using Jack's transit van. I didn't care what he did with it. Once he bought it, the car was out of my hands and nothing to do with me. Mick said he didn't have that amount of money on him at that moment but he'd pay me after the weekend.

'No problem, Mick. Do you and Peter fancy a cup of tea?'

'We're in a bit of a hurry actually Darren,' said Mick. 'We'd better get going.'

And they did, with Mick driving his Hi-Lux and Corry in the Jaguar. As soon as they'd gone I sent a message to Jim's pager. 'Tell him to call Darren, urgently,' I told the woman. A few minutes later, he called me on my mobile.

Internal Investigation Bureau, Essex Police
Transcript of Covertly Recorded Telephone Conversations.
Source: Desk Phone of DC Jim
Date: 09051996

DC Jim: Hello

Nicholls. All right. You can save some money and ring me at home if you want.

J: Oh it's the firm's phone.

N: Well he's been round. He wanted to buy my Jag. They will be back up around Tuesday 'cos they're now in possession of what they want.

J: Yeah.

N: They're coming back.

J: Right.

N: 'Cos he said to me, I'm trying to use different vehicles for everything he said 'cos of the amount of times that Jack has used the same motor to pick the gear up off the beach. They also want to use it to run some dough abroad.

J: Right. That's good that is. So really all you've got to do is steal that car when it goes abroad next time and keep the loot.

N: (pause) That wouldn't be a fucking bad idea, would it?

J: No.

N: That would be a bloody good idea. Wouldn't that be nice between us?

J: Yeah.

N: It'd be like 100 and something odd thousand pound. More than that actually, no, it'd be about 150 grand I reckon.

J: Oh.

N: There's a lot of gear down where they're going.

J: Yeah, exactly.

N: He wants to borrow my Land Rover to put the boat in. Sometime next week. Just thought I'd tell you. Urge to catch someone.

J: Oh no, no, no. Let it run 'cos you'll have a little bit of a play round here anyway.

N: Yeah. Oh blimey, you'll be able to get loads of people. I'll dish it out like sweets.

J: (laughing) Long as you get paid for it.

N: Well I'll make sure that I get the cash before I tell you.

J: Exactly.

End of Tape

NICHOLLS I was really starting to worry about Jim. He was still going on about this idea of me selling drugs to people and then him nicking them. It hadn't happened yet though. He had a weird way of working. There were some things that he'd tell me that I'm sure I was never supposed to hear and others that he would keep mum about, even if I already knew. I wondered whether everything he was saying, including all the stuff about letting Jack and Mick carry on for now, was just some kind of smoke screen. After all I couldn't work out why he wasn't jumping up and down with excitement at the prospect of bringing them in. Surely that was worth far more kudos that half a dozen small-time street dealers? Maybe he was just being cool. Or maybe he was just being crap. I was starting to lose faith that it was ever going to happen, but I'd travelled so far down the road with him there was no point in turning back. I just had to keep going.

To take my mind off things, I spent most of Friday night and a fair amount of Saturday morning working out what I was going to do with the money from the Jag. So when Mick called me up later than morning to say that he didn't want it after all I fell as though part of my world had collapsed.

In order to be capable of pulling the boat, the Jaguar needed a towbar fitted, but because it was one of the models with a digital dashboard, it needed a special module, which was going to take forever to order. Instead, Mick asked if he could borrow my Land Rover and when I agreed, he told me to come round and pick up the Jag when I dropped the Land Rover off.

I had a few things to do that day so I didn't set off for Meadow Cottage until Saturday evening. Once I arrived, Mick drove me in his Hi-Lux over to the Robin Hood pub car park where he'd left the Jaguar. He said he'd put £30 worth of petrol in the car and would also buy me a drink sometime to make up for the inconvenience. For the first time in a long time I felt a twinge of guilt. There I was trying my hardest to get this bloke nicked and, all of a sudden, he was treating me with a bit of respect.

I didn't hear from Mick again until Sunday morning, when he asked if I could do him a huge favour and give him a lift up to meet Jack that afternoon. We arranged to meet in a pub near Great Bentley village and I set off in my Jag in the middle of the afternoon. I was waiting in the car park when Mick turned up in his Toyota Rav 4 being driven by Jackie Street. Paul Gwinnett was also in the car.

Mick and Paul took a couple of bags and some fishing rods out of the Toyota and put them in the back of my car before both getting in.

'Where to, guv?' I asked Mick. It was pretty obvious I'd been magically transformed into a cab driver for the day so I thought I might as well act like one. Mick told me to go up the A12 towards the Ipswich roundabout. More than once he told me not to drive so fast and when we got to the Copdock roundabout he told me to turn right and stop at the first petrol station I saw. I did so and saw Jack already in the garage with his blue Transit towing a trailer carrying the boat.

We all got out and went into the garage while Jack filled the boat with petrol. I thought I'd be leaving them there but Mick told me he wanted me to drive him and Gwinnett to Levington marina. We stopped in a layby just outside and

Mick and Paul opened up their bags and put on a couple of dry suits. They then unstrapped the boat, removed the number plates and made it ready to go straight into the water.

National Investigation Service, Customs and Excise Surveillance Log, 12 May 1996
Mobile Surveillance Unit

At 1710 I saw a blue Transit van towing a black and orange rigid hull inflatable boat with a large blue engine mounted drive into Levington marina immediately followed by a black Jaguar, which contained three occupants.

At 1711 a man who had been identified to me as Jack Whomes parked the van near the Harbour Master's office and went in.

At 1715 the van, L98YDX, with the RHIB still attached was parked by the harbour office. The empty Jaguar was parked alongside. Jack Whomes and a man who had been identified to me as Michael Steele were standing talking together and looking down at the slipway. A third man who I would describe as stocky with curly black hair (Nicholls) was standing looking around the general area.

At 1720 the blue van and RHIB turned around and drove towards the slip.

At 1725 the RHIB was reversed down the slip with Michael Steele who was wearing a blue/red sailing suit and a fourth man (Gwinnett) who had collar-length hair and was wearing light blue waterproof trousers and a dark jacket already aboard. The engine was started immediately the boat entered the water, the vessel then manoeuvred at the bottom of the slip and exited the marina via the harbour entrance. It then headed east down the River Orwell towards the North Sea.

The blue Transit van driven by Whomes then drove up the slip and out of the marina. The third man (Nicholls) who had been standing watching the vessel launch and looking around then walked to the Jaguar and drove out of the marina at 1728. I was then involved in the mobile surveillance of the blue

Transit and empty trailer as well as the Jaguar. Both vehicles were seen to stop at a layby close to the Marina. The driver of the Jaguar then had a short conversation with Whomes who was sitting in the driver's seat of the Transit van.

End of Log

NICHOLLS I watched the boat go out to sea and then Jack told me to meet him back in the layby. He was refitting the trailer when I pulled up behind him and then got back in the transit.

'So how come you're not so involved in our business these days?' he asked me. He was sitting in the driver's seat, staring forward through the windscreen. It was like he was trying to be cool or something.

I scratched my head. 'Well, you know I don't have my passport anymore. But the main thing is it just wasn't worth it. I never really earned any money out of it.'

Jack nodded slowly, still staring straight ahead. 'Well if you invested a bit of money in it,' he continued, 'then you'd make a lot more. Mick and I were talking and we wanted you to go down to Spain and run that end of the operation for us. We think you'd be good at it. We'd pay all your expenses and everything. It's a good offer.'

'I'm not really interested. I don't really think this is the right business for me. Especially after what happened at Christmas.'

Jack's face suddenly erupted into a cheesy smile, which faded as quickly as it had appeared. Then he looked directly at me for the first time. 'Here's the thing, Darren. We want you to get more involved. If you don't, that's going to cause problems. What happened to Pat could easily happen to you. You can be replaced.'

I suddenly got this weird sensation like I was flying backwards really fast. I wanted to be sick. I felt my legs buckle and my throat dried up in an instant. I thought I was going to faint and had to hold on to the side of the Transit to steady myself. I couldn't speak. I was numb with shock. Jack had just threatened to kill me. I was speechless. 'I'll probably call you later tonight,' Jack said. 'I might need you to do us a favour. That won't be a problem, will it?'

I looked at him. His eyes were dead. There was no humour in his face at all. He was like a machine. It crossed my mind that he'd probably had exactly the same look on his face when he carried out the murders. I forced out some words. 'No, Jack. That won't be a problem at all.'

15

'I'm being fucking nicked'

NICHOLLS I was feeling a bit brave when I went to bed so I switched the phone off. I woke up at around 5 a.m. feeling like an absolute pansy and dialled 1471. Jack had called me at around 2.30 a.m. Shit. I decided to call him back and pretend I'd fallen asleep. Why? Well, I still felt involved in the whole murder thing and didn't think I could just walk away from things just like that. Oh yeah – and I was terrified of what he might do if he thought I was avoiding him. But at the back of my mind I was really hoping that Jim had done his job and they'd all been banged up.

I got through to Jack right away and he sounded really pleased to hear from me – he'd been fast asleep and needed to get up to meet the boat when it came back into the harbour.

'Is everything okay?' I asked softly.

'Yeah,' said Jack brightly. 'Everything's fine. No problems at all. You can pick up your Land Rover whenever you want. It's over at Mick's.'

'Okay, will do,' I said and put the phone down. Then I

swore to myself over and over until Sandra woke up and asked what I was going on about.

My workmate Colin was due round at any time so I thought I might as well take advantage of the extra pair of hands and pick up the Land Rover right away. Once he arrived I drove the two of us over to Mick's in the Jag and then the two of us headed back towards Braintree in our little two-car convoy.

I'm not the paranoid type, but as we were on our way back I had this feeling I was being followed. I knew it didn't make any sense. I mean, I hadn't done anything, but I just had this weird prickly sensation on the back of my neck. But every time I thought I spotted a car that was tailing me, it would turn off or something, so I guessed it was all just in my mind and soon forgot about it.

As we were heading back, just before 5.30 a.m., my phone went off. It was Mick on his mobile. 'We're fishing at sea. It's been a good night. We'll see you later on. Jack's going to get us out,' he said.

'Cheers Mick. See you later,' I replied, then I started swearing to myself again. Up until that moment I was hoping that maybe Mick had been arrested and Jack didn't know about it. No such luck.

There were so many red faces at the Monday morning police and customs briefing it looked like a clown convention. The operation had been meticulously planned, hugely expensive and swallowed valuable resources and manpower. But it also looked like being a complete failure.

Undercover officers had watched as Steele had met Whomes at G&T Commercials and picked up the boat. They had seen the boat being filled up with petrol and Steele, driven by Nicholls along with Gwinett, arriving to meet Whomes. They had followed the party down to the marina and seen the boat launched.

From there a spotter plane with a thermal-imaging camera

had followed the boat as it crossed the Channel and eventually moored off the coast of Belgium at Blankenberg. The plane had to break off to refuel (normally two would be used on this sort of operation but one had a fault) but it resumed a couple of hours later and picked up the boat on its way back to England. So far so good.

For the first time, thanks to the plane, customs were able to see where Steele landed his boat – just along from the pier at Clacton. 'We had always assumed it would have been somewhere a bit more remote,' says Bill Davidson. 'Anyone walking along the promenade would have been able to see what was going on. But the advantage to Steele was that he could see anyone coming. There was no place to park up for effective surveillance and no way of surprising him. I imagine Steele really liked the idea of being so open about it. There was always an element of bravado with everything he did. Quite a few of the officers chasing him don't mind saying they have a certain admiration for him.'

Once the landing point had been established, customs had expected the remainder of the operation to be plain sailing. They thought the most likely scenario was that the three men would unload the boat and carry the drugs up the beach to a waiting vehicle. Instead, Whomes drove the car right on to the beach itself, right up to the waterfront, and loaded the car there. Within seconds he was driving off again. A police team attempted to follow him but he was soon lost in the night. The whole operation was starting to fall apart.

'He caught us on the hop,' says Bill Davidson. 'The plan had always been to wait until the drugs were landed and arrest the vehicle loaded with the drugs and then wait until the boat came back to the harbour and pick up the rest of the gang. We could have gone in when the drugs were being unloaded but that would give Steele an easy escape route. All he would need to do is start the boat's engine and head out to sea. Even with our fastest cutters, we'd never have caught him.'

The surveillance team had worked virtually non-stop for

thirty-six hours but had nothing to show for it: they had no drugs, no idea where they were being kept, no evidence of drugs even being smuggled.

The decision was taken to put all the remaining sources on Nicholls. He had played no part in the drugs operation since the previous afternoon and both Storey and Davidson had a strong hunch that he would pick up some cannabis the following day. Easy to follow and far too lazy to bother with any of the anti-surveillance techniques that Mick had patiently taught him, Nicholls was an easy target. He was also their last hope.

NICHOLLS By the time I got back home I was so depressed about the fact that yet another drug run had been allowed to slip by that I couldn't be bothered to do any work, at least not until later. I sent Colin home and went back to bed. Mick phoned me a bit later and asked me to go round about 1 p.m. All the way there, I still got the feeling someone was watching me. I was almost 100 per cent certain that the police were watching me. Eventually it got so bad that I phoned Jim.

'Oi, am I under surveillance? Are you lot following me?'

'Nah. Don't be stupid, Darren,' came the reply. 'You're just being paranoid.'

'I don't think so mate. I'm sure I'm being surveyed. I've been paranoid before and it doesn't feel anything like this.'

'I'm telling you, Darren, you're not being followed. If you were, I'd tell you, wouldn't I? I mean, I'm not going to fuck you up, am I? You're on our side. Just relax.'

'All right. Listen though, the shipment came in last night. I'm just going over to pick up my share.'

'I know,' said Jim, 'Mick's got it in his mum's garage. He hasn't even bothered to lock it. Don't worry, everything is under control. Relax.'

I tried my best but it wasn't quite good enough. In fact I'd been so distracted I completely forgot to ask Jim how he knew where the drugs were. It almost sounded like he'd been over there himself to check it out – maybe something was going to happen after all. When I eventually arrived at Mick's he was sitting in a chair by his caravan at the front of Meadow Cottage sunning himself. He asked how much puff I wanted to take away with me. 'I've got 10 if that's okay but there's more if you want it.' Ten kilos? £22,000 worth? He obviously had it coming out of his ears. That was more than enough. I opened up the toolbox and Mick threw in the bars, counting each one off until he reached 40. As they hit the bottom of the toolbox, I rearranged them neatly in order.

I'd made Colin wait around the corner – I didn't want him getting involved – but when I returned I put the toolbox of drugs in the back of the van and let him drive it with me following behind in the Jag. We set off for home and I phoned Sandra to let her know what time I'd be back. Just as I put the phone down, Mick called. He sounded really frustrated, like he'd been working himself up into a frenzy. He asked if there had been anything in the Land Rover when I had picked it up that morning. I told him that there wasn't, that I'd checked it carefully and it was completely empty. Mick launched into a furious torrent of swear words down the line.

'What's wrong?' I asked, totally confused. 'Why did you want to know?'

I could hear Mick's breathing getting harder and harder. 'Because I've fucking lost something, that's why.' Then he hung up.

It only took me a few seconds to realise it must be some of the drugs that had gone missing. As soon as it clicked, I was overcome with a huge fear that Mick might think I was responsible, that I was trying to rip him off. What with Jack being on the warpath and having threatened me the night before, that was the last thing I wanted. I phoned Mick back immediately. 'Have you lost what I think you've lost?' He was still fuming.

'Yes, I fucking have.' I assured him that there was nothing

at all in the Land Rover. 'Okay, okay,' he said and hung up again.

I was so caught up in what Mick was saying that I barely noticed the half-dozen police cars ahead of and behind me until they switched on their sirens. A couple of them pulled right in front, forcing me and Colin to stop. All I could see around me were flashing blue lights and dozens of uniforms heading towards me.

Quick as a flash, I locked all the doors in the Jag, wound up the windows, pulled out my mobile and started dialling like a maniac. As soon as I heard Mick's voice I spoke. 'I'm being arrested,' I said. The mixture of fear and excitement must have done something to my voice because Mick didn't recognise me. 'Who's that?' he said. 'It's Darren. I'm being nicked.' There was a pause and I thought I heard him swear, then the line went dead.

By now two or three coppers were banging on the windows of the Jag, telling me to put the phone down and get out of the car. I dialled again. Sandra picked up on the second ring. 'Sandra, I won't be home after all, I'm being stopped by the police. I'll try and call you later, bye.' Outside the car, the coppers were frantically trying to get in. They had taken out their truncheons and were tapping them on the glass. They started telling me in a really nasty way what was going to happen if I didn't open the door there and then. But I had one my call to make. He wasn't at his desk so I called his pager.

'DC Jim's message service,' said the woman, 'can I take your message please?'

'Yeah, the message is: "I'm being fucking nicked."' There was a stunned silence.

'I'm sorry, sir,' the woman said. 'I don't think I can send that particular message.'

I was looking out of the window and I could see the cop nearest me contemplating breaking the glass. I had to act fast. 'All right. Just tell him that Darren has been arrested.'

The last two phone calls I have no problem with, but up until this day, I can't explain why I called Mick, let alone why I called him first. It's a complete mystery. After all, I'd been doing everything in my power to engineer him being arrested for weeks so it made no sense at all for, when I thought it was finally happening, to tip him off and give him the chance to get away. The only reason I can come up with is that I wanted to protect myself, to stop him thinking that his arrest was anything to do with me. Stupid really. But I guess I wasn't thinking straight at the time.

The second I stepped out of the car they grabbed the phone off me and handcuffed my hands behind my back while I watched Colin being led off to a police van.

'Do you know why you've been pulled up?' said the copper nearest to me.

I shook my head.

'Where have you come from?' he said.

'Colchester' I replied.

'Well,' said the policeman, trying to think on his feet, 'there have been a number of burglaries in Colchester and we've pulled you over because we'd like to search your van.'

I nodded. 'Okay. Fair enough. But everything in the van is mine. Colin is just driving it for me. He has nothing to do with anything. It's all down to me.'

It didn't take long for them to find the toolbox – there wasn't anything else in the back of the van. 'What are these then?' said the policeman. I thought I'd play the fool one last time. 'They look like chocolate bars to me. What do you think they are?' The policeman smiled. 'I think they're drugs.' And that was it, I was arrested on the spot.

Over in the neighbouring county of Suffolk, Michael Steele and Jackie Street were bombing along the A12 towards the Ipswich roundabout in their Toyota Rav 4, having left Great Bentley a little earlier in the day. Just up ahead, Peter Corry was driving Jack's blue Transit van. The trio were on their way to G&T Commercials to see Jack. The call from Nicholls had come only a few minutes earlier but Steele was still taken by surprise when a convoy of unmarked cars suddenly appeared by his side and a man in a uniform gestured at him to pull over. Steele put his foot down. Two of the pursuit cars also accelerated, weaving around the traffic to take up positions just ahead and just to the side of the Toyota.

Steele tried to drive his way out of trouble but was out-classed. Then the unmarked Escort deliberately drove across his path, crashing into him and forcing him to a halt. A man leaped out and ran towards the driver's window. 'I am DC Chappel from Essex police and I am arresting you both for sus-picion of being concerned in the importation of controlled drugs.' Steele stepped out and glanced at the front of his car. 'Has he fucking damaged my bumper?' he said. One of the younger, keener officers stepped forward and put his hand on Steele's shoulder to guide him towards the car that would take him to the station. Steele's ice-blue eyes burned a hole right through the youngster's head. 'Take your fucking hands off me, boy,' said Steele.

Never one to miss an opportunity, Steele would later lodge an official complaint about his arrest. He claimed the officers responsible had 'driven in a malicious manner' which could have resulted in serious injury or even the death of him and his partner of twenty-five years. Steele also complained that when Jackie Street was finally released she was horrified to discover their home had been 'abused and damaged' by the police. Money loaned to the couple from relatives was allegedly taken and Street's vehicle was seized. 'She has been maliciously penalised by over-zealous officers,' wrote Steele. 'She is now unable to perform normal, daytime duties. She has no one to turn to.'

A few feet further down the road, the door of Jack's Transit van was opened by DC Sanders, who slapped his palm down on the quivering shoulder of Peter Corry. 'You're nicked,' he said triumphantly. 'You are under arrest for conspiracy to supply controlled drugs.' Corry stepped down to be cautioned and handcuffed, and glanced over at Michael Steele and Jackie Street, both surrounded by equal numbers of police officers. He swallowed hard and then spoke. 'I don't know what you mean, mate.'

Jack Whomes was at G&T Commercials cleaning an engine when Bill Davidson, others customs officers and a few members of the police armed-response unit approached him.

'Okay, Jack,' said Davidson. 'Put down the power washer.'

Jack's brow became a mass of furrows. 'Actually, it's a pressure washer.' Then Jack slowly looked around at the hordes of officers and gunmen surrounding him. 'Fucking hell, Bill, this is a bit heavy ain't it?'

As he was driven away in handcuffs, Darren Nicholls kept an eye out for a familiar face.

NICHOLLS They took me down to Chelmsford police station. All the way there and when we arrived, I kept looking out for Jim. I kept expecting him to pop up at any moment and say, "No, this one's okay. He's on our side." I was sure this was all down to him, that he'd finally swooped and the reason I'd been arrested was to stop Mick and Jack from suspecting that I'd grassed them up.

They let Colin go home after a couple of hours – they realised he had nothing to do with anything illegal – but he wasn't allowed to make any phone calls or see anyone for ages. They interviewed me for the first time just before 11.30 p.m. and they were asking me loads of questions about the cannabis that they'd found in my van and where it had come from. I was just going, "No comment," to the whole lot, no matter what they said. I'd only been selling the drugs because Jim had told me to keep in with Mick. In my mind, at least, I hadn't really done anything wrong. I was sure it was all going to be fine. But then they played their trump card.

Essex Police
Record of Tape-Recorded Interview
Chelmsford Police Station
130596 2326HRS

Det. Con. Winstone: We believe that you were in convoy today and you were playing an active part in the transportation of 10 kilos of cannabis resin and you are being asked to make some form of comment about that. Do you wish to say anything about that?

Darren Nicholls: No comment.

DC: Again, I draw your attention to the fact that if you refuse to answer this question it may affect any other answers you give at your trial. Do you understand that?

DN: No comment.

DC: Right, and lastly that a record is being made as I've said of this tape and should you later be prosecuted this will be brought up at your trial. Do you understand that?

DN: No comment.

DC: Right, okay, well if that is it, you've got the notice. I don't intend to say anymore about the possession with intent to supply at the moment. The time by my watch is now 2335 hours and you're now going to be arrested for being involved in the murder of Pat Tate, Craig Rolfe and Tony Tucker. Do you wish to make any comment to the fact that you've now been arrested for that murder?

(A slight pause. Almost imperceptible.)

DN: No comment.

> Nicolls They were doing it to gauge a reaction and I didn't make one. But as soon as they switched the tape off I went mad. 'What the fuck do you think you're doing, arresting me for that?' I said. This was my worst nightmare coming true. And where the fuck was Jim?

The following day, the evidence against him was starting to mount up. Nicholls was beginning to realise how hopeless his

situation was. In addition to all the police and customs surveillance records, which now included still pictures and video
footage, the police also had access to the phone records of
both Nicholls and Steele. Again, Nicholls took the 'No comment' road but it was obvious he was being backed into a
corner. In fact, with neither Steele or Whomes being caught in
possession of drugs, there was more evidence against him than
anyone else. And then, once again, just when things were
looking at their blackest, they got even worse.

Essex Police
Record of Tape-Recorded Interview
Chelmsford Police Station
140596 1551HRS

DC: Just to put it in a nutshell here, Darren, what we're actually
saying is that there has been a large importation of cannabis
resin to this country. You have now been shown to have been
privy immediately before this importation came about by your
association with Steele and the others. You have then subsequently in the very early hours of the next morning been
involved directly in the importation of these drugs. Your vehicle has subsequently been forensically examined and there is
salt water and a large amount of sand consistent with this
having been used on the beach consistent with the importation
taking place. You have been shown by surveillance to have
been involved in the collection of a consignment of 10 kilos of
cannabis resin. As far as I'm concerned you're a large player in
all the goings-on that have happened. You were so concerned
at the time you were stopped that your first thought was to try
to tell Mr Steele that it had all come on top as far as you were
concerned. I feel in the light of that summary you should
reconsider your situation. I want you to understand the enor-
mity of what we are saying to you. Do you understand that?

DN: No comment.

DC: Fine. Now I have here a copy of your custody record from
last night. This entry is timed at 2116 hrs. It says: 'Whilst car-

rying out the review Mr Nicholls asked if he could speak to a
nominated police officer known to him. I passed this to
Superintendent Storey who declined this and Nicholls was
informed of the above.' Would you like to make any comment
about that?

DN: No comment.

DC: Would you like to tell me who the police officer was that
you wished to have some dialogue with at the time?

DN: No comment.

DC: All right. I can tell you that at the moment, two police
officers from Essex have been arrested and are currently in
custody.

DN: Oh fuck. I don't fucking believe it . . .

DC: The officers have been charged with a number of offences
including some linked to the possession of controlled drugs.
We have evidence that you have had numerous dealings with
one of the officers. Is there any comment you wish to make
now?

DN: No. No fucking comment.

As soon as the interview was over, Nicholls asked to see the
most senior officer available. What happened next was
recorded by DC Winstone in his pocket book. 'I was in company with Detective Superintendent Barrington when we
spoke to Darren Nicholls in an interview room. Nicholls had
signed the Custody Record to agree to be seen without a
Solicitor. This meeting had been requested by Mr Nicholls who
was introduced to Mr Barrington. Nicholls asked Mr
Barrington if he named the arrested police officer would he
confirm it. Mr Barrington agreed and Mr Nicholls said, 'Is it
DC Jim?' Mr Barrington confirmed this and then he [Nicholls]
went on to say that this was how he had gotten into trouble
and wanted to say he'd been set up. Mr Barrington explained
that regardless of what information Mr Nicholls gave that he
would be responsible and have to accept any sentence passed
on him by the legal system. Mr Nicholls accepted this and

asked about what protection would be given to him and his family. Mr Barrington said that Mr Nicholls must be totally honest in all details given so that an accurate judgement could be made regarding the level of protection offered. Mr Nicholls asked about protection in prison and was told about the system of protection that was available for registered informants. Mr Nicholls said he would be giving information regarding illegal activities of Policemen and said that he did not say anything to DC Winstone because he did not know if he could trust him. Mr Barrington said that Mr Nicholls could trust him fully and that he should tell him the whole truth of what his involvement was. Mr Nicholls stated that he was a registered informant of DC Jim and Mr Barrington acknowledged this by stating that he knew all about that and that he had sanctioned the payment to him and that DC Winstone had no involvement with DC Jim at all. Mr Nicholls said that for the last six months he felt he was being used and that drugs jobs were not his main concern and that other more serious things would be disclosed.'

NICHOLLS I knew I didn't have any choice. I tried to put myself in Jack and Mick's shoes, to wonder what was going through their minds and pretty soon I realised I was totally fucked. Two days earlier Jack had threatened to kill me. The next day he gets arrested. In Mick's case, I come round to collect some drugs, and an hour later he gets arrested. It was a good bet that by now they would also have been told that a couple of policemen had been nicked and that I had been talking to one of them. It wouldn't take long for them to put two and two together. And even if they didn't work out I was giving information about the smuggling side of things, I was still the weak link in the murder case. And now the cops were talking about remanding me in custody in Chelmsford prison. That's exactly where they were going to put Jack and Mick and the others. I wouldn't last five minutes. It was time to start talking.

16

'Do you want to be with me?'

SANDRA I hadn't heard a single word from Darren for nearly three days. When I got the phone call saying he was going to be late home because he'd been stopped by the police, I thought to myself, 'Ah, he's being done for speeding,' 'cos he always drives like a lunatic. But then a friend of mine, Angela, came round to the house about half an hour after he called and said that she'd seen him surrounded by dozens of police and with his arms behind his back and that some of the cops had got guns. It was obviously more than a traffic offence so I jumped in Angela's car and we went over to where she'd last seen him. The Transit van was still there, parked up on the side of the road, so I knew he'd been wheeled off somewhere, but I had no idea where. And for a while I didn't care.

I got home and just sat around waiting for the raid. It was horrible. There were so many police there, at least thirty of them, and they had dogs and guns and everything. Luckily Angela was still there otherwise I might not have got through it. They went through everything for hours and hours. They know every possession I own. They emptied my entire house and threw most of it in boxes to take away with them. And some stuff they just kept going through again and again. I sent my sister to the school to pick up the kids so they wouldn't have to see it. The police were all very nice about it – I made them all a cup of tea – but I just had to have a proper drink. I sat there trying to blot it all out with vodka.

After they'd gone, I went over to the police station but they wouldn't let me see Darren. So I went back home and phoned, but they wouldn't let me speak to him either. I tried a couple more times, but I soon realised it was a waste of my time. Then on Thursday, just before midnight, I got a phone call. He didn't say hello, he didn't ask how I was or how the kids were managing without him. All he asked was whether I was alone. I wasn't – Angela had been staying over. 'Get rid of her,' he said. 'I'll call back in half an hour.' And that was it. He was gone again.

Angela was in bed at the time so I had to go wake her up, tell her that Darren had called and that I didn't know why but she'd have to leave right there and then. She'd been a huge source of strength since Darren had gone and I felt really guilty as I pushed her out of the door but then the phone started ringing again.

'Sandra. Do you want to be with me?'

'What are you talking about Darren?'

'Do you want to be with me?'

'Well. Of course. Of course I want to be with you.'

'Okay. Just pack enough clothes for you and the kids for a couple of days and someone will be round to pick you up.'

'What's going on Darren, what have you done?'

'I can't talk now. Just get yourselves ready. I've got to go.'

I assumed – that was my mistake, I know now you should never assume anything when it comes to the police – but I assumed that they were going to take me somewhere to be with Darren. I packed all the stuff up, woke the kids and waited. Then this van turned up at about three in the morning. The kid were so tired, so dopey they didn't really know what was going on. And neither did I. We drove to some kind of student boarding house and they put us up for the night. The guy who was driving said he couldn't say anything about anything. 'As soon as you see your husband, everything will be clear,' he said. 'Yes,' I replied, 'but when will that be?' The driver didn't even look at me. 'I'm afraid I can't say.'

They woke us up at 7 a.m. the next morning and said we had to move straightaway. All the students would be waking up and they didn't want anyone to know where we had stayed. I was getting more and more confused by the second – no one was telling me anything and I still hadn't spoken to Darren – then they took us to a kind of safe house they use for interviewing rape victims. We stayed there all day and all night and for the whole time I wasn't allowed outside the front door. There were police everywhere looking after us, but none of them could tell me anything about what was going on. All they'd say was, 'It's down to your husband, it's down to your husband.' But that wasn't any bloody good because my husband wasn't around either.

Then this tough little woman called Sue turned up at the house and said, 'I'll take you to see him now.' She took me down to the cells at Chelmsford police station and Darren was waiting for me. I sat down, he took my hand and told me the whole story from start to finish. He told me about the night of the murder, about how he'd been giving information to Jim, about how Jack had threatened to kill him – the whole lot. I remember that at first I didn't feel anything, but the more he spoke the more I started to shake. Then I got this sick, numb feeling inside, the kind you get when you're about to do something really scary like jump off the top board at the swimming pool.

That feeling stayed with me all that night. Later they took me and the kids to another safe house and explained that I'd be able to see Darren every day. Whenever I did see him, he was always so calm, so relaxed. He kept telling me, 'Don't worry, it's all going to be okay.' So I believed him. I really wanted to believe him.

Sue gave me the impression it was all going to be fine as well. 'Don't worry,' she'd say to me cheerfully. 'Two weeks and you'll be back to normal. It will be just like nothing ever happened.' It was obvious she was talking bollocks. I don't know why she bothered. I really didn't like her much at all.

Few, if any, of the forty or so people who sign up on witness protection programmes in the United Kingdom each year have any idea of just what they are letting themselves in for. Although it inevitably involves a major, often traumatic change in their circumstances, the decisions almost always have to be taken in a matter of minutes, overnight at most.

Although they are generally lumped together, there are, in fact, two distinct categories of protected witness. The first is the innocent bystander, for example the housewife who sees a gangland execution from her living-room window. Should such a witness agree to give evidence, they will first be moved into a hotel, all expenses paid, and have statements taken. They will be assigned one or sometimes two police handlers whose job is to ensure their comfort and safety at all times. In the run-up to the trial, they will be asked to choose where they would like to live. If they are a home-owner, the police will arrange the purchase of a new property and the sale of the old. If they rent from a council, the police will arrange for them to move to a new area with the minimum of fuss. Until they are settled in a new job, they will be paid a 'salary' equivalent to whatever they were earning prior to joining the programme (in addition to any reward). They will, of course, still be restricted from seeing their friends and families ever again but because the crooks generally have little idea who they are or who they associate with, the danger to those around them is fairly minimal. Depending on the severity of the threat against them, such witnesses can even choose to relocate to a number of countries around the world.

Witnesses are often awarded large sums from public funds and, in the case of those who inform on robberies or major thefts, they can receive tens of thousands of pounds from banks or insurance companies. When truck driver Chris Brooker was asked to drive a shipment of heroin worth £2 million into the United Kingdom, he went straight to the police. His evidence saw the gang of three sent to prison and Brooker was given a new identity and rewards and payments totalling more than £80,000.

When it comes to testifying in court, any jury in the land will have little difficulty understanding what an enormous sacrifice the person has made, all in the interests of justice, and their evidence will be treated with the utmost respect. They have no criminal connections, they have no ulterior motive. Even the defence barristers will shy away from attacking such a witness too harshly for fear of turning the jury against their own clients.

The second category of protected witness enjoys no such privileges. They are, like Nicholls, professional criminals who turn grass because it is the only choice they have. Failure to co-operate with the police would either lead to a long prison sentence or, in the worst case scenario, certain death.

The major difference between the first and second categories is that the police will never let the second – no matter how crucial their evidence, no matter how key their role in the forthcoming trial – forget that they are criminals. Rather than being kept in a hotel or a safe house, they are more likely to spend their first three months being moved from special prison units to police stations as they make their statements. Even a glimpse of someone they think they recognise means that they will instantly be moved.

Rather than being given some form of income equivalent to what you had before, you are reduced to living on benefits. The idea is that if you admit to having made some money from crime in the past, all your past earnings are tainted with the same brush. Only by reducing your income to virtually nothing can the police hope to counter any accusations of bribery or favouritism.

Furthermore, in order to ensure that the subject comes across as a witness with nothing to hide they must first confess to every single crime they have ever committed, even the crimes they were never caught for. Not only must they confess, but they must agree to plead guilty to the crimes in court and accept whatever sentence the judge wishes to hand out to them. Failure to do this can invalidate their place on the programme. The last thing the police want, mid-trial, is for the defence to suddenly bring up the fact that their key witness was involved in organising an armed robbery with one of the defendants five years earlier.

There are no guarantees, no promises. Protected witness status merely means that police will inform the judge that you have been of assistance to them. It is up to the judge to gauge how valuable that assistance has been and whether or not the subject deserves a reduction in their sentence. There are plenty of cases where witnesses have been given longer sentences than those they are giving evidence against, particularly in cases where the trial has collapsed and all the accused have walked free.

It wasn't always that way. The phrase 'supergrass' was first coined in 1973 when Derek 'Bertie' Smalls, an active armed robber who had been involved in a £138,000 robbery in Wembley, was tracked to his Northampton hide-out through his au pair girl. Caught bang to rights and facing a long sentence, Smalls offered to strike a deal. If the Home Secretary gave him a written guarantee that he himself would be immune from prosecution for every crime he had ever committed, then he would happily give evidence against everyone he had ever worked with.

Within a year Smalls's evidence had led to more than 150 arrests and 21 of his former associates were jailed for a total of 308 years. Bertie Smalls never served a single day.

Panic spread throughout the underworld like wildfire.

Dozens of hardened villains, worried about what Smalls might be saying about them, began to give evidence themselves and the spectacle of one member of a gang appearing as the star witness in a trial of the others became a regular one. The numbers increased further still after stories of the treatment provided to self-professed 'King Squealer' Maurice O'Mahoney began to emerge. While being held at Chiswick police station, he would get his favourite paper every morning along with his tea and toast. When it came to meal times, food was brought in from local restaurants and served with linen napkins and silver-plated cutlery. To prevent him going stir-crazy he would be taken from his cell every now and then for a boozing session or a slap-up meal or a day at the races. It was even said that prostitutes were provided on a regular basis.

Little wonder then that some of the most violent, vicious, vile men in criminal history suddenly came forward wanting to tell all, knowing that regardless of what they had done they would not face prosecution themselves.

A bad taste started to develop in the mouths of the public by the early eighties when characters like John Childs, the head of Britain's only known 'Murder Incorporated' style contract-killing company, decided to implicate former colleagues in six murders rather than face the rap for a huge series of robberies. Childs was rewarded with a single life sentence and no recommended minimum term, at a time when the memory of the Kray Twins – who had each killed one person but received thirty-year minimum sentences – was still fresh in many minds.

Within a few years, after a number of trials started to collapse, the whole notion of the supergrass had completely fallen out of favour with both police and juries. Today, under the new name of protected witnesses, they are rarely if ever granted full immunity from prosecution and the levels of comfort they are allowed to receive are strictly monitored.

NICHOLLS I don't know what I was expecting. Joining the

witness protection programme, becoming a supergrass – it all sounds quite glamorous and exciting. The truth is it's nothing of the sort. A couple of days after I'd agreed to co-operate, I was taken out of my cell into a little interview room and had this sheet of paper shoved in front of me. It had my full name at the top and then a list of conditions I had to agree to. The first was that I had to promise to plead guilty to three offences – possession of 10 kilos of cannabis, supplying a firearm to a prohibited person and conspiracy to import drugs. The gun and the conspiracy charges really pissed me off. I had never been caught doing either and there was no real evidence that I had been involved at all. I was only being charged because I had admitted it to them. But that was part of the deal, that I had to admit everything I'd ever done. Being honest meant that if it all went pear-shaped I was risking a sentence at least double that I would have got for the drugs alone.

The next condition was that I had to agree to attend court and testify in all cases that involved Whomes, Steele and Corry.

The next paragraph was about what the police were going to do for me. I started to concentrate really hard because I was keen to find out exactly what they said, but as I started reading I realised that they weren't really saying anything. They promised to provide me with a new name and new identity, and then to put me back in the position I was in before my arrest.

I remember I called one of the cops over and pointed to the last condition. 'Does that mean you're going to stick me in a battered old Jag with 10 kilos of puff in the back?' He didn't find it funny. I asked about my council house. I'd been living there for five years and, having earned a nice discount, I was thinking of trying to buy it. Would they be able to arrange for me to get the same discount once I moved? The answer was no. Okay, would they be able to help me to get a job? The answer was maybe. It was all very vague, nothing specific. They explained that it had to be like that because if there was anything in the contract that was rock solid, it might be deemed an inducement to me testifying. So that was it. One and a half sides of A4, a couple of signatures and then nothing to do but start telling everything that I knew and then wait to see if I could trust them.

At first Darren Nicholls talked only about Jim. How he'd met him, how he'd led him to the drugs in the lake, how they'd fabricated a story about where the drugs had come from and how they'd shared the reward. Then he moved on to talk about what he'd told Jim about Mickey Steele. How he'd passed on details of all the importations he'd known about and how Jim had failed to do anything about any of them. When the tape ran out they started again, talking about how Steele had imported drugs since the beginning of the year and how he'd given Jim his 'theory' on the reasons behind the killing of Tate, Tucker and Rolfe.

When it came to Nicholls' own involvement in smuggling and selling drugs, he began to stray from reality. He'd only gone abroad once and then his passport had run out; he never spoke to Dopey Harris, just sat in the bar drinking beers; he'd never made any money from selling drugs. He deliberately fudged the truth to make himself look good, to look like some concerned citizen who just happened to be friendly with a couple of drugs dealers and had decided to help bring them to justice. At the time it seemed the best option – the only policeman he had ever spoken to before that had betrayed him. He simply didn't know who to trust. Eventually, as the interviews moved on and focused more and more on the murder, so Nicholls began to open up and be more honest. His full involvement in Steele's importations became clear, as did his role in distributing and selling drugs around Braintree and other Essex towns. But there was no going back over the first interviews and his early reticence and lies would turn out to be a mistake that would come back to haunt him. With a vengeance.

NICHOLLS Once I'd decided to co-operate and tell everything that I knew, the police didn't seem to know what to do with me. They were holding me in the female cell unit at Chelmsford police station for ages but they had armed guards at the entrance in case anyone tried to get to me. That made it bloody obvious to every visiting solicitor and prisoner that something special was going on. Eventually they moved me to Colchester and kept the whole thing on a much lower profile.

Because I was just in a police station rather than a proper prison, they didn't have any of the proper facilities. For months I was still under caution and all I was doing was making statements about the murders and the drugs. It meant I couldn't really have any visitors or talk to anyone about anything so I quickly started to get really bored. They gave me a TV and a fridge and I got Sandra to send over a video recorder and a Nintendo game console. Food was the biggest problem. There was no canteen at the nick so they had to send out for pizza or McDonald's or Kentucky Fried Chicken. As for hot drinks, all they had was one of those pre-pack vending machines that makes everything taste like water with a bit of dirt floating in it. The coffee was disgusting, even with sugar. The tea was even worse and I don't even want to think about the soups. The only thing I could bear was the hot chocolate so whenever they used to offer me something, I used to go for that.

I thought I'd stay there, in the police cells, until the trial, but then, once all the statements were over, they said I had to go to prison. At first I was terrified. I was sure I'd be attacked and killed within a few days, but then they explained that there was somewhere very special, somewhere very safe, just for people like me. It sounded dreadful.

Officially, the Protected Witness Unit does not exist. For many years it was based at HMP Woodhill in Bedfordshire but recently it moved to another prison in the south of England, the location of which is a closely guarded secret. Used to house criminals who have agreed to provide 'valuable assistance' to police and other law enforcement agencies – in other words, supergrasses – the PWU is intended to offer them absolute protection from other prisoners by ensuring that no one knows who they really are. The inmates are even told to keep their true identities secret from one another and from prison staff. Instead of their real names, every one of the dozen inmates is referred to as Bloggs followed by a number. Darren Nicholls was Bloggs 19.

The PWU is a prison within a prison. The idea is not so much to prevent the inmates from escaping – the vast majority know only too well they are far safer inside than out – but to prevent anyone from breaking in.

NICHOLLS They told me everything is secret but the first day I got there everyone was saying to me, 'Oi, you're that geezer whose grassing up the blokes over the triple murder ain't you?' Then they all sat around me like it was fucking *Listen With Mother* and wanted to know all the details. At first I didn't want to say anything. I didn't know who any of these people were and it really pissed me off that they all knew about me. But after a while I started to get into it. You had to. You do feel like you're part of a special club and sitting around with everyone, chatting about what you have and haven't done is all part of the fun. It's also a club where you get to call each other names that in any other prison would see you get your face smashed in. There is one joke you hear in the unit at least ten times a day, but even then we still all laugh. It happens when someone asks to borrow some milk or cigarettes and promises to pay the other person back. 'How can I trust you?' someone will say. 'You're a fucking grass!'

It was no Hollesley Bay, but it was good fun at times. It wasn't all laughs though. I know that prison is not supposed to be a holiday camp, but the simple truth is that even though we are at least partly supposed to be good guys, doing the decent thing and all that, we actually got treated far worse than other prisoners. We had to cook our own food because they couldn't trust anyone else to cook for us in case someone tried to poison someone. That's all very well in principle but we only got the same food budget as other inmates. It works fine if you're buying stuff in bulk but when you're only shopping for twelve, it doesn't go very far at all.

We also spent a lot more time locked up in our cells, just to make things easier when they were changing shifts. They started locking us up at 7.30 p.m. whereas the rest of the prison were not having to go back to their cells for at least another hour. We couldn't have any education or special activities because there weren't enough of us; we couldn't use the rest of the exercise facilities in case we got attacked so we had to make do with some really second-rate equipment.

The funny thing was they had all these measures to stop people getting to us but all anyone ever had to do was turn up during visiting time and just walk straight in. Because we were supposed to be a 'secret' and no one knew which prison we were being kept in, the idea was that only visitors who knew people in the unit would ever turn up. So rather than being searched or having to provide identification like other visitors, all my friends and family had to do was turn up at the front gate, say, 'Bloggs 19,' and they be walked straight through.

The security was also pretty lax during visits to the unit itself. We didn't have a proper visiting room so people just used to come into the main unit and hang about on the landing. We were not supposed to go into our cells but no one ever paid any attention to that and people got up to all sorts. They finally tightened it up when one of the inmates, Eaton, got his girlfriend pregnant during one of her visits. He obviously didn't have any money he could give her so she tried suing the governor, saying it was his fault for letting her into Eaton's cell unsupervised.

They say prisons are universities of crime. If that's true, some of the people in the Bloggs unit were studying for their Ph.Ds. A couple of the drug smugglers I was in there with had actually done it all on purpose. They knew it was all coming on top for the gang so one of them had volunteered to turn grass, give some evidence against a couple of others to take the heat off the main operation. They get a reduced sentence, a couple of nobodies go away for decades and the drugs still keep on coming in.

These guys had so much money it was untrue. I remember once one of them was looking through some car magazines and he started asking me about what car he should get for his wife. The choice was between a brand new Mercedes or a Porsche. There was another guy, a chemist, who had been making amphetamine and ecstasy for a big north London criminal gang. He had made millions. He'd actually bought an island – he showed us pictures of it – along with his houses, boats, aeroplanes. He had so much money that he used to pay people £10,000 a time just to leave the country with a suitcase full of money to take to Switzerland and pay into his private account.

I learned a lot from my time in the Bloggs unit but the main thing I was told was never to trust the police. The other people that were there – some of them had been stitched up really badly. I'd find myself talking to people who had been in the unit for five years. They would tell me what the police had said to them at the start and I'd realise it was exactly the same things that the police had told me a couple of days earlier.

One guy, Paul, was serving fifteen years. His story scared me the most. I remember him telling me not to trust the police. 'Right now,' he said, 'they need you. They really need you. Believe me Darren, they'll treat you like a God right up until the day of the verdict and they they'll drop you like a stone.'

Paul had good reason to be bitter. He had been on

remand in another prison after being caught with a gang of armed robbers in Ireland. He had been a bit of a weak link but was happy to keep his mouth shut and do his time. His mates didn't believe it, though, and they arranged to have him killed. One day, while he was out in the exercise yard, he was told to go towards the wall because he was going to be helped to escape. As he made his way over there, something told him it wasn't right. He decided to follow his hunch and went straight back inside and asked to be put in isolation. He soon found out that he was actually being set up to be shot. He turned supergrass the very next day.

When it came to the trial, the police had done a shit job of gathering evidence and everyone else got off. That only left Paul and, because he'd admitted all this stuff that he'd been involved in, the judge gave him fifteen years. I couldn't believe it. I wanted to cry for him. Not only that, it made me think I'd made the biggest mistake of my life by joining the scheme and agreeing to give evidence. But by then it was too late. If Mick and Jack got off, then the judge might decide it was because I didn't do a good enough job and decide to sentence me to the full amount, for the drugs, the guns, everything. For the first time I realised that I could get ten years, while Mick and Jack would both walk free.

17

'If only I'd kept my big mouth shut . . .'

By February 1997 Darren Nicholls had been in custody for the best part of a year and had, for the first time ever, failed to spend Christmas with his wife and family. Sandra was by now firmly ensconced in the new safe house, but despite repeated requests the police ruled that for his own protection Nicholls had to remain in custody until after the trial.

After his initial arrest, when Nicholls was being held in numerous police stations across Essex, Sandra saw him every couple of weeks and the pair would tip the custody sergeant to turn a blind eye while they had frantic sex on his cell bed. But once Nicholls moved to the Bloggs unit, Sandra could no longer bring herself to go.

SANDRA I'd visited prison a few times when Darren had been inside for the counterfeit money thing and I always hated every single second of it. I could never make it through the gates on my own – I always had to have someone with me otherwise I would have just collapsed or something. I'd wake up on the morning of the visit and I'd have this terrible splitting headache. Really painful. And the nearer we got to the time we were leaving, the worse I would feel. And then the closer we got to the prison, the more I'd just want to throw up. I'd feel so terrible that I'd start taking it out on the kids, being really horrible to them, which meant they'd end up dreading every visiting day every bit as much as I did.

The whole point of going is that you're supposed to give the person you're seeing loads of moral support and cheer them up. But with me and Darren it never happened. I'd be feeling tense all the way there and by the time we got inside it would be completely impossible for me to relax. I'd sit there drinking tea and wouldn't say a word. I couldn't even raise a smile. By the time the visit was over, Darren would be more miserable than before he'd seen me. I much preferred staying at home and waiting for him to call. Somehow that made it seem more normal and it was a lot easier to communicate. So, after a couple of months, that was what we did. And as soon as I knew he was going back to prison for the murder inquiry, I knew that we'd end up doing that again.

But this time round, Sandra didn't have her friends and family around to help and support her during the separation. In fact, she felt completely isolated and was terrified of saying anything that could accidentally put her life in jeopardy.

SANDRA The neighbours were the worst thing. Out of all innocence they'd ask you questions about your life. Where you come from, what you do, that sort of thing. They didn't mean anything by it but they had no idea how difficult it was. I'm no good at inventing things. Other people can talk and talk about all sorts of rubbish, but I couldn't talk to anybody. It was like I didn't have a past any more. If someone asked me a question – even a really simple, stupid question – I'd just go completely blank. I was just so worried that I'd going to give something away that I hid away from the world. I couldn't face anyone, anything. And I started to get really angry at Darren. I was really starting to hate him for what he'd put me through.

I just wanted to go back to Essex. I just didn't want to have to play this stupid game any more. I was going to leave Darren and just go back to the life I used to have. I told Sue, the police handler, that one day and she said that I couldn't go back. I could never go back because of the danger I was in. Then she told me that if I tried to go back, they would say that I was putting my children in danger and my kids would be taken away from me. I couldn't believe what I was hearing. There I was, feeling crap and scared about everything and instead of offering me any support they were threatening to take my kids away. I told Darren I couldn't handle it. I told him I didn't want to be with him anymore, that he'd got into the mess and he had no right to drag me and the kids into it. I even started putting money aside and making plans to just vanish in the middle of the night to somewhere they'd never find me. It was a nightmare.

As the gulf between him and his wife widened, Darren Nicholls spent weeks arguing with the police and the courts that the only way to save his family was to allow him to live with them. After all, the family would be living in the same safe house once the trial had finished. How could it be unsafe one day but then magically safe the next?

At first the police were reluctant to give any ground but Nicholls started threatening to withdraw his statements, to refuse to take the stand. Eventually the police agreed to refer Sandra to an expert psychiatrist and place the decision in his hands.

The report by Dr Robert Fox, published on February 5 1997, was damning: 'Since Mrs Nicholls was taken with her children suddenly and without initial explanation in the middle of the night into police custody last May, she has had three disrupting moves of home. She weeps quite often and has the wish to just go to sleep until it is all over . . . The changes have involved domicile, school and identities and exclusion from all contacts of significance to her. "I can't even tell the neighbours my real name, the whole thing's a farce." What hurts most is probably separation from her husband with whom she has had a good relationship: no contact for four months except by daily five-minute phone call.

'"Lonely is the only thing I feel. I can't make friends, like other people have friends. Never could. Paula tells me to go and talk to other mothers at school but I just can't. Paula's not sympathetic. She's got no understanding of what I'm going through. It's just a job to her, she doesn't get involved emotionally."'

'Mrs Nicholls wept a good deal during the interview. How does she sleep? "Under a rug on a sofa in front of the TV mostly. As soon as you get into bed, you're awake. You toss and turn and think about it all." Appetite is negligible by day but excessive to the point of bulimia once the children are in bed. She has also started drinking a bottle of wine a night, 'for something to do, for oblivion".' The report concluded: 'The sooner the family can be reunited with their father, the better.'

On 24 February 1997 Darren Nicholls was granted bail on condition that he reside at the safe house with his family and adhere to certain guidelines. There was to be a strict curfew, which meant he was only able to leave his home between 8 a.m. and 8 p.m., he was never allowed to travel more than twenty-five miles from his front door and he was not allowed to seek any form employment. Any breach would mean an immediate return to prison.

At first Sandra enjoyed having her husband back, but the dream quickly turned into a nightmare. The murder trial was set to begin at the Old Bailey on 1 September and, as the weeks went by, Sandra watched her husband become more and more frustrated, more and more stressed and increasingly bitter and angry about his situation and what the future held for him.

SANDRA Darren wasn't allowed to work because he didn't have a National Insurance number or a tax code. He didn't even have a bank account. Back in Essex, he'd be out of the house during the day and I'd look after the kids. But now, suddenly, he was around all the time. The police would come round once a week and give him some money – about the same that he'd get if he was on the dole – and he'd go straight down the pub and spend the lot getting pissed. Things had been pretty tight when he'd been inside but somehow I'd just about managed. But now I was having to feed one extra mouth with no extra money.

It got to the stage when we were arguing about absolutely everything. Any little excuse would set us off. It must have crossed my mind a thousand times that the best thing to do would be to leave but I guess I knew that Darren really needed me, no matter how badly he was treating me. And I needed him too. It seemed that all of the police promises that they were going to look after us when it was all over were nothing more than a sweetener to ensure Darren gave evidence at the trial. We never expected much. It wasn't like we were expecting a foreign villa and a life of luxury. But they gave us nothing. Less than nothing. They took away everything we had and didn't give us anything back.

The police were absolutely terrified of being accused of bribing their main witnesses. If there was any hint of someone benefiting in some way after being made a supergrass, the defence would jump all over it and the case would collapse. What the police love best is being able to stand in front of a judge and say, 'Look your honour, we did absolutely nothing for this bloke and he still gave evidence. In fact, we've actually made his life much worse than it was before and he still turned up. He must be telling the truth.' And that's just what they wanted to do with Darren.

As the trial loomed ever nearer, Darren Nicholls became more and more nervous about what might happen. In particular, the prospect of Mick and Jack going free played on his mind. He found it impossible to talk about it with his wife who was becoming increasingly bitter about the enforced separation from her family. His police handlers had no time for him unless he was making statements. Desperate for an outlet, Nicholls decided to make a video diary of his thoughts and feelings. He began filming himself at home. Such was his relief at being able to offload his anxieties he even smuggled the camera into his prison cell to help him cope with the stresses and strains in the final days before the trial.

The following transcripts reveal much about the reality of life on the witness protection programme.

Thursday 22 May 1997, thirteen weeks before the trial.
I'm getting really paranoid, I just can't help it. Some days are better than others.

Sometimes I have a drink and it makes me more relaxed. Other times I have a drink and it just brings my paranoia out even more. I lie in bed and I can't sleep because I can hear all these people in the street outside walking their dogs and stuff and I'm convinced that it's them coming for me. Since I've been here, in the safe house, I've had constant sleepless nights. Sometimes there's a noise, just a small noise, and it sets me off. If a cat meows outside, I'm up in an instant, looking out the window wide awake or I'm creeping down the stairs to check out the house. I've even started sleeping with a knife under my pillow. Sometimes when I walking down the road, I see people looking at me and I'm convinced that they recognise me. I'm always on edge.

I'm drinking a lot. I suppose everyone expects you to be an alcoholic by now and I don't think I'm going to disappoint them. It's causing a lot of problems because I'm being very selfish but I don't know I'm doing it.

After a little while I just sit there and go into my own little world of Red Stripe lager. But I need it. I'm not allowed sleeping tablets in case the defence end up using it against me in court – they might say that my testimony isn't valid because I've been under the influence of drugs. I don't feel like I'm a person any more – I feel like a piece of evidence, exhibit number one. I feel like I've been sealed up and I'm not allowed to get contaminated.

It's weird but the only time I really feel I can sleep is when my wife is awake. I suppose it's because then I feel like she's watching over me, protecting me. But if she's asleep, I can't sleep. So it's back to drinking again. If I get pissed enough, I can always get to sleep.

Wednesday 11 June
Right now, I wouldn't recommend that anyone accepts witness protection. The police are just being completely out of order. I've given them all the information they asked for but they still refuse to say exactly what they're going to do for me. They say wait and see, wait and see. That's no good to me. I'm really worried about things.

I'm not allowed to work at the moment – it's too much of a risk. So the police come round to visit me once a week and give me £48 because that's how much I'd get if I was on the dole. It doesn't go very far. But it's really stupid because the police gave Sandra a cover story which doesn't make any sense. Apparently I'm this really successful builder who spends loads of time working on big money contracts abroad. That was fine while I was away but now I'm back and I haven't got a pot to piss in, it must make it really obvious that we're living a lie.

If I could go back in time to when I was arrested, I'd never go down this route again. I wouldn't even consider it. I'd much rather be locked up with them and risk getting killed. In fact, I'd probably end up killing myself. I must have thought about it a hundred times in the last year. The way they've treated me, I'd just never do it again. I don't think anyone would.

The way I see it, if you get put away for eight years you do four, but when you come out you can hold your head up high. You don't have to spend your life looking over your shoulder like I'm going to have to. I did it the first time – did the crime and then did the time and it was okay. I came out and was able to start my life again. But this way, it just never ends. It just goes on and on and I'll always regret doing it. I'm looking forward to playing these tapes back when it's all over because I hope I am going to be wrong. I hope the police will keep their promises and help me start my life over. But I don't feel very confident. When I was in the supergrass unit, the one thing you hear from all the people there is 'Don't trust the police, don't trust the police'. I'm convinced that I'm going to be shat on from a great height.

Tuesday 17 June
I asked the police for money to put extra locks on the doors and windows. They said they couldn't afford it. I was trying to tell them how worried about things I was but they just didn't seem to understand. I started telling them that I was going to make my own arrangements. I told them that when I got my new identity, I was going to apply for a shotgun licence so that I'd have some way of taking care of myself. They just looked at me and said there was no way they would ever let me have one.

I tried to explain that the people who were going to be coming after me were hardly going to turn up with lumps of wood or knives; they were going to turn up armed to the teeth. If I didn't get a shotgun then at least I wanted them to give me a bulletproof jacket so that if it did all come on top at least I could throw it on and perhaps survive it. They said they couldn't afford it.

They gave me a car for emergencies but then they took it off me. They said I was abusing it, that I was doing too many miles and that I wasn't keeping it clean. Now the car's gone but one of my bail conditions is that I should have a vehicle as a means of getaway. It's really fucking stupid. So now if anyone comes to shoot me, I'll have to hope the bus is going by.

Saturday 28 June
The police said they'd arrange a holiday so that my family could come and see me. I don't believe them. All the things they have told me so far have turned out to be lies. They really don't want to do anything for you because they're so terrified that when you go to court it will end up being used against them. That's all very well, I understand it, I really do – but it's no good to me right now, is it? It's not very promising at all. If I do ever get a holiday I know it's not going to be much fun anyway. Some caravan in the middle of nowhere with twenty armed guards and me mum.

They keep saying that I have to wait until after the trial and that's when they'll start helping me out. But they won't tell me what to expect. The contract I have with the police says they have to put me back in the position I was in before I became a witness. I'm never sure whether that means getting me a job and somewhere to live or putting me into a town that needs a good drug dealer. I might get a nice little sweeping job down at Fords or a job digging holes for the council and they'll say to me go on, enjoy your new life.

I have seen the things that the papers are writing about me. They make it seem like I've got a private jet and a million pounds in the bank. Even if the police had that kind of cash to throw away, I don't think I'd get it. At the end of the day, police and criminals are pretty much the same really. So even the cops hate a grass. I don't think they like me at all. Sometimes, in my heart, I wish I'd never become a witness. When I first got arrested, I met with my solicitor and he said that if I hadn't said anything, he could probably have got me off. After all, I only bought the drugs because Jim wanted me to keep in with Jack and Mick. I was a registered police informant. If only I'd kept my big mouth shut, I'd still be living in Braintree and none of this would be happening.

Friday 11 July

Sandra's gone out for the night so I'm here on my own looking after the kids.

I'll probably have to tell my children the whole story one day. I'm not looking forward to that. They'll want to get married or something one day and the whole name change thing can cause big problems. I don't know how they'll feel about their dad when I tell them. I'll just have to wait and see. To an extent they know already. My eldest boy, he's too young to know what's going on, but he knows it's not right. He asks me lots of awkward questions. He wouldn't know what a supergrass was but I'm always telling him off for telling tales on people, and if I explained what I have done that's exactly what he'd think I've been doing.

My kids think the reason that we had to move out of our house in the middle of the night was because some old World War Two bomb had been discovered and was about to go off in our street. It was the only excuse the police could come up with straightaway. The first night they had to put them in a police training school. My eldest isn't stupid; he can read. He kept asking Sandra, 'Why are we in a police station, Mummy?'

The first time I went to prison, the kids were told that Daddy was being sent away because he had been naughty and made the Queen angry. They were really upset by the whole thing. They slept with their mum every night. Ever since then my eldest has been really clingy. When I've had to go into custody just for a few days at a time to make statements or something, he's acted in a really odd way. I've gone to say goodbye and he's said to me, 'You are coming back aren't you?' as if he just knows that something's not right. It really gets to you. When I was away, I got all these letters and pictures and things saying 'Daddy we love you' and 'We think you're the best daddy in the world'. And I'm there thinking, no I'm not, I'm full of shit. I've got all these kids telling me I'm wonderful and I just don't deserve it.

Monday 4 August

Let's talk about the Old Bailey. They took me there last week for a look around and I can tell you it's not a very nice place. The trial is going to be held in Court No. 2, which is very, very overpowering to say the least. When I was at the old-style committal, I was at least 35 feet from the dock where Whomes and Steele were. This time I'm probably 10 feet at the most. They're gonna be there in my face and there's nowhere to hide from them. It's made me pretty scared because it seems such a small room for the number of people that are going to be in there. They made me walk the route that I'll take into court every morning. I was expecting at least some kind of dedicated facility for special witnesses, but I was wrong. I go into the Bailey through the back doors and then me and my armed escort walk through the cells. Then we went along the corridor, up a few flights of stairs and finally ended up in a toilet outside the court. 'What's this?' I said. 'This is where we'll be keeping you,' said one of the coppers. And that was it. That's where I'm gonna be every morning; it's where I'll eat my lunch and where I'll be sent to every time there's a bit of legal argument. A fucking toilet. Mind you, with the amount of nerves I'm likely to have, it's probably the best place for me to be.

Thursday 14 August

I don't think me and Sandra are going to make it. She keeps saying that she wants to go back to Essex, to go back to living a normal life. Sometimes I think it might just be the best thing for her. But when I start to think about my future without her, all I see is problems.

Basically we're just living a lie at the moment. And we have to spend our lives remembering all the lies we've been telling so we don't get caught out. It would be so nice, just such a relief, to be able to tell someone. It would be brilliant if there was someone out there who could understand why I am the way that I am. I feel that I must come across really weird to quite a few people. But I don't know whether I'll ever feel comfortable enough to tell any of my new friends the truth. The paranoia is always there. What happens if I run into someone I knew in the old days and I'm with my kids? What do I do – not let the children speak? It's an impossible situation.

My biggest worry is what might happen if Sandra and I don't get back together. What happens if I start seeing someone else and fall in love. Do I sit her down and say, 'By the way, I'm a supergrass and there's a quarter of a million on my head? But we'll be okay as long as you don't tell anyone.' What happens if you don't tell her? What if you do tell a girl then you split up, if she tells her next boyfriend and he tells someone? But if you don't tell her, then how would you feel if they burst in for me and she's there?

Tuesday 19 August

I don't want to do it. It's only a week or so away but I really don't want to go through with it. I've been sitting here trying to work out what they might ask me. I know they're going to try to trick me and that's what really does your head in. I guess I've been trying to work out the answers in advance but my barrister says the one thing you shouldn't do is try to work out what they'll ask because they'll always come up with something different and then you'll be stuck. I'm trying not to do it, but I can't help it. It's not just a case of me going there and telling the truth. The whole case rests on me. Without me there is no case. So they are going to try to do absolutely everything they can to destroy me because it's their only chance of getting off. Are they going to call me a liar? Are they going to try to rip my character apart? Are they going to let me speak at all? I'll just have to wait and see.

I'm not looking forward to going back into custody. I'll be back in the police stations again, but this time no one will be allowed to see me. No visits at all. They are scared that if anyone sees me when the trial is on the defence will say I'm being coached or I'm being given ideas. So I'm going to be spending a lot of time on my own. I'm not looking forward to it. All you can do is watch TV. I'll be fully up to date with *Neighbours*, *EastEnders*, *Coronation Street*, the lot. But that doesn't make up for much. And it's not like I'm in some peaceful place where I can think. Because it's a police station, it's full of drunks who are up for a fight, especially on Friday and Saturday nights. They scream and kick the doors all night long. It's horrible and I'm not looking forward to it one little bit.

I'm not the same person that I was when all this started. I used to laugh at people who cried at soppy films. But now, at everything, even when I hear a song that's slightly sad, I tend to cry. I don't know why. I have thought about my dad a lot, that keeps going through my mind. I lay there and it's as if he's there, but he's not. Difficult. They want me to see a psychiatrist, to see if I'm cracking up. When they first said it I felt good because I thought they were actually worried about me. Now I realise they were just worried that I might not be able to give evidence in the case.

Friday 29 August (three days before the trial)
Sandra isn't speaking to me anymore. Last night I told her I was popping out for a quick drink. I didn't get back until 3 a.m. and when I did I was completely out of my tree. My neighbours are really on her side. They were all having a go at me today saying, 'How can you go out drinking every night when you're about to go off to Germany for two months?' That's the story everyone's been given – that I'm off abroad to work on some kind of building contract. They're all saying I should be spending more time with my wife. They have no idea just how much stress I'm under. If Sandra doesn't start talking to me again soon, I'm just going to go out back down the pub. As far as I'm concerned, any excuse to get pissed is a good one.

Saturday 30 August (back in custody)
First night back in the cells. Not very good. I can't sleep. I'm
very nervous. I'm bloody nervous. I've only been back sixteen
hours but I've had my first big row with the wife already. We
actually fell out over a difference of things that she said to
one of our neighbours and something that I said to one of
our neighbours. We forgot to confer. You tell so many lies in
this game that it just happens automatically. You don't think,
you don't ask.

I'll just have to take it in my stride. People say don't worry,
but I can't help it. This is the beginning of my whole life and
it's a life of worrying about everything and having to be extra
careful who I make friends with. I even have to make sure my
kids don't slip up. At the end of the day, I can handle going
to court and giving evidence. What I can't handle is the rest
of my life. The rest of my life is going to be horrible, no
matter which way the verdict goes. I spoke to my mum a
little while ago. That wasn't very good either. She just told
me to tell the truth.

Sunday 31 August
I feel like shit.

It's my second night back in custody and I've just had the
biggest scare of my life. Sandra was really depressed when I
left and scared about being on her own. When I phoned her
back last night, she was pretty miserable because of the row
but after a while things seemed pretty much okay. But when I
phoned her tonight, there was no answer. So I paged her. No
answer. So I phoned her mobile. It was turned off. I started to
panic. I didn't know what to do. So I told the police and they
started to panic. They sent a car round to the house and she
wasn't there and neither were the kids so they started
searching for her and put out an alert on her car. And the
whole time I was just sitting there feeling absolutely useless. I
really wanted to do something to help but I was locked up. I
really started to believe that they'd got to her. They knew the

trial was about to start and they'd snatched her away. I was ready to retract every statement I'd ever made. There was no way I was going to get in the witness box. I really believed my family had been abducted and killed. The police were getting really nervous, checking on all my other relatives and with the families of the accused to make sure they knew where they were.

Then at about 3 a.m. the police said they'd found her. It had just all go to be too much for her and she'd gone off on some bender and left the kids with a friend. I know I keep going on about how tough things are for me, but I know it's fucking hard for Sandra as well. All this shit, somehow it affects the innocent more than the guilty. I was so relieved that she was safe. I wanted to tell her that I loved her and cared for her but I just ended up shouting at her down the phone, calling her all the names under the sun. I was really having a go at her and left her even more upset. Then I just sat on the bed and cried.

Tuesday 2 September
Everyone back in Braintree has got it in for me. If anyone gets arrested for anything, even if they get stopped by the police for speeding, the story is that I must have grassed them up. I'm getting the blame for absolutely every problem that anyone's ever had. I'm the ultimate scapegoat. Okay, so I'm an informer. I've informed on people. But I'm trying to make amends. I feel like more of a criminal now than ever before. I've been condemned to a life of misery. I want to sleep but I can't. It's getting too close for comfort now. Someone told me today that they want to use me in another trial next September, the one where Russell Tate and that lot are up for smuggling the drugs they found in Mick's mum's garage. I'm really fucked off about it. I was hoping that, after this trial was over, that would be it. They wouldn't have any more hold over me and I'd be able to get sentenced and then get on with my life. But now they say I have to wait until the second

trial is over. They've got me by the nuts. If I don't agree to give evidence, it's gonna look really bad and the police won't petition the judge to give me a discount on my sentence. If I do give evidence, it means another whole year of living in limbo. It's all down to me. Sometimes I feel like a performing dog. The more tricks I do, the more dog biscuits I get.

Friday 5 September.
I think I'm going to die of some stress-related illness before I get into court. There's another delay now so I won't be in the box until next week. It's doing my head in. I got a letter from my sister today. She said she is really proud of me for doing what I'm doing. She's proud that I'm her brother. No one has ever said that to me before. Normally my family are really angry at being related to me because of the things I've done in the past. It's nice to think at least one person thinks I'm doing the right thing.

Saturday 6 September
I've been reading statements all day. Yesterday the police told me to expect to be in the dock for at least a month. I'm bloody worried about it. I can't help it. What scares me most is the fact that if there's just one mistake, they could get off. Not because they didn't do it but because there is some stupid technicality. Why am I so scared? How can they be sitting in court smiling? I hear they're very confident, they think they've got a good case. But if they get off it's a bloody travesty.

People say you can't destroy the truth, but you don't get to be one of the top barristers in the country without knowing a thing or two. If they get off, I will be distressed. They won't get off. They did it. They are guilty men. If they get off then I don't know what will happen. They will try to throw lots of doubt. I hope I can survive the onslaught of questions. I hope the truth is enough. What a situation to be in, eh?

Monday, 8 September,
First day in court. I sat there all day, in the toilet, but never
got to go on. I was talking to the guys on the protection
squad. They just say tell the truth, don't worry, take deep
breaths. I must have heard that ten times. It got to be a real
pain in the arse. I feel numb.

Tuesday 9 September
Today was my first day. I was really nervous this morning,
nearly sick. I think part of it was the drive down from Essex to
the Old Bailey in the back of this armoured Range Rover. It
was like being in a boat in the middle of a storm. Then after
that I had to be in court all day. I started giving my evidence.
I just kept looking straight forward. I got brave at one point
and had a quick glance to my side but Mick and Jack were
both engrossed in reading, they didn't notice me. It's all
pretty good at the moment. I'm just standing there telling
my story.

Thursday 11 September
I started being cross-examined today. The bloke is good. Very
good. He made me think that I'm a liar. He made me think
that they were innocent and that I made the whole thing up.
He's making me look like a complete idiot out there and I'm
not getting a chance to say why I did it or how the whole
thing happened. He's bloody good, but that's why he earns
the money he does. You don't hire rubbish if you're fighting
for your life. I feel like a kebab. I'm being grilled in the
courtroom and I'm just waiting for Steele's barrister to start
slicing away. I can just imagine what the press are saying
about it all. They're going to pick up on all the bad stuff
because it makes a better story for them. I don't think the
press like me at all. I don't think anyone likes a grass. I feel
like the most unpopular man in the world.

It's just like that joke. This bloke who really hates Arabs
decides to join the French Foreign Legion so that he could kill

as many of them as he wants. And when he goes to the interview they ask him why he wants to join and he says, 'I hate Arabs. I really fucking hate Arabs. I want to kill loads of them.' And they say to him that's great, you're in. Then on his first day he gets put on guard duty. And in the middle of the night another Legionnaire comes up to him and says, 'Look over there, there are four Arabs hiding behind that rock.' So quick as a flash, the bloke runs over and shoots the four Arabs and then comes back and shoots the Legionnaire who told him where they were. Later on his boss calls him over. 'Well done for killing the Arabs, but why did you shoot the other Legionnaire?' And the geezer says, 'Well I hate Arabs. I really fucking hate Arabs. But I hate people who grass even more.'

18

'I could do that, I could shoot someone'

The first suspicion that the police might have arrested the wrong men – that Michael Steele and Jack Whomes were not the killers and that the testimony of Darren Nicholls was a complete pack of lies – came less than two weeks after the opening of the five-month murder trial.

Through the auspices of the Police and Criminal Evidence Act (PACE) 1984, there are strict guidelines that prevent officers from discussing any evidence or any aspect of a case with someone in custody, except during formal, recorded interviews. Officers are, however, allowed to make 'welfare visits' to ensure the suspect is being properly looked after. Ideally, the officers responsible for such visits should not be the same officers responsible for conducting interviews with the suspect.

As the triple murder trial unfolded, it emerged that during his first week in custody the detectives responsible for interviewing Nicholls had made some thirty-six hours' worth of welfare visits, including one single visit lasting a mammoth seven hours and forty-three minutes.

Even the solicitor acting for Nicholls, Lee Craddock, expressed surprise at the length of the meetings and agreed with the court that it was an 'undesirable' situation for his client to have found himself in.

Graham Parkins QC, the highly experienced barrister acting on behalf of Michael Steele, confidently explained to the jury exactly what had happened: Essex police, desperate to convict Steele, had used the visits to give Nicholls a 'script' containing what would later become his 'evidence'. The whole story Nicholls had given was, in fact, a fabrication and Nicholls was playing along purely to save himself from more serious charges.

Parkins accused Detective Constable Chris Winstone – who interviewed Nicholls after his initial arrest – of 'helping him, prompting him' and suggesting things that he hadn't said in order to make his story sound more convincing.

The evidence of this was everywhere. Parkins showed that during one recorded interview, the tape was turned off for twenty minutes while Nicholls went to the toilet. When he returned, Lee Craddock confirmed that no discussions had taken place while the tape had been switched off. In fact, Craddock had been out of the room making telephone calls at the time and had no idea what might have been said.

Extracts of other taped interviews were played. In one Nicholls was talking eloquently about a particular sequence of events and then stumbled: 'I've fucked the story up here again,' he said. 'No, you're all right mate. Go on,' came Winstone's reply. In another, Nicholls paused when he had trouble recalling the name of an associate. In the background, a faint sound like someone else's voice was heard – a prompt? – immediately before Nicholls began speaking again. In other tapes, Nicholls sounded distinctly as though he was reading something out rather than speaking his own words.

Parkins showed the jury the early statements Nicholls had made and pointed out how they told a very different story to the one that later formed the bulk of the prosecution case. Parkins also pointed out that Nicholls only began speaking and naming Whomes and Steele as the killers *after* he himself had been charged with the murders.

While giving evidence for the prosecution, Nicholls had been poised and confident. But under cross-examination, as cracks in his story began to appear, so his answers became less precise, less convincing, less specific.

'Has anyone told you to keep it vague?' Parkins asked one day, frustrated with the inability of Nicholls to answer a straight question. 'I put it to you that the final version of what the jury has heard is not your own work. You have been prompted, helped and guided by other police officers.

'That's not true.'

'Mr Nicholls, are you a truthful man by nature?'

'I don't think you could say I am.' Pause. 'But I'm telling the truth now.'

'But Mr Nicholls, how does one know when you are lying and when you are not? You are both a blatant and persistent liar. An opportunist, I suggest, grasping at straws to save yourself. By December 6 you knew Mr Steele very well and had the means to make up a plausible story about him and his colleagues.'

'Yes, if I wished to do so, but they did do the killings.'

'Are you falsely accusing these men when you know who was really responsible?'

'They did it.'

'Do you want to protect yourself and others who are not before this court?'

'No, they did it.'

'Were you involved in these murders yourself, with other men?

'Look, I've told you, I picked them up from the murders they committed. I was badly affected by it,' Nicholls replied angrily.

'Were you indeed? You told those officers you didn't really want anything to do with Mr Steele after the killings. You had been duped into the ferrying the men to and from a triple shooting. If you are telling the truth, an awful, evil thing has been done to you.'

'Yes, that's right.'

'Mr Steele would hardly be on your Christmas card list.'

'No.'

'Can you explain then why you sent his family a card for Christmas 1995?'

Nicholls said nothing. Steele, sitting in the dock, allowed himself a wry smile.

Parkins continued. 'You also gave this man you claim was a killer a case of canned beer and a bottle of wine.'

Nicholls shuffled uneasily in the witness box. 'Yes,' he mumbled, 'but only because he gave my children a present.'

'Ah yes. A radio-controlled aeroplane. Which you went flying at Mr Steele's house. Isn't it true that you then took your children to the house of this triple killer so they could watch the rabbits running in the garden?'

'Yes,' said Nicholls softly.

A few days later, Graham Parkins began examining the mysterious, threatening phone calls that Steele had received from Ireland and uncovered the most dramatic twist yet to the murder saga. It emerged that Billy and John, the gruesome twosome who had called both Michael Steele and Sarah Saunders, were nothing more than a figment of Detective Superintendent Ivan Dibley's imagination.

'The idea behind it was to try to flush Steele out through an undercover police operation and to try and meet with him,' says Dibley. 'We took a bit of a gamble because we didn't know whether Steele knew for sure who Tucker and Tate were supplying their drugs to. We chose Ireland because it was outside Steele's immediate circle – we didn't want to be operating somewhere where he might have contacts – and because the terrorist link added a bit of extra pressure. Also, if we had made the team somewhere else in this country, Steele could just have told them to find another supplier. Being across the water made it more understandable why they were keen to keep the established supply chain going.

'We hoped it would run as a long-term project, that through a series of meetings we might eventually gain his trust and that, some months down the line, he might just say to us, "Yeah, I was the guy who did the murders." As it happens he didn't take the bait. Right from the start he denied that he was involved so we got nowhere. But I still supported the operation. We switched to Sarah because it seemed clear there was some sort of close relationship between the two, but that wasn't successful either and the operation was shut down.'

In one of his early interviews, Nicholls had mixed up the order of events. Knowing that Tate had borrowed some money off the Joneses and knowing that Tate had later threatened to kill Steele, Nicholls implied that the threatening calls from Ireland had come *before* the murders and were part of the reason Steele decided to kill Tate.

Graham Parkins was quick to seize on the error as further evidence of police colluding with Nicholls to concoct the perfect story.

'You now know the Irish threat was in reality two policemen; you were told that by other officers weren't you?'

'No, no, no.'

'You made a massive blunder when you put them forward as the motive and that claim didn't appear in your later witness statements. Was that because the officers interviewing you said, "Hold on, the Irish brothers were policemen and they only rang up after the killings?"'

'No. You would have to be in my situation to understand. You try and explain it to someone when you have been a witness to a murder. I was very confused.'

NICHOLLS I hated every minute of being in the witness box. It made me feel ill for hours afterwards. The worst part was the walk in each morning, from the toilet to the courtroom, knowing that all those eyes were on me and knowing what

was to come. It didn't take long for me to realise that it
didn't matter what I actually said, I still got a hard time. Yes
was always going to be wrong. No was always going to be
wrong. Every word was used against me. Whatever I said, I
was a liar. I heard it all the time. Liar, liar, liar. It made me
really angry every time they doubted that what I was saying
was the truth – they even argued the things that weren't in
any doubt – but that's just what they wanted. I think they
wanted me to lose it, to go out of control because then they
would be able to go for the jugular and make me look like
some kind of thug in front of the jury.

Full credit to Parkins – he did a fucking wonderful job.
He'd tie me up in knots, make me think the sun was shining
even though it was pissing down with rain. I remember one
time I said to him: 'Listen, you don't know what happened. I
do, I was there.' He just laughed and called me a liar again. I
suppose you have to expect it because they are fighting for
their lives but it was still a horrible thing to have to go
through. Innocent or guilty, it doesn't matter what you are –
as soon as you step foot in that witness box, it's only you
that's on trial, no one else.

On 3 November, after ten weeks of sitting quietly and taking
in all that was being said about him, Michael Steele himself
rose and, under heavy escort, moved to the witness box. Under
cross-examination, the first thing he would have been asked
about was his criminal record so, with attack being the best
form of defence, he decided to get it out in the open straightaway.

'Is it true that you are content for the jury to know things
about your past?' asked Parkins.

'I would like the jury to know everything there is to know
about me,' Steele replied.

Parkins then cleared his throat and read out a list of previous convictions: in March 1964 Steele went to prison for
twelve months for stealing property and driving while dis-

qualified; February 1966, six months for stealing property and assault causing actual bodily harm; June 1966, twelve-month conditional discharge for stealing from a vehicle; April 1968, fine for possession of an offensive weapon (a motorcycle chain); February 1969, eighteen months for trying to cheat customs of oil duty (the red diesel scam); March 1972, five years for theft from a vehicle; February 1980, six months suspended for theft; September 1980, twelve months for theft; August 1986, conditional discharge for criminal damage; June 1990, nine years for importing cannabis.

'Do not hold the past against him,' Graham Parkins told the jury after he finished reading the list of his convictions. 'He has paid his debt to society and should not be branded a triple killer. Judge him solely on this case.'

That Steele's account of the events leading up to the death of Tate, Tucker and Rolfe would be somewhat different to that of Darren Nicholls was a given. But just how different came as a shock to everyone.

'Nicholls is what you call a suicide jockey. He's a major drug smuggler who travels abroad regularly to bring shipments of cannabis into the country. The cannabis is loaded into the boots of cars in France or Belgium and driven on to a ferry and then through customs. That's where the name comes from because the chances of being caught are so high. What you do is bring in three cars at a time. That way, if one goes down, you still make money,' Steele told the hushed courtroom.

According to Steele, by the time the pair met in prison, Steele, stunned at the length of his prison sentence, had decided to give up smuggling for good. Nicholls, on the other hand, was fascinated and eager to start up a drugs-based business of his own. Once both men were released, Nicholls would visit Steele regularly, eager to pick up advice. 'Nicholls had the room next door to mine so I saw him every day. My first impression was that he was a fool. I didn't like the man at all, but after a while he grew on me.

'I was released in June 1993. He got my number and rang

on a regular basis just to chat, even though he never seemed to have much to say. You'd pick up the phone and say, "Yes Darren?" and there would be a pause. It would always be you that would have to make conversation.

'He's what I would call a habitual, always turning up on my doorstep. Sometimes I would say anything just to get rid of him. I found there were two sides to him: a very silly side and a very educated side.'

In the early hours of one morning in November 1994, Steele said he had received a phone call at home. He let Jackie answer it, thinking it was her brother who, because of his job as an all-night taxi driver, often called at odd hours. In fact the call was for him. It was Sarah Saunders explaining that Pat Tate had been shot and was in hospital. According to Steele, Nicholls called a few days afterwards for one of his usual chats and knew nothing about the shooting. When Steele told him, he immediately demanded Tate's phone number. Steele called Tate at the hospital to ensure it was okay to pass it on and then called Nicholls back. A few days after that, Nicholls turned up at Steele's house looking miserable.

'He had been to visit Pat Tate in hospital and he and his friends had taken the piss out of him, bullying him quite badly and making him run around like an errand boy,' Steele explained. 'He was obviously very upset by the visit. He was standing with his hands in his pockets and his head bowed. He looked like a child that had been scolded. Then Nicholls said something very odd. Something I'll never forget. He said, "I could do that. I could shoot someone. I have often spoken to myself about it." I'll always remember it because of the way he said it, that thing about having spoken to himself about it. You see, when you got to know Nicholls, he was a schizophrenic.'

After that, Steele kept in touch with Nicholls because he needed lots of electrical work done, first on his business unit and eventually in his new home, and Nicholls was cheaper than anyone else.

Over the next year or so Nicholls and Steele spent a great

deal of time socialising. Much of the story Nicholls had put before the court, reported Steele, was either a twisting of the true facts or a simple switch, where Nicholls had substituted Steele's name for his own. It was Nicholls who was the 'phonebox' man, not him. It was Nicholls who was in contact with drug suppliers in Amsterdam, not him. It was Nicholls who had panicked when Leah Betts had died, not him. It was Nicholls who had made the comment about looking in the phone book and picking the killers, not him. During his first two days in the witness box, Steele systematically countered or rubbished every single one of the allegations Nicholls had made against him. If anyone had killed Tate, Tucker and Rolfe, it had to be Nicholls. How else would he know so much about what happened and how they died? But his friendship with Steele made it easy for him to pin the crime on a man who, because of his criminal background, must have seemed a soft target. It was particularly hurtful to hear Nicholls lying about him and accusing him of triple murder as, throughout their friendship, Steele had been nothing but a friend to Nicholls and had never shown him any malice.

'Over the months, Darren Nicholls had got to know everything there was to know about me,' Steele told the court. 'He knew all my habits, all my background, all about my friends. He would come round my house, he would hang round my workshop and he would also join in our social outings. For example, we were in a pub one day with Jackie near Point Clear and I told him about a friend of mine who had got into a bit of trouble with a Range Rover when he tried to take it down to the beach. The differential lock got stuck on some pole sticking out of the sand. I was telling Nicholls about all the things he tried and how he eventually got it out. Nicholls then twisted that story around and claimed it happened to me and Jack when we were coming back from a smuggling run. But it never happened, not to me. Never.

'As for smuggling drugs across the Channel, I would say the easiest way to do it would have been with a plane. That was what I used to do and if I was ever going to do it again, that is how I would do it now. I am experienced as a pilot. I qualified in 1970 and am multi-engine rated, which means I can fly any propeller aircraft.

'Darren Nicholls has never been in my boat in his life. I don't think he's ever been in any boat. You can tell from the way he speaks about it. He claimed that during the time we supposedly crossed the channel at night with a load of drugs, I had the GPS on. That's nonsense. When you're out at night, it's crucial that you have good night vision, that your eyes are accustomed to the dark. If you have the GPS, which is basically a small, bright TV screen, then you wouldn't be able to see anything. You'd be effectively blinded. It just wouldn't happen. It proves he's a liar.'

Steele spoke about his friendship with Pat Tate, how the pair had been so close that they had even taken foreign holidays together on a number of occasions. The jury were shown pictures of the pair laughing and joking together. Steele's partner Jackie Street was also firm friends with Sarah Saunders and the pair would call each other most nights. 'When I first met Pat, he had a magnetic personality. He was lovely to be with. He never changed with me but over the years he became more and more of a junkie. It was sad to watch what was happening. Towards the end, 70 per cent of me disliked him but the other 30 per cent of me loved him.

'When he and Sarah split up, he was getting out of control. He said a lot of things I sure he did not mean. He told Sarah that we didn't want to see her any more. He said to her, "Mickey and Jackie, they're not your friends, they're my friends and they're only putting up with you because I want it, because I say so." He started telling her lies that we were saying about her. He was doing anything to upset her and it worked.

He was still giving her money to look after their son but when things got really bad he started being cruel about it. Rather than giving her money once a week, he'd let it go ten or fifteen days. Sometimes she was desperate. I lent her £100 once, just to help her get through. Sarah is very nice. She's a very, very nice person. She took to me. I was like a father to her. It's total rubbish about an affair though. Nonsense. She is a woman of twenty-four, I am a man of fifty-five.'

Steele told the jury that the bullying incident in the hospital was one of a number that, over time, increased the tension between Nicholls and Tate. The situation broke down completely after Nicholls brought over some dodgy cannabis and sold it on to the Firm. With Tate on the warpath, furious at being made to look a fool, Nicholls went round to see Steele once more. 'Pat wanted to meet Nicholls – but Nicholls wouldn't go near him, he was terrified of the man,' Steele told the court. 'I ended up being the go-between. Pat would call me and I'd call Nicholls, and vice versa. Pat asked me to chaperone Nicholls to Amsterdam, where I was told he was going to retrieve some money. I didn't know who he was getting the money back from and I never saw it handed over. Nicholls gave me Tate's share and then made himself scarce while I gave it to Tate, who took £2,000 out of it as my fee for going along. That was all I had to do with it.'

As for the gun that had been found in the loft of his house, the one that Nicholls claimed he had asked him to buy shortly before the murder, the truth was that he had never seen it before in his life, he said. When the gun was originally recovered, Steele quickly made the following statement: 'During the search of my premises, a firearm has been recovered. Because of the death of two or three persons known to me I have now been charged with those killings. Forensic science will prevail and totally exempt the weapon found at my premises.'

In court he explained that he had once had a neighbour, an old man who was a bit strange and paranoid, who kept a gun in his loft that wasn't found until after he died. Having only moved into the bungalow a few months earlier, Steele was convinced the gun had a similar origin. He knew he had nothing to worry about.

That Court No. 2 at the Old Bailey might be witnessing an

almighty miscarriage of justice seemed even more likely when, on his third day in the witness box, Michael Steele finally shared his alibi for the night of the murder.

At 5.01 p.m. on 6 December 1995, the exact same time that Nicholls claimed Steele had pulled up outside the motorcycle shop in Marks Tey in his red Toyota Hi-Lux, Steele had concrete proof that he was somewhere else.

Graham Parkins produced a credit card receipt signed by Steele showing he was buying petrol from a Texaco garage on the A120 some eight miles and at least 20 minutes away. Furthermore, the till receipt showed that Steele was buying four-star petrol. The Hi-Lux – the vehicle in which Nicholls claimed he arrived at the rendezvous – ran on diesel. As far as alibis go, it was about as strong as they come and Steele knew it. 'It's shockproof, rockproof and everything else,' he said.

'We then drove to Tesco's and I waited in the car while Jackie went in and bought a couple of bottles of wine. From then were drove to the village of Bulphan near Brentwood, where we picked up the boat trailer from the house of Dennis Whomes, Jack's uncle. We arrived at the house and knocked several times but there was no answer so I hitched up the trailer and drove home.'

Steele told the jury that he and Jackie Street arrived home at Oaklands at 7.25 p.m. Five minutes later, Steele's sister-in-law and her daughter arrived to view the property with a view to possibly buying it.

'Did you go to Rettendon on that night?' asked Parkins.

'Nowhere near Rettendon,' Steele replied confidently. 'We came straight home.'

Jackie Street did not appear at the Old Bailey. Doctors confirmed that she had been suffering from severe depression since Steele's arrest and was therefore not fit to attend court in person.

After a round of legal argument, the judge agreed that the statement she had given before becoming ill could be read out. It confirmed everything Steele had said.

Further corroboration came from postwoman Phyllis Stambrook, Steele's sister-in-law from his first marriage, who told the court that the night of the murders was the night she and her daughter Gemma went to view Steele's home. 'When we arrived they were having a celebration. They had signed a contract that day for a new property and we had champagne.' She confirmed that she had arrived at the house in Great Bentley at 7.30 p.m. and that Steele was already there. Parkins explained that with the murders said to have taken place between 6.45 and 7 p.m., it would have been impossible for Steele to have been in the two places that night. He could not possibly be responsible for the killings.

Like Michael Steele, Jack Whomes had originally been advised against appearing in the dock. During the trial, particularly when he saw how well Steele was managing to defend himself, he changed his mind. It proved to be an emotional experience.

Speaking to his defence barrister, David Lederman QC, Whomes agreed that he had been in prison at the same time as Pat Tate and also agreed that he was an expert shot, having used his father's twelve-bore shotguns from the time he was a young boy to shoot rabbits and dead branches off trees. When Lederman put it to him that the prosecution would say he cold-bloodedly killed Tate along with Tucker and Rolfe, Whomes could no longer hold back his feelings. 'I could not even kill a sparrow. Anyone who knows me knows I am not capable of killing. To say I killed these men is ridiculous. I did not know Mr Tucker and I did not know Mr Rolfe. The last time I saw Pat Tate was when he was being transferred from a prison near Haverhill, Suffolk with my brother Johnny. He was a friend.'

Lederman then suggested that Whomes was put up for the shooting by Steele. Whomes raised his voice again. 'I would not do it for anybody. I could not do it. Why would I want to do it? I deny it. I deny any suggestion that I had anything to do with drugs or murder. All the stuff about the duff drugs deal is rubbish. I would much rather put money into motors. I would never deal in drugs.' Whomes told the jury how, while working as a bouncer, he had seen a girl high on drugs take her clothes off and dance naked. 'There was a girl like Leah Betts. She'd had some bad gear and was foaming at the mouth. That worried me sick and I called an ambulance for her. I told undercover police to come in and search for drugs.' Then, without warning, Whomes burst into tears and began sobbing uncontrollably in the witness box. 'I did not do anything like that. What they are suggesting is ridiculous. You don't now what I am going through, being locked up. They won't even let me cuddle my own son.'

Under cross-examination by Andrew Munday QC, Whomes admitted that he had indeed been in the Rettendon area at the time of the killings, but that it was a 'pure and unfortunate coincidence'. He claimed that Nicholls had called him and asked him to pick up a broken-down Volkswagen Passat from outside a pub on the A130, just a few hundred yards from the murder scene. That, said Whomes, explained his brief mobile phone call to Nicholls – he was letting him know he'd got the car.

Munday pointed out that his phone had also been 'spotted' in the area the day before the killings and suggested that he was scouting the murder scene. Whomes shook his head and told Munday that, with the greatest of respect, he could not be more wrong. The day before the killings he had simply gone to see his uncle in the village of Bulphan, also close to Rettendon, to pick up Steele's boat trailer. 'I banged on the door. I remember the letterbox in the middle of the door. I held it open with my fingers and shouted through it, but there was no one about. Finally I left a note.' Dennis Whomes, Jack's uncle, was brought in to corroborate the story. He agreed with Jack's version of events completely. He remembered that his nephew had indeed left a note to say that he'd called but, not surprisingly, he had long since thrown it away.

Ian Bristowe of the Forensic Engineers' Association seemed

to confirm this version of events when he told the court that Whomes could not have made the call logged on his mobile at 6.59 – when Whomes was alleged to have told Nicholls to 'come and get us' – because his mobile signal would not work on either of the two aerials covering the crime scene. However if he had been on the nearby A130 he could have.

Other witnesses, some of them former friends of Nicholls, testified to the poor state of the Passat. It had no heater, a noisy exhaust and to all intents a clutch that was unusable. The idea that anyone would use it as a getaway car for a triple murder was laughable. Finally there was only a single footprint found on the ground by the offside back door of the Range Rover where the killer would have stood. It was identified as coming from a size 8 or 9 Hi-Tech training shoe. Lederman pointed out that Jack Whomes wore a size 11 and, according to Nicholls, was wearing Wellington boots at the time of the murder. In a nutshell there was nothing, absolutely nothing, to suggest that Jack Whomes had ever been down the lane itself. If the jury looked at the facts, said Lederman, he could not possibly be responsible for the murders.

Graham Parkins and David Lederman had made convincing cases for the innocence of their clients. If Steele and Whomes were truly the victims of a cruel fantasy created by Darren Nicholls, if the evidence against them had been concocted, dreamed up and falsified with the help of the Essex police, if the lack of forensic and other evidence of their guilt was purely down to the fact that they had no guilt, it left only one question: if Steele and Whomes had not murdered Tate, Tucker and Rolfe, then who did?

As the weeks had passed, the defence had offered up some tantalising possibilities without ever spelling out the allegations fully. It had emerged, for example, that the shotgun cartridges used in the murder were a type popular with clay pigeon shooters. DC Jim, who had been heard on tape discussing with Nicholls ways of ripping Steele off by stealing his

Jaguar while it was carrying £150,000, was a regular clay-pigeon shooter. Jim was now under arrest. The implication was obvious.

The mysterious Jones brothers from whom Tate had supposedly borrowed £40,000 were vaguely touted as another possibility, as were literally dozens of other members of the Essex and London underworld.

But it wasn't until early December when the trial was in its fourth month that a full, practical and detailed alternative explanation for the deaths came to court. And when it did, it was absolute dynamite.

No one expected much the day that William George Jasper took the stand. A shaven-headed, square shouldered bruiser of an East End hard man, he spoke mostly in sentences of five words or less in a sullen, monotone voice. But as his incredible story unfolded, the entire courtroom ended up hanging on his every syllable.

Jasper had been arrested on theft and drugs charges on 16 January 1996, a little more than a month after the murders. During his initial interviews at Rayleigh police station, he said little but after a few hours he began to relate the tale of the 'five large ones' he'd earned for 'a bit of driving' he'd done the month before.

The saga began in a Mexican restaurant in Canning Town in the middle of December. Jasper, along with two leading members of a East End crime syndicate, were discussing what to do about a gang from the Essex who had arranged to purchase some cocaine. The word on the street was that the Essex boys were not planning to hand over any cash, but instead had bought a machine gun and were going to rip off the London team. The Essex firm in question was, of course, none other than Tucker, Tate and Rolfe.

The East End gang was run by Jesse Gale and a man known only as Mr D. For Gale the discussion had a personal element: he had been ripped off by Tucker before, to the tune of £20,000 and there was no way he was going to let it happen again. As the beers flowed and the enchiladas went down, so the conversation got more serious.

'Why don't *we* rob *them*?' said Gale.

Mr D. shook his head. 'We can't do that, there would be too many comebacks. We'd be better off taking them out of the game. Put them out of their misery.'

Now it was Gale's turn to shake his head. 'Nah, just rob 'em,' he said.

Mr D. then turned to Jasper and asked if he wanted to earn £5,000 for a night's driving.

On the evening of 6 December 1995, the night of the murder, Jasper picked up a grey Fiat Uno turbo from outside the Peacock Gym in east London. He drove to a bar near Hornchurch, where he picked up Mr D. who was carrying a sports bag. Jasper soon learned the bag contained a sawn-off shotgun and a 9-millimetre Browning pistol. From there the pair travelled to a cab office where they found Jesse Gale waiting outside. Jasper waited in the car while Mr D. got out, taking the bag with him, and disappeared with Gale down an alleyway.

Ten minutes or so later, Mr D. returned and told Jasper to drive him to Rettendon, pulling up alongside a lane close to a garden centre. Mr D. got out, again with the bag, and told Jasper he was going to pick up 4 kilos of cocaine. He returned around forty minutes later carrying the sports bag and also a foot-square rucksack. As the pair drove back to London, Mr D. called Jesse Gale and told him everything was 'sorted'.

It was only when he saw the news of the murders the following day that he realised what had happened. He had already arranged to meet Jesse Gale the following evening at Moreton's Bar in order to pick up his fee and he turned up just before 10 p.m. 'I thought they were just going to do a deal but somewhere along the line they changed their mind. When I got to Moreton's the next night, Gale was already there. He asked me what I wanted to drink, I said Jack Daniels and Coke, and he got me a large one. I had a couple of mouthfuls then he said he was going to the toilet and for me to wait a couple of minutes and then follow him in. I found him in a cubicle cutting up some cocaine. I had a couple of snorts then he gave me the money. I said something like, "You cunt, you fucking took them out the game." He gave me a little grin, a smirk and said, "Don't ask questions. What are you? A cozzer?" And that was me intro to shut up.'

Jasper's testimony seemed to be the final piece in the jigsaw as far as the defence were concerned. They had surely proved beyond doubt that Darren Nicholls was a liar – he had admitted as much himself – that Steele and Whomes had solid alibis for where they were and what they were doing the night that Tucker, Tate and Rolfe had died, and they had also provided a highly convincing alternative explanation of how the men met their death. In the public gallery relatives of the family of Jack Whomes were starting to feel confident that things would go their way, while the relatives of the dead men were starting to shuffle around uneasily. 'The whole case has been unnerving for all the family,' said Marie Tate, 'but Billy Jasper's evidence was the most unnerving of all.' They were not the only ones suffering.

SANDRA While the trial was going on Darren was completely impossible to live with. He never actually got violent with me or the kids but there were loads of times when I really thought he was about to. Every now and then, for no reason, he'd suddenly get really angry about something really stupid and storm off or try to smash something. He'd never been like it before. The stress was clearly getting to him but he point blank refused to talk about it, not to anyone, so it all just bottled up inside him. When it came out it was terrifying. More than once I thought about running away but the threat to take my kids away always held me back.

When you're in a couple, I always think the most important thing is to be able to talk about the future. Whether it's what you want to be doing in five years time or where you're going on holiday, you always have to have something to look forward to or know where you're going. At that moment we couldn't do that. We had no idea what the future held. It all depended on which way the trial went. I remember I couldn't even bring myself to think about what might happen if they got off. I had never been so unhappy in all my life.

When you sign up for the witness protection programme, they try to tell you what to expect, but it never comes close to the truth. It does nothing to prepare you for what it's really going to be like. I guess if they actually told you exactly how difficult it was, how little money you'd have to live on, how often you'd be separated and how much your family, relationships and friendships would suffer, then nobody would ever want to get involved. If Darren had asked me what to do at the time, I would have told him to go for it, to sign up just the way he did. Now, looking back, I'm not at all sure.

In September 1996, five months after their arrest and exactly a year before the trial had begun, Michael Steele and Jack Whomes had appeared at Belmarsh Magistrates' Court for a committal hearing. After a week of evidence, the trial was passed on to the Crown Court and the trio were told they had seven days to file notice of alibi. If they had witnesses or evidence that proved they could not be responsible for the murder, they had only a week to submit it.

The rule is a simple extension of the caution given to anyone who is arrested: that while they have the right to remain silent, if they later in court rely on something that they have not previously mentioned, the jury can be made aware of this. In other words, if rather than explaining their actions or whereabouts straightaway, they appear to have gone away and had a good think about the best possible excuse, then the jury has a right to know.

For Steele and Whomes, their alibis had seemed straightforward enough, if slightly weakened by the fact that their only witnesses were relatives. What weakened them far more was the revelation that the pair had not submitted their alibis until July 1997, more than ten months late and just eight weeks before the start of the trial.

Not only that, but under close scrutiny, Steele's 'shockproof, rockproof' alibi quickly began to crumble. The till receipt didn't necessarily relate to the credit card slip. Anyone could have bought the petrol at that garage at 5 p.m. It also transpired that Steele's former sister-in-law, Phyllis Stambrook, whose evidence that he had been home around the supposed time of the murders did so much to support his version of events, had not been asked to give evidence or make a statement until a few months before the trial. She was clearly crucial, so why wasn't she contacted sooner? That question was intriguing enough on its own, but when Andrew Munday QC began to question her about how she could be so sure of the date she and her daughter visited Steele's house, her answer surprised everyone.

'That's the day the solicitor told me it was,' she admitted.

'Let's say he spoke to you on March 1,' said Munday. 'If I had asked you on February 28 on what date you went round to see Mr Steele, what would you have said?

Mrs Stambrook paused for a moment then replied, 'I would have said I can't recall.'

When it came to Jack Whomes, his recollection of shouting through the letterbox of his Uncle's home seemed equally flawed. While in the witness box, he repeatedly told in great detail how he bent down, held the slot open with his hands and shouted through the door. Andrew Munday then showed Whomes and the jury pictures of the door in question. It had no letterbox.

And as for the supposedly broken-down Passat that Whomes had picked up for Darren Nicholls, the court heard from a local car breaker who gave a very different version of events. The day after the murder, Whomes had *driven* the vehicle to the man's scrapyard and told him, 'Do what you like with it, just so long as there's nothing that could come back to me.' Rather than destroying it, the man checked the vehicle out and found it still had some life left in it. He sold it on.

Then there was the evidence of Billy Jasper. Soon after his arrest, police in Chelmsford had contacted Ivan Dibley with the news that a man in custody was confessing an involvement with the triple murder. By mid-January, Dibley and his team had already gathered a wealth of evidence against Michael Steele that pointed to him being the killer. Jasper's story was intriguing but failed to fit in with much of the evidence gathered thus far. A quick check into Jasper's background provided an answer. He had a history of 'confessing' to crimes that he had nothing to do with. A self-confessed drug addict who admitted that he spent £400 per day on heroin and crack cocaine, he clearly found it difficult to distinguish between fantasy and reality.

'He was such a Walter Mitty we just couldn't take anything he said seriously,' says Ivan Dibley. 'We looked into his claims, but there wasn't much substance. We told Chelmsford police to continue the investigation and to let us know if anything came of it. Nothing ever did.'

That only left the mystery of why, if Jasper was lying, the members of the East End gang he had fingered for the crime had done nothing to shut him up. Although he had named them during his original police interviews, Jasper refused to name any of his accomplices in court, claiming he was too scared of reprisals. But even when their names eventually came out in the open, Jesse Gale (who later died in a car crash in May 1998) and Mr D. did not seem overly worried about being linked to the crime. In fact, dozens of villains all across the country were happy for people to think they might have been involved. In a world where double-crosses and rip-offs are becoming increasingly common, the kudos of having wiped out three of the country's most dangerous men – and having gotten away with it – is undoubtedly the best protection of all.

*

Just after midday on Thursday 15 January, the jury of eight women and four men retired to consider its verdict. As Steele and Whomes waited anxiously in the cells below, the news came just before 4 p.m. that they had failed to reach a verdict. The jury were sent to a hotel and told to return to court the following day.

The next day it happened again and the jury were told to return to the court on Saturday to see if they could reach a verdict. By the middle of Saturday afternoon it was clear that they would not and their stay at the hotel was extended yet again. Mr Justice Hidden decided to give them Sunday off, hoping to give the jury the chance to relax by taking them all on an organised trip. They returned on Monday happy but still unable to agree and stayed at the hotel yet again.

In any criminal case, reading a jury is almost impossible. Some say the longer the deliberations go on, the more likely the verdict will be not guilty. Others say extended deliberations show that not all the members of the jury are in agreement and are attempting to convince one another of their version of the truth. But often, as was the case with the Rettendon trial, it is simply that the jury are going over every item of evidence before taking their vote. They asked for additional material, to see certain pictures, to read transcripts of certain interviews once more.

On Tuesday 20 January 1998, after five full days of deliberation, the jury returned its unanimous verdict.

Guilty.

NICHOLLS I think I got the phone call within ten seconds of the verdict going out. All I could think was, 'Yes, yes, yes, it's all over. Thank fuck for that.' But it faded really quickly once I started to think about it properly. You wait and wait and wait for the end of a trial, but once it's over you realise that it's not really over at all. There was another trial coming up and I knew that Mick and Jack would put an appeal in straightaway. It was a victory, knowing that the jury saw through their lies and believed me, but it was pretty hollow. Deep down I was really pleased, of course I was, but I couldn't show it. I actually felt really bad about the whole thing. There was a time when I really looked up to Mick. He was almost a father figure to me and I felt like I'd really let him down. It's so stupid, all this nonsense about the criminal code and all that. None of it makes any sense, but when you've been mixing in those circles for a while, it does start to get to you.

Back in the court, Whomes and Steele glanced at each other for a moment, then both shrugged their shoulders, then looked back to the judge. 'There is no other sentence I can pass on you for these horrifying murders of which you have been convicted than that of life imprisonment,' Mr Justice Hidden told the pair. 'There is little that can be said usefully about either of you at this stage. You two were responsible in my view for taking away the lives of these three victims in a summary way. You lured them to a quiet farm track and executed them. They had crossed your path and you showed them no mercy. There is about these killings a hard and ruthless edge, which can only horrify and stagger the non-criminal mind. You are extremely dangerous men and you have not the slightest compunction for resorting to extreme violence when you thought it was necessary.'

Both men were told that they would serve a minimum of fifteen years.

It took a while for the shock to settle in, but as the pair travelled back to Belmarsh, Steele tried to look on the bright side.

'Don't worry Jack. I'll make sure that wherever we end up, we'll do the time together. At least we'll have that.'

Whomes turned to face Steele, holding his stare for a second or two before he spoke. 'Fuck off. I never want to see you again.'

19

'The contract is out . . . he's finished'

The name of the man responsible for putting the gang behind bars appeared, neatly painted in black block capitals, on the side of London's Blackfriars Bridge in the early hours of the morning. Right beside the name, in the same neat black lettering, was the ultimate underworld insult: Grass.

Later that same day, 10 February 1998, James Lawson, a wealthy forty-one-year-old car dealer, heard a knock at the door of his home in Hook, Hampshire. He had been sitting in his plush living room enjoying a drink with his friend Sven Hamer and hoped the caller was his girlfriend, Lynn, who had stormed off the previous day after a furious row. He jumped up and rushed to greet her, leaving his friend to finish a tumbler of whisky.

Before he had time for another sip, Hamer heard a scream followed by a loud crack. He craned his neck towards the door and saw Lawson fall backwards and collapse on the floor, blood spurting from a gaping hole in his shoulder. He then saw a man emerge, dressed from black head to toe in motorcycle leathers and wearing a full-face helmet with a tinted visor, and step into the hallway. In the man's right hand was a heavy black pistol with a tiny wisp of smoke drifting out of the barrel. Another shot was fired, this time into the centre of Lawson's chest, and then the gunman stepped forward again and aimed a third bullet through his victim's forehead. Hamer, speechless with shock and terrified for his own life, dropped his glass. The gunman turned and vanished.

Although they had never met, James Lawson and Darren Nicholls had something in common.

Lawson's real name was Peter McNeil and ten years earlier he had given evidence at the Old Bailey against three drugs barons who were planning a £70 million cocaine deal. The stakes were high: the drugs barons were linked to the American Mafia and among those lined up to receive the cocaine were the IRA and numerous London-based gangs. McNeil had been intimately involved in the operation, supervising the movement of tons of cocaine on routes throughout Europe and even travelling to Colombia to arrange the initial shipments, all the time enjoying a millionaire playboy lifestyle. He was initially arrested in Colombia and offered a deal by Customs and Excise when they discovered his gang was behind some £20 million worth of cocaine being smuggled into the United Kingdom each year. The deal was simple, straightforward and non-negotiable: if he would reveal the details of plans to smuggle drugs through to Britain and the routes used, he would be offered immunity from prosecution and a new identity once the trial was over. McNeil jumped at the chance.

Acting on his information, police swooped and captured three men and a substantial quantity of cocaine at a rendezvous in Essex. The trio were jailed for a total of thirty-eight years and Peter McNeil of Southall, west London, became James Lawson of Hook, Hampshire. Like Nicholls, Lawson was not entitled to any reward money because he had been involved in the crimes and had decided to turn supergrass only after being caught red handed, so once the case had finished he went to Fleet Street hoping to sell his story for big bucks.

Frank Thorne, a former reporter on the *Daily Mirror*, was one of those whom he contacted. 'During our first cloak-and-dagger meeting he handed me a bullet and, in somewhat melodramatic terms told me, "I know that somewhere, there's one of these with my name on it. You're looking at a dead man. The Mafia cannot let me live." He would make a point of checking the men's room several times and would sit with his back to the bar so he could watch the comings and goings. Sometimes he would point out perfectly innocent advertising executives or lawyers on their lunch breaks and panic that they were following him. He feared IRA or Mafia hit men were everywhere.'

It was tempting bait but none of the newspapers were biting. The trial had rumbled on far too long for anyone to remember what it was all about, let alone remember the role of the supergrass who made it all possible. As a result, the price the press were willing to pay for Lawson's story was nothing like he had hoped for and he walked away bitter and disappointed.

When, a decade later, Lawson's cold-blooded execution finally saw him make headlines once more, it didn't take long for the truth about his background to emerge. But what surprised many was that the life he had been living in the years since he took on a new identity was every bit as dramatic as the manner in which it had all come to an end.

After settling in Hampshire, Lawson had set up a company – in partnership with local businessmen – selling prestige cars, using his charm and gift of the gab to shift dozens of medium motors at top prices. As the profits rolled in, so he began to enjoy the trappings of his new-found success and establishing a reputation as a big spender. He drove a Rolls-Royce, rarely drank anything apart from vintage champagne and developed a first-class cocaine habit.

Although he was making money, it wasn't anything like as

much as he was making before he was first arrested and it was only a matter of time before he was back to his old ways, importing and dealing in sizeable quantities of cocaine.

Careless and big-mouthed, Lawson was soon caught but this time he had an ace card to play. Lawson offered to become an informer for Hampshire police, providing information about local goings-on in return for being allowed to carry on dealing – purely to ensure he was in touch with the underworld, of course.

The police agreed and Lawson's new position quickly went to his head. He began boasting to anyone who would listen that he was beyond the law, untouchable. To prove it he ran his drugs business in an increasingly blatant style. He would hire taxis and hand the drivers £40,000 in cash to take to the bank for him; he would buy drinks for everyone in a bar to celebrate one of his couriers getting through customs; he would go to restaurants and simply ask for the most expensive items on the menu.

The money, the champagne and the fine food were all very well but Lawson's true great passion was for sex. And as with all his activities, his appetite proved almost insatiable. If he couldn't seduce the wives and girlfriends of those around him – and most of the time he could – then he would hire prostitutes, often shelling out enormous sums on taxi fares to have them shipped to his home from London. But his carefree attitude to money went only so far. When a woman on the books of the Saints and Sinners escort agency in Surrey was dispatched to his home, she returned hysterical. She explained that an argument over the cost of her services had erupted and Lawson had threatened her with a swordstick and a gun.

The police were called and Lawson's house was searched. No gun was ever found and he was not charged. The agency put his name on their blacklist but a month or so later, Lawson hired another woman under a different name. She complained that he refused to pay her the agreed fee. When the owner of the agency phoned to complain, Lawson recorded her increasingly angry conversation. The woman, Donna Cannon, soon found herself in court accused of threatening to blackmail him.

Lawson himself gave evidence and, in July 1992, Cannon received a community service sentence. The jury were not told that Lawson had a history as a police informer. Nor were they told he had picked up convictions for assault, criminal damage, attempted burglary and numerous driving offences since he had assumed his new identity.

His arrogance, boasting and lack of morals outraged many of his neighbours. When he died, police attempting to find witnesses heard the same refrain over and over again as they interviewed those who knew him. 'It wasn't me, but I'm not sorry he's dead.'

SUPERGRASS SHOT. The words in neat black block capitals on the front page of the *Sun* sent a chill down the spine of Darren Nicholls and sent his friends and family rushing to the phone.

NICHOLLS There was no picture on the front page. No one knew where I was living or what name I was living under so loads of people thought it was me. I got dozens of calls on my mobile and messages on my pager from people who were convinced I was dead.

I think it drove it home to a lot of people just how serious my situation is. And it really worried me as well. It's all very well having someone tell you there's a contract out on your head, that people are looking for you because they want to kill you, but you can't really take it seriously. But when this happened, it made me think. Fuck, supergrasses do get shot; there are people out there who will spend years trying to track you down and then put a couple of bullets in your head.

If I was stunned by the news then Sandra was completely devastated. It was horrible. She just sat there and didn't say a word for ages and ages. Then we had this really serious discussion about what we would do if there was an emergency, whether we needed more locks on the windows and that kind of thing. We were both trying to stay calm and keep it together for the sake of the kids, but inside we were both absolutely shitting ourselves. And the worst part was that I had another trial coming up. There were going to be seven more people who would be totally pissed off with me; who would want their names to go on the list of people who'd like to see me dead. It wasn't much of a summer, I can tell you.

In March 1999, James Clelland, a car dealer, stood trial for the murder of Peter McNeil, aka James Lawson. Clelland couldn't be accused of actually pulling the trigger himself as he had the perfect alibi – he was in prison at the time of the shooting. Instead Clelland was accused of passing on details of McNeil's whereabouts to his enemies, allowing them to finally track him down.

Bournemouth Crown Court heard that Clelland had become obsessed with the idea that McNeil would win back the affections of his former girlfriend. McNeil's lover at the time of his death, Lynn McDonald, had been Clelland's partner for nine years and he had convinced himself that McNeil was also seeing Rebecca Chappell, with whom Clelland had split a month or so before the shooting.

On 13 December, a furious Clelland arrived at McNeil's house in the early hours and demanded to be let in to check whether Chappell was there. He kicked repeatedly at the doors and windows and swore that McNeil would be made to pay. He screamed out that he had been offered £30,000 to pass McNeil's address on to the underworld. 'We were in fear of our lives,' McDonald told the court. 'I was in fear that Peter was going to be killed that night.'

Soon after Clelland found himself on remand at Winchester prison for making threats to kill McNeil. While there he allegedly told Chappell that he had phoned a pair of gangsters known as the Brothers Grim and told them to sort McNeil out.

Tapes of telephone calls made by Clelland from prison were played in court. In one he could be heard telling a friend that McNeil 'was going to get his comeuppance' and that he would 'put paid to him for once and for all'.

There were also answerphone messages left at Chappell's house in which an emotional Clelland could be heard begging her to take him back. In one he said softly, 'The contract is out. McNeil is finished.'

The problem with the case was that Lawson/McNeil had made so many enemies and had been so indiscreet about his past that there was simply no way to prove that Clelland had anything to do with it. After a three-week trial, Clelland was acquitted of all charges and walked out of court without a stain on his character.

Lawson's killer may never be found but his death taught Nicholls a lesson he will never be able to forget.

> NICHOLLS I've always known that I would have to spend the rest of my life looking over my shoulder, but I always assumed that with time, the threat would start to fade. Now I know better. No matter what I'm doing, where I am or who I'm with, I know I can never completely relax.'

In September 1998, Darren Nicholls found himself back in custody as he gave evidence at Woolwich Crown Court as Russell Tate and six others faced trial for drug smuggling. Although they were intimately involved in bringing the cannabis across the English Channel and transporting it to the garage owned by Steele's mother, it had long been decided that Steele and Whomes would not face trial themselves. They were already serving fifteen years for murder and, even if they were convicted, the additional sentence would be concurrent. It would be a pointless exercise and the cost of the security operation needed to bring them to the court, let alone to keep Steele and Russell Tate separate in the dock, made the whole thing pointless.

There was also the fact that, if Steele and Whomes had appeared, the jury would not have been able to know about their previous convictions. All the evidence gathered as a result of the murder investigation would not be admissible.

As the legal arguments rumbled on, Nicholls got more and more bitter about his own involvement and more and more frustrated about the delay in his sentencing.

NICHOLLS I wasn't interested in the second trial. I didn't want to go through it all again. The only reason I became a witness in the first place was to put away those two for saying that they were going to kill me. Then all of a sudden everyone seemed to think that I wanted to grass the world up, that I was getting some kind of kick out of it. The truth was that I hated what I had become and I wanted to get on with my life.

As it was the customs trial turned out to be something of a non-event, with Nicholls appearing in the witness box for less than two days. Even without his testimony, the evidence was overwhelming: there was film of meetings between Steele, Tate and others; there were mobile phone records showing the convoy had travelled down to Spain through France and then returned to Blankenberg on at least three occasions; there was footage from a thermal-imaging camera that had followed Steele's boat as it left the Suffolk coast, picked up the drugs in Belgium and then returned; there were surveillance reports of Whomes's Range Rover meeting the boat and removing the cannabis. Finally there was the £500,000 worth of cannabis that had been found in Steele's possession, under a blanket in his mum's garage.

The only excitement came when Russell Tate himself took the stand. Faced with a mass of rock solid evidence that he had been wholly aware of and intimately involved in the plot to smuggle cannabis, his defence had to be a stunning one. And it was.

In front of an astonished court, Tate explained that he knew all along that Steele had killed his brother and had only got involved with him to help bring him to justice. Tate believed that by befriending Steele through the joint smuggling venture he might eventually leave some clue or drop some hint that gave away his involvement in the murders. Then, and only then, did Tate plan to go to the police.

It was a great tale but one that no one could be expected to take seriously. As Mr Justice Jeffrey Rucker said during his sentencing after the six-week trial, Tate had prepared 'an ingenious story as a way of explaining his involvement in the conspiracy but it did not simply bear the scrutiny of common sense and day-to-day experience of life – it was wholly untrue. In listening to the evidence, I do not for a moment believe that Tate had ever suspected Steele of murdering his brother.'

After being found guilty, Tate was jailed for five years. Paul Gwinnett was given four years while Craig Androliakos received two. Tate's lover, Sarah Darlaston, her childhood friend Tracey Roulstone and Ian Kerr were each jailed for thirty months. Michael James, who had been filmed meeting with Steele on at least one occasion, was acquitted.

On Friday 13 November 1998, Darren Nicholls returned to custody one last time before making a brief appearance at Woolwich Crown Court before Judge Hidden for his sentencing. 'I have no doubt that without the evidence provided by this man, a terrible crime would never have been solved and two killers would still be walking the streets. In return, Mr Nicholls will undoubtedly have to spend the rest of his life in fear. I have no hesitation in awarding him full credit for the assistance he provided both police and customs in this matter.' Nicholls was sentenced to fifteen months. The time he had already served in prison while awaiting trial more than covered it. He had paid his debt to society. He had finally become a free man.

On 26 January 1999, representatives of Michael Steele and Jack Whomes appeared at the High Court to ask for leave to appeal against their convictions. Outside the court friends and families fixed banners to the railings declaring their innocence, but it was not to be. After a five-hour hearing, Lord Bingham, the Lord Chief Justice, Mr Justice Kennedy and Mr Justice Jackson concluded there was no evidence to suggest the convictions were unsafe.

As their supporters chanted, 'Fix,' relatives of Whomes spoke to the ranks of waiting reports and photographers. 'He'll cry for a week when we tell him,' said John Whomes. 'We will carry on campaigning and the campaign will get bigger.'

And indeed it has. In May 1999, Jackie Street finally broke her silence and told the *Basildon Echo* that she was investigating every avenue in her fight to get her common-law husband released. 'We are looking at every possible channel,' she said. 'They did not commit these murders and both Michael Steele and Jack Whomes protest their innocence. Michael is determined and absolutely resolute that the truth will eventually come out and he will never give up.'

With other avenues exhausted, Steele was trying new tactics, putting the blame on his representation in court and complaining to the legal ombudsman. 'If it is found that he was not properly represented, then he will automatically have leave to go to appeal,' Street added. An application was also being made to the Criminal Cases Review Committee, the European Court of Human Rights and Steele was even looking at taking out private prosecutions against some of the police officers involved in the case.

'I know he's no saint but he did not murder these three men,' Street continued. 'He has committed a number of crimes in the past and he has paid for them. The evidence is there that he is innocent but we just need someone to listen. I have had everything taken away from me. I had no means of support and I am living on benefits. My main aim in life is to get Michael home and I will never give up. In order to be free he would have to admit his guilt. He will never do that. He would rather die in prison than admit to something that he did not do.

On 14 May 1996, Darren Nicholls, a little known petty criminal from Braintree, Essex, disappeared from the face of the earth. But it wasn't until 2 March 1999 that he finally, officially, became someone else.

There was no ceremony or celebration the day that the police turned up with his new passport and driving licence – just a quick handshake and a request that in future, he stay out of trouble. And that was that.

Today Darren Nicholls lives somewhere in the United Kingdom, in an average house on an average street where nothing, least of all Nicholls himself, stands out from the crowd. He and his wife both work in reasonably interesting jobs, have a growing circle of friends and are slowly saving up for a second car. No one has any real idea about his past, what he has been through and the things he has seen. And that's just the way he intends to keep it.

Epilogue

'I feel my problems are only just beginning'

NICHOLLS That's pretty much all there is to it: that's the whole story of how I went from living in a shitty little town with a shitty car and not much of a future to where I am today – living in a different shitty little town, with a different shitty car, not much of a future and a passport that, no matter how many times I look at it, still seems to belong to someone else.

I really don't know what I think or how I feel about it, all the stuff that happened. I guess that with the two trials finished and Steele, Whomes and the others banged up I should be happy, but I'm not. No way. I have this terrible guilt. I feel like I've been a right bastard. I know I shouldn't feel guilty, but I just can't help it. It's going to be a long, long time before I can feel good about myself.

When I went to court for the last time to have the judge hand down my sentence, the usher asked me what the toughest part of being a protected witness was. He guessed it was going to be giving up the good life. I had to laugh. I wasn't much of a criminal – I never had the wads of cash to spend or got the best tables in the local bars and restaurants or even came close to dripping with gold. Leaving my old life behind was easy. The real challenge has been trying to cope with the new one.

The nightmares about the murder, the time I spent in prison, the fear that someone was going to try to track me or my family down – it's all a cakewalk compared to the strain of living a lie. It means I can never really relax, never lower my guard. I just spend the whole time on edge, waiting for someone to say, 'Hey, don't I know you from Braintree? Hang on, you're Darren Nicholls.'

A couple of weeks ago I was in the local pub with a bunch of friends and there was a telephone call at the bar. The landlord called out, 'Is there a Darren in here?' so I jumped up, said yes and started walking over. I was almost at the phone when I remembered that I didn't have that name any more, that I'd become someone else. I had to pretend that I was drunk and making a joke. I think I got away with it, but I can't help thinking that for at least one of my friends it has sown the seeds of doubt. There are people around here who already think there's something a bit strange about me, that my background doesn't quite add up. All it will take now is for another piece of the jigsaw puzzle to fall into place and I could find myself having to move on all over again. In truth, I feel my problems are only just beginning.

There's one other question that people always want an answer to – just what do you get for becoming a supergrass? I know there are people out there – most of them relatives of Steele and Whomes – who still believe that I've been paid some vast amount of money and that I'm now living in the lap of luxury.

Well it's time I came clean. Forget the rumours about £300,000 in my bank account, my Villa in Spain, my brand-new sport cars and all the other benefits. That's nothing. The truth of being a supergrass, of signing your soul over to the police, is that you get much more than that. In fact, there's so much, it would take another book to list it all, so I'll just tell you about three things, the ones that matter most:

I get to never see my parents again.

I get to spend the rest of my life lying to my kids.

I get to never, ever feel completely safe.

And then there's the money. During the trial and when I was out on bail, I got exactly £48 per week because that's what I would have got if I was on the dole. And since the trials finished? I haven't had a penny.

Don't get me wrong – I'm not complaining. I've got my freedom and I'm thankful for that. I also get the chance to start over with a clean record, but that's where it ends. I know there are people out there who think that I only said what I said in court because of the deal that I struck with the police. Well surprise, surprise, that's absolutely right. But that doesn't mean I wasn't telling the truth.

The biggest difference between my new life and my old life is that there's no safety net. If I run out of money before the month runs out, I can't think about selling a few ounces of puff to make up the difference or getting involved in some dodgy money scam. From now on I have to do things by the book. I have to be a whole new clean-living person, and that's not easy at all, especially if you've spent your whole life bending the rules. So the only thing to do with my old life is to put it behind me, to forget about it completely. I don't think about it. I don't look at the photographs, and I don't ever talk about it, not even to Sandra. It's just too dangerous. Because with all the shit that happened, with all the weird crazy stuff that went on, there were still some good times. And thinking about the good times just scares the shit out of me.

I might start to miss them.